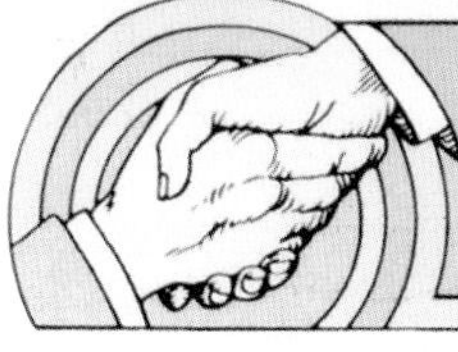

The Ford-UAW deal

— Story, Page 3A

A 2d Front Page on 3A today

World Series edition

Detroit Free Press

Volume 154, Number 164 | ON GUARD FOR 153 YEARS | Monday, October 15, 1984

metro final

Gr-r-reat!

The culmination of an incredible season, the high point of a still-young career: Kirk Gibson after his second home run Sunday.

Free Press Photo by MARY SCHROEDER

Fans go wild over Tigers

By MARTIN F. KOHN
Free Press Staff Writer

Five or so ounces of cork wound in twine and wrapped in sewn white leather settled into the glove of a man named Larry Herndon, and the baseball season of 1984 settled into the massive mitt of History.

The Tigers, the come-from-ahead ball club from the coming-from-behind town, won the World Series, beating the San Diego Padres 8-4 before Vice-President George Bush and a home crowd of 51,901 who hollered themselves hoarse and waved themselves silly and, years from now, can show their ticket stubs to their grandchildren and say they were there.

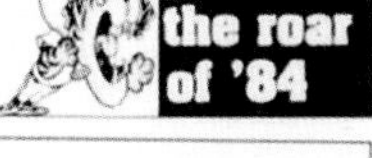

■ *Game story and special Series Report. Section F.*
■ *More pictures. Page 12F.*
■ *Talbert's Tiger diary. 7E.*
■ *Series Sidelights. 1E.*

Playing no favorites, President Reagan telephoned both locker rooms after the game to congratulate the players.

For Detroit, for Michigan, for the Midwest, for everybody who has been with the Tigers in spirit, the victory was a moment to cherish in a season to savor.

Starting in the Tigers locker room and spreading out in immeasurable waves wherever fans of the home team gathered, it was "cel-e-brate good times, come on!" and dancing in the streets.

BUT IT wasn't all fun. At least four police cars were damaged at Michigan and Trumbull; another was set afire and destroyed, and a private car also was set afire.

Emergency Medical Services ambulances had trouble reaching at least one accident victim, police said.

Souvenir vendors near the stadium had their remaining wares stolen.

Many bottles were thrown at police officers. No serious injuries had been reported within the first couple of hours after the game.

For the most part, though, just as it happened 16 years ago, when the Tigers last won the Series, hearts swelled and spirits lifted. Banished for the moment were thoughts of crime and unemployment, recession and soup kitchens. The Tigers were world champions, and all things good suddenly had become possible, or even likely.

See **WORLD SERIES**, Page 15A

The naturals win in maverick way

Mike Downey

They won it, just the way everybody in Detroit thought they would.

They won it, in a way nobody thought they could.

They won it on a sacrifice fly ... *to second base.*

They won it on a pinch-hit, bases-loaded pop-up ... *by Rusty Kuntz.*

They won it on a wild run for the money by Kirk Gibson, who tagged up and scored on a ball that might not have gone 25 feet onto the outfield grass.

They did it with two Gibson home runs, one of which opened the scoring, one of which closed it.

They won it.

The World Series.

THE DETROIT Tigers became the undisputed best team in baseball Sunday, beating the San Diego Padres, 8-4, for their fourth world championship since joining the American League in 1901. When Willie Hernandez got Tony Gwynn on a short fly to left field for the final out, the crowd of 51,901 stormed onto the Tiger Stadium field, as did thousands of non-paying customers outside the park who didn't want to be left out.

They couldn't restrain themselves. The Tigers had won it.

They won it with Gibson tying into a Mark Thurmond pitch in the first inning and sending it halfway to Hamtramck. The two-run homer landed in the upper deck in right-center.

They won it because another San Diego pitcher failed to last beyond the first inning. Thurmond threw only 15 pitches and faced only six batters.

They won it even though the Padres put together a rally that knocked out Dan Petry and tied the game at 3-all.

See **DOWNEY**, Page 15A

The Corner

A century of memories at Michigan and Trumbull

By Richard Bak, Charlie Vincent and the Free Press staff

Detroit Free Press

Triumph Books
Chicago

Memories

Contents

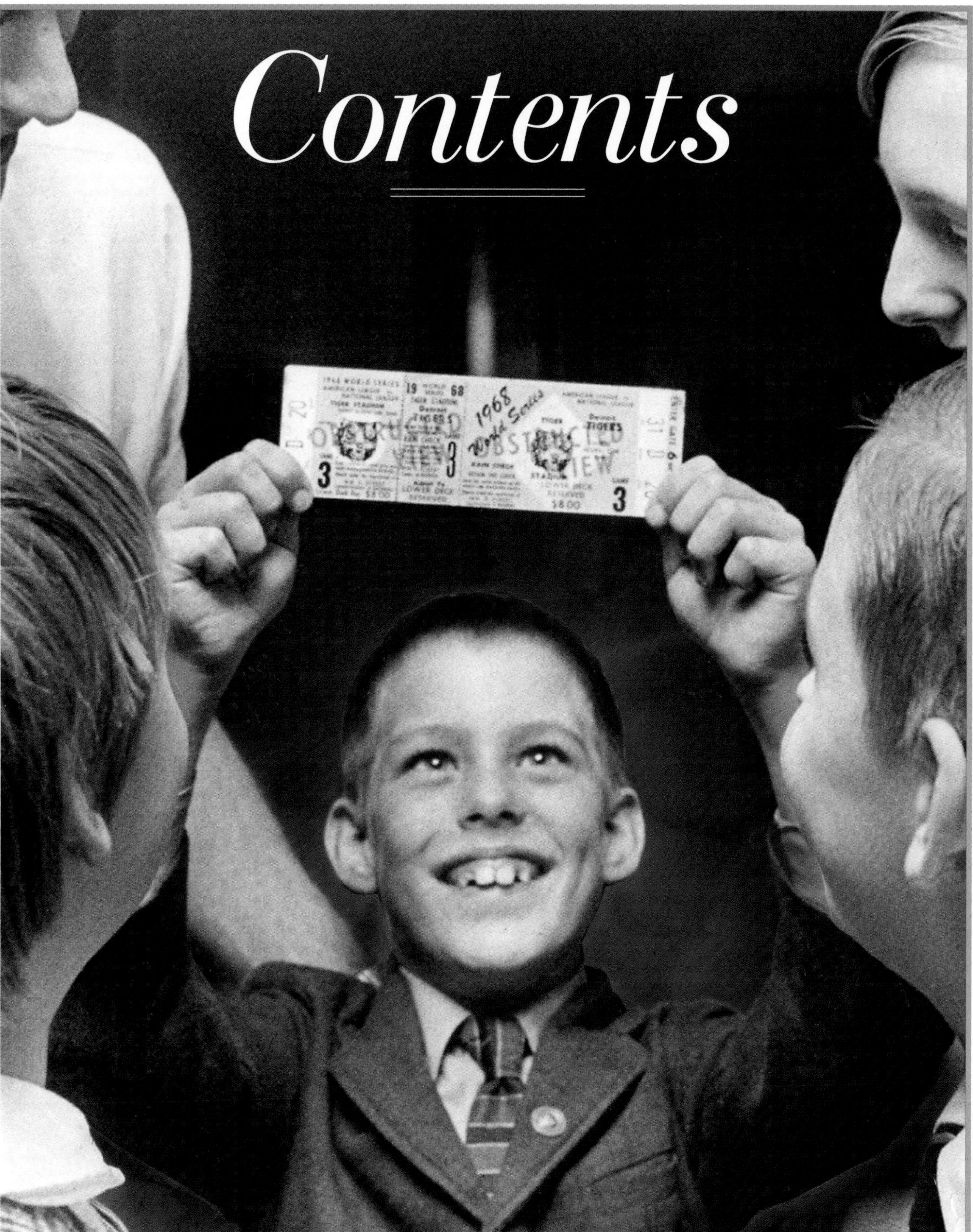
1968 World Series
19 68
TIGER STADIUM
Detroit TIGERS
3
LOWER DECK
3
$8.00

Editor Tom Panzenhagen
Designer Steve Anderson
Photo editor Alan R. Kamuda
Photo technician Rose Ann McKean
Cover designs Rick Nease
Technical advisers Bob Ellis, Andrew J. Hartley
Copy editors Bill Collison, Reid Creager, Bob Ellis, Ken Kraemer, Tim Marcinkoski, Karen Park
Research assistant Bill Dow
Special thanks Bill McGraw, Gene Myers, Dave Robinson and the Free Press sports staff

Printed in the United States.

This book is available in quantity at special discounts for your group or organization. For more information, contact:

Triumph Books
601 South LaSalle Street
Suite 500
Chicago, Illinois 60605
(312) 939-3330
Fax: (312) 663-3557

ISBN 1-57243-337-X

Cover: Opening Day 1984. (Tony Spina / Detroit Free Press) **Title page:** Opening Day 1993. (Action Image)
Contents page: A boy holds his ticket to a lifetime of memories. (Fred Plofchan / Detroit Free Press)

Editor's note: Statistics in this book current through July 5, 1999.

It has been handed down

from generation to generation, this deep affinity we share for the yard at Michigan and Trumbull. They started playing baseball there on April 28, 1896. Now – 103 years later, as "The Corner" goes to press – it's the bottom of the ninth. Come 2000, like rookies, we'll wander the corridors of a new park for the first time. ◆ Tiger Stadium – and, before it, Briggs Stadium, Navin Field and Bennett Park – evokes feelings within each of us. Most are good, but not all. You could freeze at The Corner in spring or broil in summer, or find yourself sitting behind a post or stranded for innings outside a restroom or in the beer line. Or excluded entirely by a team that didn't employ its first black player until 11 years after Jackie Robinson broke the color barrier in 1947. ◆ And yet it's the warmest feelings that endure – and fill this book – as the sun sets on The Corner. After all, it's where Ty Cobb played. And Gehringer, Greenberg, Newhouser, Kaline, Horton, the Bird, Gibby, Tram and Lou. More important, it's where we played, where we grew up. We were at home there, and – win or lose, from generation to generation – memories of days shared with loved ones at The Corner will last forever. ◆ This book is about players who found fame and teams that won championships. More important, it's about us. Enjoy the memories. – *The editors*

It happens every spring. Manager Steve O'Neill accepts the Detroit Fire Department's traditional floral horseshoe on behalf of the defending world champs in 1946.

Richard Bak Collection

CHAPTER 1

For openers

Opening Day always has been extra special in Detroit. It's the one afternoon when everything from the immaculately groomed grass at the ballpark to the team's unblemished record is free of failure and alive with the optimism of a fresh start. Its annual observance – part circus, part rite of spring – was staged at the northwest corner of Michigan and Trumbull every year since 1896, a comforting stretch of continuity that spanned five generations in the life of the city.

Think of it. Three years before Detroit had an auto plant, four years before there was an American League and seven years before the first modern World Series was played, wimpy-armed politicians were bouncing ceremonial pitches 10 feet in front of the plate at The Corner.

For those whose memories stretch only as far back as Chris Pittaro, a primer is in order. Between 1894 and 1899, the Tigers played in the Western League, a minor circuit of Midwestern clubs that in 1900 formed the nucleus of the American League. After playing the summers of 1894-95 at Boulevard Park, near the Belle Isle bridge, club owner George Vanderbeck built Bennett Park on the former site of a municipal haymarket.

The wooden 5,000-seat facility officially opened April 28, 1896, with the Tigers clobbering Columbus, 17-2, in the first Opening Day at The Corner. Although the names of the players and the parks (Navin Field in 1912, Briggs Stadium in 1938, Tiger Stadium in 1961) changed, The Corner remained the oldest playing address in professional sports. And Opening Day continued as the city's oldest and grandest sporting tradition.

"Opening Day in Detroit is an event," longtime play-by-play broadcaster Ernie Harwell said. "It's New Year's, Easter and Christmas all rolled into one unique afternoon.

"Ritual and ceremony are an integral part of the day. There's festive music from the band in deep centerfield. The firefighters present wreaths of flowers to the manager. The governor and mayor perform as the ceremonial battery."

Tony Spina / Detroit Free Press

William Milliken, Michigan's governor, throws out the first pitch on Opening Day 1976.

Even the players get caught up in the hoopla. Dave Rozema was the starting pitcher for three of four home openers in 1979-82. Although he didn't make it past the sixth inning in any of them, the irrepressible Rosie preferred to dwell on the positive vibes emanating from the packed grandstands.

Ed Haun / Detroit Free Press

Bill Freehan, who grew up in Royal Oak, became a fixture behind the plate in 1963.

"It was a beautiful scene coming up from Florida and seeing 50,000 people all geeked up and ready to go," he said. "I still go down for the opening game every year. I have a big tailgate party. There's a lot of memories there."

More than a few belong to Bill Freehan. The big catcher's emotional recollection of the 1963 opener against Chicago is at odds with the stoic, solid-as-a-cinder-block image he projected during his 15 seasons as a Tiger.

"I had been with the team before, but never for Opening Day," said Freehan, who recalled hitchhiking from his Royal Oak home to Briggs Stadium during the 1950s. He usually sat in the bleachers, a wide-eyed schoolboy who dreamed of one day joining the larger-than-life figures on the felt-like expanse below.

"I stood there crying with my mask off during the national anthem. … The fantasy has become real."
Bill Freehan

"I stood there crying with my mask off during the national anthem," he said. "My parents were in the stands, and I was standing there thinking, 'Wow! The fantasy has become real.' One day you're a kid, and all of a sudden you're 20 or 21 years old and you're the starting catcher in your hometown. How many kids are ever able to say that?"

Burton Historical Collection

Davy Jones peers through the flurries during the final opener at Bennett Park on a snowy April day in 1911.

Opening Day sellouts are not a recent phenomenon, though the weather and the state of the local team and economy historically have been factors in determining how often the turnstiles spin.

Another factor was introduced in 1957, when the game was televised locally for the first time. The fact that it drizzled also hurt the gate. The result was a half-filled stadium. "I won't say television killed us," general manager Spike Briggs said. "But we won't televise next year's opener." Or the next. It would be another 20 years before fans could count on seeing the opener every year on the tube.

For the record, the largest crowd was in 1938, when 54,500 attended the dedication of Briggs Stadium. Close behind were the openers in 1971 (54,089) and 1969 (53,572). The four puniest gates occurred in successive years, 1897-1900, with the 1898 game drawing an all-time low of 2,700. People had better things to do on a 63-degree afternoon.

Of course, the size of the crowd doesn't dictate the size of the thrill. Some of the most entertaining home openers were played before those small but enthusiastic turn-of-the-century audiences.

In 1897, the Tigers dropped a 5-4, 10-inning decision to Indianapolis that so enraged the locals that the umpire, an unfortunate fellow named Ebright, barely escaped with his life. One Tiger, upset with Ebright's calls, sucker-punched him in the head after the game, further inciting the crowd. "Kill him!" some yelled. "Put a rope around his neck!"

A phalanx of bat-swinging Indianapolis players kept the mob at bay while Ebright was hustled into a waiting carriage, where he

GOOSED

Here's how the Free Press reported the Tigers' first American League game, at Bennett Park. The "basket of fresh goose eggs" in the headline refers to the succession of zeroes chalked on the hand-operated scoreboard as the Tigers failed to get either a run or a hit that afternoon.

BASKET OF FRESH GOOSE EGGS

BUFFALO PRESENTED IT TO THE UNWILLING TIGERS

DETROITERS HAD ALL SORTS OF THINGS DONE TO THEM

DIDN'T EVEN HAVE THE FUN OF REGISTERING A HIT

DOC AMOLE PITCHED A WONDERFUL GAME OF BALL

GIVEN GILT-EDGED SUPPORT BY HIS TEAM MATES

CROWD OF 5,000 HAD NO CHANCE TO CHEER THE TEAM

Mayor Maybury and Charlie Bennett Opened the Season of 1900

If there is anything in that old gag about a bad beginning ensuring a good ending, then Ban Johnson might just as well pack up the pennant and express it to James D. Burns on the first train. For the Tigers made a start yesterday such as was never equaled in the history of baseball. It is impossible to imagine anything more harrowing than the calamity that befell the Detroit players in the opening game with Buffalo, and if the familiar saying holds good, when they get fairly on their stride it should be like finding money to walk away with the championship of the American League.

Think of it! The biggest crowd that ever attended an opening game in Detroit since the days of the famous Big Four gathered in the grand stand, on the bleachers, in carriages, and swarmed around the outskirts of the gardens. It was distinctively a Detroit crowd. They came there to cheer and root for the Tigers, filled to the brim with enthusiasm, but not once after greeting the players as they came upon the field and paying a graceful and hearty tribute to that great catcher of seasons gone by, Charlie Bennett, did they have even a slight opportunity to turn loose that pent-up loyalty of the noisy and unmistakable variety. For the Buffalo club, Ald. Jim Franklin's pennant winners, not only won the game, but shut the Tigers out, the final score being 8 to 0.

BENNETT PARK AS IT LOOKED ON OPENING DAY 1901, A YEAR AFTER THE FIRST AMERICAN LEAGUE GAME AT THE CORNER.

That was an awful blow – "it nearly killed" Burns and Stallings, while the players did not feel exactly jubilant – but the loss could have been borne much more easily had insult not been added to injury. Doc Amole, a young man who throws with the wrong hand, was the direct cause of the insult. He was in grand form, had all sorts of curves and speed and kept the Tigers guessing so effectually that only once in the game was there anything that approached a base hit. It is sad to lose the opening game of the season; sadder still to be shut out, and positively mournful to be sent back to the club house with the batting average of each and every man badly punctured; but that is exactly what Doc Amole did, and the act will never be forgotten so long as baseball lives. Perhaps the wound will heal sufficiently to allow forgiveness to be granted and due credit allowed the twirler for his wonderful feat; but forgotten, never!

AMOLE'S WORK WAS GILT-EDGED

No-hit games are events that are seldom seen, and when such a feat is accomplished, it is generally along in the middle of the season, when the pitchers have rounded into the finest kind of form. For that reason, the performance of Southpaw Amole will go on record as one of the seven wonders of the national game and Manager Hanlon, of the Brooklyn team, will wonder what caused him to release a man with an arm that is capable of such deeds the day the flag falls for the long drawn-out race. While it is quite true that the Detroit men were handicapped by lack of practice and have not found their "batting eyes" as yet, it is equally true that such gilt-edged work is not expected of a pitcher, and too much credit

Richard Bak Collection

cannot be given Amole for his masterly effort of Thursday, April 19, 1900.

A more desirable day could not have been made to order than was Thursday, with its bright sunshine and balmy spring breezes, and the streets were thronged when the parade moved away from the Russell House. The players of the Detroit club, wearing their new and neat white uniforms with black trimmings, were seated on one coach, while the plain gray of the Buffalo men adorned the top of another coach. City officials and newspaper men were in carriages, while Frank McDonald's "Hot Air" club was a feature of the street display, with the little German band to assist the tin horns of the rooters in the noise making. On Woodward Avenue the Elks joined in, about 400 strong, and when the park was reached, fully an hour before the game commenced, the gates had already been thrown open and the seats were being rapidly filled.

At 1 o'clock the Bisons took the field for preliminary practice and fifteen minutes later the Tigers scampered out to their positions and did some pretty work. When the gong announced the hour for play to commence, the players of both teams marched to the plate, in company front, with Magnate Burns at the head of his team and Magnate Franklin accompanying the Bisons. At the sight of Charlie Bennett, accompanying Mayor Maybury to the home plate, the crowd could not restrain a cheer, but quickly quieted down and listened attentively to the brief address of the chief executive of the city. In a few well-chosen words, Mayor Maybury referred to the popularity of the game, the loyalty of Detroit people to their team, and the necessity of clean baseball, expressing the hope that no fault would be found with the Detroits along that line this season. The patrons were complimented on their fairness to visiting teams, and then the formality of introducing the famous catcher was gone through with.

PITCHER MAYBURY – CATCHER BENNETT

When Charlie Bennett doffed his hat, cheer after cheer was lustily given, the mayor paying a deserved and handsome tribute to the man Detroit learned to love so well in the National League days. Bennett then took his place behind the plate, and the mayor, with a new ball in his hand, started for the pitcher's slab. He wanted to pitch the short distance, but was urged to take the regular position, and that proved his undoing as a twirler. His speed was good, but he was shy on control, and after failing to pitch it within Bennett's reach in four attempts, he moved up several feet closer to the plate. The first trial from that distance was also a failure, but the sixth ball pitched went straight into Bennett's hands, and the season was officially opened. ◆

OPENING STATEMENTS

Who was the greatest Opening Day performer at The Corner? While such players as Germany Schaefer, Walt Dropo, Al Kaline and Alan Trammell all demonstrated a knack for excelling in the curtain-raiser, the most consistently brilliant Bengal was a stocky right-handed pitcher named Wabash George Mullin.

Mullin, a Toledo native, started nine of 10 openers between 1903 and 1912. As his pitching totals indicate, Mullin had an arm of rubber and a heart of oak. He completed all of his opening starts, including four extra-inning affairs, and won five of eight decisions. (A 12-inning tie in 1904 resulted in no decision.)

Burton Historical Collection

Mullin was a man of extremes. He shut out Cleveland in 1907 and Chicago in 1909, the latter a one-hitter that took 82 minutes. Between was a 12-inning loss to the Indians in 1908, in which he surrendered 20 hits but was still going strong at the end. In 1912, the 31-year-old warhorse was selected to open brand-new Navin Field. Mullin responded by going all the way in an 11-inning, 6-5 victory. And who knocked in the winning run with a single? Why, George, of course.

Mullin wasn't too shabby the rest of the schedule, either. His 29 victories in 1909 led the majors, and his 209 career wins are 12 shy of leader George (Hooks) Dauss on the Tigers' all-time list. Mullin also split six World Series decisions and pitched a no-hitter on July 4, 1912, at Navin Field. It was his 32nd birthday – a special occasion, to be sure, but no more so than Opening Day in Detroit.

Open and shut

◆ The earliest openers occurred in 1971, 1987 and 1992, all of which were played on April 6. The latest opener took place May 3, 1897, a 5-4 loss to Indianapolis.

◆ Roughly one-third of all openers were played in rain or near-freezing temperatures.

◆ The warmest opener was April 27, 1899, when Columbus topped Detroit, 4-3, on an afternoon when the temperature reached 80 degrees. Close behind were the 1941 and 1960 games, when it hit 75.

◆ The biggest slugfest was the 1901 game, when Detroit and Milwaukee combined for 27 runs and 35 hits.

◆ The Tigers' biggest blowouts were in 1993, when they hammered Oakland by 16 runs (20-4), and in 1896, when they bombed Columbus by 15 (17-2).

◆ The worst defeat pinned on the Tigers was a 10-0 thrashing at the hands of Baltimore in 1975. After being shut out only twice in their first 78 openers, the Tigers were blanked three straight times, 1974-76.

◆ There were 33 one-run games, the Tigers winning 18.

◆ Fourteen openers stretched into extra innings, the Tigers winning only two: 6-5 over Cleveland in 1912 and 3-2 over St. Louis in 1914. The 1904 game was called a 4-4 tie after 12 innings because of darkness, the only opener never played to a decision.

◆ The 1959 opener against Chicago was the longest played: 4 hours, 25 minutes. By contrast, the 1909 game – a 2-0 blanking of the White Sox – took 82 minutes.

◆ There were four 1-0 games: Tommy Bridges pitched a four-hitter against St. Louis in 1931; Hank Aguirre and Larry Sherry combined on a five-hitter against Kansas City in 1965; Milwaukee's Jim Slaton two-hit the Tigers in 1976; and three Twins pitchers shut down the Tigers on three hits in 1999.

◆ Only three players hit grand slams on Opening Day: Cleveland's Roger Maris in 1957, Dick McAuliffe in 1966 against Washington and Cecil Fielder in 1996 against Seattle. ◆

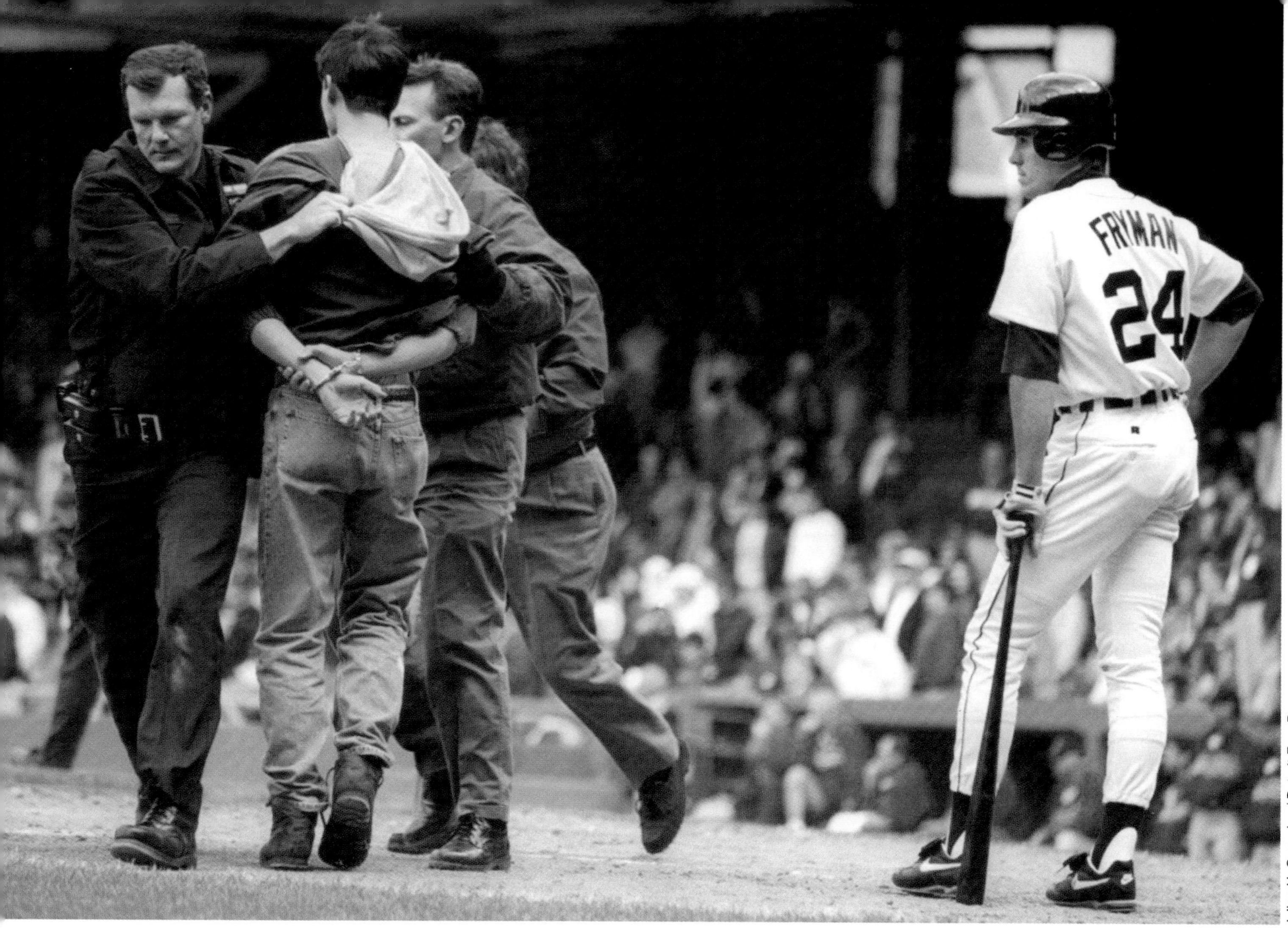

Julian H. Gonzalez / Detroit Free Press

SPANNING THE CENTURY: TRAVIS FRYMAN WAITS PATIENTLY AS AN UNRULY FAN IS CORRALLED DURING THE RAMBUNCTIOUS 1995 OPENER.

crouched in terror on the floor. "The mob did not discover where Ebright was hidden for a moment," one observer reported. "Then they gave chase. It would have fared worse with Ebright had they caught him."

(Before becoming too critical of our riotous ancestors, it should be remembered that nearly a century later, at the 1995 opener, play was continually disrupted by rowdies throwing bottles and racing onto the field. In all, 34 people were arrested, including one inebriated fellow who lumbered all the way from centerfield to make a swan dive across home plate.)

The 1900 curtain-raiser was calamitous in its own way. Buffalo's Doc Amole pitched an 8-0 decision over the home boys in their American League debut. To make matters worse, the Tigers didn't get a hit and committed seven errors.

Just to show how things can change from year to year, however, the following April the Tigers beat Milwaukee in their most rousing comeback. The American League now considered itself a major league, and the Tigers made their big-league debut a doozy, scoring 10 runs in the ninth inning, erasing a 13-4 deficit. The last-licks rally was aided by the rambunctious overflow crowd, which pressed in on the Milwaukee outfielders, resulting in several ground-rule doubles.

Pop Dillon collected four doubles, including the winner. "Dillon was the hero of the day and pandemonium broke loose when he made his last hit," the Free Press reported. "The big first baseman was almost torn to pieces by the fans, and finally he was picked up and carried around on the shoulders of some of the excited spectators."

The 1901 opener signaled the beginning of Detroit's emergence as a big-league town. Attendance picked up in the first three decades of the new century. During this period of unprecedented prosperity and population growth, Opening Day often resulted in overflows ringing the outfield and more foolhardy fans clinging from neighboring trees,

Burton Historical Collection

POP DILLON'S FOURTH DOUBLE OF THE DAY WON THE OPENER IN 1901.

rooftops and utility poles. During the Roaring '20s, attendance averaged about 34,000 per opener, a figure that didn't drop until the Great Depression of the 1930s.

The first 50,000-plus gates were recorded in the enlarged Briggs Stadium in 1938, 1946 and 1949, but World War II and the Tigers' mediocre teams of the 1950s kept attendance in the low 40,000s until 1960, when a postcard-perfect day produced a near-record crowd of 53,563. From 1961 to 1979, however, attendance again leveled off to the 40,000 range and topped 50,000 just three times.

All: Richard Bak Collection

Time out for trivia: Ray Boone homered as a Tiger in the 1954 opener; on Opening Day 1953, he homered against the Tigers while with Cleveland.

GEORGE UHLE, STAR PITCHER OF THE TIGERS, GETTING A GOOD GRIP ON A CURVE BALL

Then came the 1980s, when the Tigers fielded consistently competitive teams under manager Sparky Anderson. Even though the game was televised locally, the magical 50-grand mark was reached each opener during the decade.

The gate slumped to an average of roughly 45,000 during the gray '90s, the result of noncompetitive teams and lingering fan rancor over the labor dispute that killed the last part of the 1994 season. But as expected, the 1999 opener, promoted by the club as the last at The Corner, was a big hit.

Logistics dictated Detroit's Opening Day opponent for more than a half-century. Because of the time and expense involved in traveling by train, nearly every April from 1902 to 1961, the Tigers opened against one of three geographically convenient "Western" clubs: Cleveland, Chicago or St. Louis.

The only exceptions during this period were in 1954, when they played Baltimore, which had inherited the St. Louis franchise; and in 1956 against Kansas City, another Western club that a year earlier had moved from Philadelphia. Both openers are a treat for trivia buffs.

In 1954, Hamtramck native Steve Gromek beat Baltimore, 3-0. Nine years earlier, Gromek – then with Cleveland – pitched the Indians past Detroit, 4-1. Only four other pitchers have recorded a decision as a Tiger and a visitor on Opening Day. Rube Waddell lost the 1898 game with Detroit, then returned the following year to beat the Tigers as a member of the Columbus team. George Uhle pitched complete-game victories with Cleveland (1926) and Detroit (1930), and Orlando Pena was the loser for Kansas City in 1964 but won the 1966 contest for Detroit. Jack Morris won three of four decisions in the 1980s before winning again in 1992 as a Toronto Blue Jay.

Tigers third baseman Ray Boone added another twist of turncoat trivia when he reached the seats in the '54 opener. Having led off the previous season's opener with a homer while playing for the Indians, Boone became the first player to hit Opening Day home runs as a member of the opposition

Pitchers George Uhle (top) and Hall of Famer Rube Waddell turned similar Opening Day tricks – Uhle beat the Tigers in 1926 and was Detroit's winning pitcher in 1930; Waddell was the starter in 1898 with Detroit and the following year with Columbus. He later played for St. Louis.

MEMORIES MARK FIDRYCH

Jim Campbell was always saying, 'Mark, you've got to get better clothes'

Opening Day. That's what I'll always remember about Tiger Stadium.

I remember standing there, a rookie, getting introduced and looking around and thinking, "Wow, all the hard work that's been done, everything that I've gone through has paid off. I'm as far as I can get." And I was thinking about friends that I had played with in the minor leagues that hadn't seen this, the guys I'd been to camp with who stayed behind.

I don't think I even pitched in the month of April that first season, 1976. At that time, Joe Coleman, Dave Roberts, Vern Ruhle and Dave Lemanczyk were the starting rotation. I sat in the bullpen and watched, and I played the exhibition game against Cincinnati. Remember how they always played them? Then Joe Coleman got sick, and I got my first start.

That summer was a happy time. It was a year when I didn't want anything to change. I just wanted to pitch and play baseball.

People would say to me, "Aren't you concerned about people putting your picture on T-shirts?" And I'd say, "No, I'm not worried about that." People would say, "You're losing money," and I'd say, "No, I'm not. I've got what I want."

All that other stuff, let it slide. Once I went into a clothing store in Birmingham – Jim Campbell was always saying, "Mark, you've got to get better clothes" – well, because I'm a T-shirt freak, I walked up to this rack of T-shirts and they've all got that Big Bird logo on them. It was an iron-on thing that had run in the Free Press. The guy who owned this store bought thousands of papers for a dime apiece and ironed them on the T-shirts and was selling 'em for like $5. When he saw me, he said, "Oh, I guess I'm in trouble."

Alan R. Kamuda / Detroit Free Press

But I told him I didn't care, and he gave me a little discount on the clothes I bought.

I'll always be grateful to Detroit and to the Tiger fans. They were great to me. They still are.

I flew into Detroit once a couple of years ago and one of the luggage handlers at the airport came up to me as I was getting off the plane. He had some things for me to sign for him and for a couple of other guys, too. He thanked me for signing, but I told him, "Hey, you made my day." And I meant it. I mean, after all of these years.

I don't get to Detroit all that often, or to Tiger Stadium all that often, but I have seats there. I have for more than 20 years.

One time in 1976 my mother and father came out to a game. They'd driven out on their vacation to see me pitch, and when they got to the window and asked for the tickets for Mr. Fidrych, the guy told him somebody had already picked them up. Well, you can imagine. They corrected it quickly – I mean, the Tigers really took care of it – but in 1977 I bought four tickets behind the dugout and I've still got them.

I plan to keep them at the new stadium. ◆

Mark Fidrych was a green and hyperactive kid from Massachusetts who made magic in the summer of '76.

Courtesy Dick Clark

VISIBLE IN THE SNAPSHOT FROM THE 1946 OPENER IS THE OUTFIELD WARNING TRACK, WHICH MADE ITS FIRST APPEARANCE AT THE CORNER THAT DAY.

and as a Tiger. He later was joined by Rob Deer, who belted one in the 1989 game with Milwaukee, then clubbed homers as a Tiger in 1992-93.

Finally, the 1954 game also was notable in that it was the first time Harwell, then the radio voice of the Orioles, sat behind a microphone at The Corner. Harwell covered his first opener as the Tigers' broadcaster in 1960.

In 1956, Kansas City squeezed past Detroit, 2-1, with two seventh-inning runs off Frank Lary. Detroit's star pitcher, nicknamed "Taters," accounted for the Tigers' only tally with an inside-the-park home run. Besides Taters' rare tater, the game featured a bit of trivia that is practically guaranteed to win a bar bet: What future Dodgers manager retired Earl Torgeson for the final out, earning his only big-league save? It was Tommy Lasorda, a pudgy ex-Dodger making his American League debut.

Today, because of the glut of teams and ease of travel, it's possible for the Tigers to open the home schedule against any team from Seattle to Tampa Bay. But it wasn't until teams switched to air travel that visits from Eastern clubs like Boston and New York became convenient. In 1962, the Tigers finally opened against their bitterest rival, the Yankees.

Richard Bak Collection

TWO OF DETROIT'S GREATEST SPORTS IDOLS, JOE LOUIS AND MICKEY COCHRANE, MEET BEFORE THE 1936 OPENER.

The game, played on Friday the 13th, marked the beginning of the end of Lary's "Yankee Killer" days. Detroit won, 5-3, as Lary ran his record against the perennial champions to 28-10. Lary pitched seven

MEMORIES ERNIE HARWELL

When the mayor tried to crawl down that ladder, he dropped the cheese

We're all going to miss Tiger Stadium, but we just have to keep the old ballpark in our minds and our souls and look at it that way rather than as a building that's been knocked down.

But there are a lot of memories. Opening Days, for one thing, have always been special. It was a snowy opener in '62 when Frank Lary hit a triple against the Yankees and hurt his leg going into third base. He had to favor his arm from then on and never regained the effectiveness he once had. In '82, we had the opening series snowed out with Toronto. We had about 10 inches of snow in April, and they couldn't get it out of the stadium. And it was an Opening Day when Kirk Gibson got hit in the head by a fly ball when he was playing rightfield.

Julian H. Gonzalez / Detroit Free Press

ERNIE HARWELL AND PAUL CAREY SHARED A MIKE FOR 19 SUMMERS, BEGINNING IN 1973.

Opening Day was always a terrible day for us because we were coming into the stadium for the first time and everybody wanted something. J.P. McCarthy did his show down on the field and in our booth, and most of the time we hardly got into the booth until the first pitch. It was just such a mess and there were so many things that could go wrong.

The broadcast booth is like home, and the view has always been great. People who come in from out of town love the view. The booth is closer to the field than in any other park except old Griffith Stadium in Washington.

We had the mayor of Chesaning come down one time. To get to the old booth – before they rebuilt it after that fire in the '70s – you had to crawl down a ladder. The booth was hung from the upper deck between home and first and had a slanting roof. That day an usher came down and said, "The mayor has a wheel of cheese he wants to present to you and George Kell."

Well, when the mayor tried to crawl down that ladder, he dropped the cheese on the slanted roof and it went right down into the box seats and almost hit an 8-year-old kid. It hit the concrete and flew all over the place. You know those big cheese wheels – they're heavy. It would've killed that kid if it had hit him.

One of the worst things that happened was around 1972. We had a Friday night game with the California Angels, and it was raining. We got a phone call from Hal Middlesworth, the publicity director, and he said, "If the game's called, we'll have a doubleheader Saturday. But don't announce it until you hear from me."

So Stits (engineer Howard Stitzel) and Ray Lane and I were in the booth when we heard this voice on the intercom: "Game postponed; doubleheader Saturday." So I put it on the air.

My wife, Lulu, came to the game and we were going to hear a friend sing in Plymouth. As we were going out of the ballpark, I noticed a lot of people weren't leaving. I figured that was kind of strange but thought they just didn't want to get wet. So we went out and got on the expressway and tuned into Ray Lane doing the postgame show, giving the scores.

All of a sudden he said, "Wait a minute, folks, that announcement Ernie made wasn't right. The game is still on. Ernie! Ernie! Wherever you are, come on back." So I turned around and came back to the booth and we did the game. ◆

Ernie Harwell has been calling games at The Corner since 1954.

strong innings, but was forced out of the game after legging out a triple.

"There was rain and sleet," he said. "I remember hitting the ball, and as I was rounding first base, I could feel the mud sticking to my shoes. I ended up pulling a leg muscle. As a pitcher, when you have an injury like that, it's possible that you favor it and do something to your delivery."

Lary's leg injury caused him to alter his pitching motion, leading to a series of arm and shoulder problems that forced him to retire.

Lary, living in his native Alabama, maintained his sense of humor about his Opening Day hitting exploits. "I led the American League in home runs that year," he said of the '56 dinger, "for about 10 minutes."

Speaking of dingers: The ball hasn't always jumped out of the park on Opening Day. In fact, between 1897 and 1910 – a span of 14 openers – neither the home team nor the visitors hit a round-tripper. And it wasn't until Chicago's Oscar (Happy) Felsch touched them all in 1916 that an opposing player homered.

The slugging has picked up considerably since those dead-ball days of yore, however, with Al Kaline accounting for five Opening Day shots. Deer, Norm Cash, Johnny Groth and Cleveland's Ken Keltner are the only others to hit as many as three round-trippers. For the record, Cleveland's Roger Maris hit the first grand slam in 1957, followed by Detroit's Dick McAuliffe in 1966 and Cecil Fielder in 1996.

Tony Spina / Detroit Free Press

The downside to having played 104 openers at The Corner is trying to compile a short list of the most memorable games. Certainly the 1993 annihilation of Oakland has to be included. Three-run homers by Deer, Travis Fryman and Mickey Tettleton helped the Tigers build a 16-4 cushion after four innings. Fielder had four singles and Fryman five RBIs in the 20-4 thrashing.

Many are partial to the 1960 game, which had all the elements of a classic day at the park: a packed house, shirtsleeve weather and a dramatic ending. Lou Berberet capped a perfect afternoon by spanking a two-out, bases-loaded single in the ninth, driving in the winning run in a 6-5 victory over Chicago. Newly acquired Rocky Colavito homered in his first at-bat and received a standing ovation when he took his outfield position.

This was revenge for the previous year's opener between the same teams. The light-hitting "Go-Go" Sox, on their way to an unexpected pennant, edged the Tigers, 9-7, on a rare home run by Nellie Fox in the 14th inning off Don Mossi. This came after Charlie Maxwell's pinch-hit, three-run homer in the eighth knotted the score at 7. The marathon lasted four hours, 25 minutes, saw 43 players used, and fell one inning short of the big-league record for the longest opener.

Old-timers can recollect the 1937 game

Richard Bak Collection

Al Kaline hit five Opening Day homers, more than anyone.

Sparky Anderson, who replaced Les Moss as manager during the '79 season, basked in Opening Day sunshine at The Corner for the first time in 1980. The Tigers lost to Kansas City that day but won 10 of the next 15 home openers during Anderson's tenure.

against Cleveland, when the aging and slow-footed Goose Goslin, never known for his defense, made a spectacular outfield catch with two on in the eighth inning, preserving a 4-3 victory. It was practically a replay of the 1929 game against the Indians, when centerfielder Harry Rice made a diving, game-ending catch with the tying run on third base.

There's a dwindling handful who can recall Ty Cobb single-handedly taking over the 1914 opener against St. Louis. Asked to name the pitcher who gave him the most trouble in his career, Cobb always said Carl Weilman. On this day, however, Cobb tagged the Browns' starter for a two-run triple in the 13th inning after St. Louis had broken a scoreless tie with two runs in the top of the inning. Cobb then roared home with the winning run on Bobby Veach's fly ball to center.

Of more recent vintage was the 5-1 victory over Texas, kicking off the 1984 home schedule. Detroit improved to 6-0 as it exploded for four first-inning runs. Free-agent acquisition Darrell Evans slammed a three-run home run off Dave Stewart in his first Tiger Stadium at-bat. Dan Petry pitched a four-hitter for the win, part of the Tigers' torrid 35-5 start to their championship season.

Evans always prized this day.

"There was so much expected because I was one of the first free agents the Tigers really went after," he recalled. "I hit a home run the first time up and, wow, I mean, you couldn't have a better script than that.

"It was just an instant feel-good place."

Another Evans home run – this one by Boston's Dwight Evans – made the 1986 opener unique. Evans smacked Morris' first pitch of the season into the centerfield seats. However, Evans' unprecedented blast was outdone by Kirk Gibson's heroics. Gibby cracked two-run homers in the fifth and seventh innings, the last giving the Tigers a 6-5 lead they never relinquished. He finished 4-for-4, with five RBIs and a stolen base.

In 1972, a two-week players strike forced the Tigers to open on a Saturday for the first time since Navin Field was dedicated in 1912. Only 31,510 fans showed up. Light-hitting Eddie Brinkman got them on their feet early with a two-run homer before Freehan's single scored Cash with the winning run in the seventh. The 3-2 victory proved more significant than it seemed at the time. Had the score been reversed, the Red Sox – not the Tigers – would have wound up winning the American League East by a half-game.

In the 1978 opener, Mark Fidrych demonstrated to worried fans that he had bounced back, at least for a day, from the arm problems that were threatening his livelihood. On a warm and pleasant afternoon, the mop-topped folk hero spun a five-hitter in a 6-2 victory over Toronto. Alan Trammell and Lou Whitaker made their first Opening Day starts, and Jason Thompson reached the rightfield roof with a long homer.

Afterward, the biggest crowd in seven years rocked the stadium with the familiar chant, "We want the Bird!" Fidrych bounded out of the dugout, giving the gathered faithful one of the last curtain calls of his brief, storied career.

Harwell, who has witnessed some 40 openers at The Corner, has trouble sorting them all out. In any event, he has always insisted that every baseball game, no matter where it falls on the schedule, is unique.

He has no problem choosing his favorite Opening Day yarn, though. It dates back many years, when Rick Ferrell was the general manager.

Ferrell was leaving the park after the Tigers lost their opener when he bumped into a close friend. The fellow knew nothing about baseball, but like many sunshine patriots, he'd come down to The Corner to make his annual appearance.

Noticing Ferrell's hangdog expression, he did his best to cheer him.

"Don't worry about it, Rick," he said with an encouraging slap on the back. "We'll get 'em next year." ◆

Julian H. Gonzalez / Detroit Free Press

Kirthmon F. Dozier / Detroit Free Press

OPENING DAY: APRIL 12, 1999

THE LAST HELLO

BY MITCH ALBOM

It was like climbing to the tree house one last time. Through the narrow turnstiles and dimly lit corridors, then up into the sunlight – like straddling a big branch with your feet dangling happily. That's the feeling. A ballpark in springtime always makes you young.

Which brings us to the strange juxtaposition of the final opener at The Corner. How, in one day, can you feel both youthful and ancient? How do you say hello and good-bye? Normally, Opening Day in Detroit is all about firsts. The first home game. The first rush of summer. The first bleacher hot dog. This time, it was also about lasts. Fans stood in the aisles, soaking in the view as if watching a loved one board an airplane. There will be no more Opening Days at Michigan and Trumbull.

"I remember the first time I saw this place," said Lance Parrish, sighing. Parrish, who played at The Corner for a decade, won a World Series and is a Tigers coach. "To be honest, I was disappointed. I had grown up in southern California, with Dodger Stadium and places like that. So

"OPENING DAY IN DETROIT IS AN EVENT," ERNIE HARWELL ONCE SAID. "IT'S NEW YEAR'S, EASTER AND CHRISTMAS ALL ROLLED INTO ONE UNIQUE AFTERNOON." IN 1999, DETROITERS CONVERGED ON THE CORNER FOR THE FINAL OPENER, ALTHOUGH NOT EVERY FAN WAS THERE FOR THE FINISH.

Julian H. Gonzalez / Detroit Free Press

Both: Julian H. Gonzalez / Detroit Free Press

WILLIE BLAIR STARTED THE FINAL HOME OPENER AND PITCHED EIGHT STRONG INNINGS. TEAMMATE DOUG BROCAIL (ABOVE) PITCHED WELL IN RELIEF BUT WAS TRYING NOT TO WATCH FROM THE SIDELINES WHEN THE TWINS SCORED THE GAME'S ONLY RUN IN THE 12TH.

when the cab driver came off the highway, I said, 'Where's Tiger Stadium?' And he said, 'It's right there.'

"And I said, 'Where?'

"And he pointed at it, and I thought, 'That's it? It looks like a warehouse!' "

He laughed. "But that all left the moment I stepped inside. Inside this place" – he motioned around him – "inside this place, there's nothing like it."

The Tigers, especially the new ones, may not understand why Opening Day 1999 was less about them than it was about their house. But it takes time to make memories with a team. A stadium, one that has been around since 1912, one that has housed World Series champions and All-Star games, a single deck, then a double deck, an open outfield, then an enclosed outfield with seats for 23,000, then 36,000, then 53,000; performances by names like Cobb, Greenberg, Ruth, Gehrig, DiMaggio, Jackson, Gibson, Clemens; a stadium that has been visited by grandparents and their grandchildren who, in turn, come with grandchildren of their own – a stadium like that, well, the memories are already there.

And every spring we are beckoned inside to strum those memories, to remind us where we came from. Now that is ending. The Ballpark of the Century. The oldest stadium in major league baseball. Time to say good-bye.

"The first time I saw this place was a picture," said Dan Petry, who arrived in 1979 and pitched for the Tigers through most of the next decade. "I was signed as a kid in California, and the scout gave me a program with a picture of Tiger Stadium in the front, and he said, 'This is your goal now. To get here. Look at this picture and dream about it.' "

How many of us can relate, in a distant way, to that story? How many children over the years have taken the image of Tiger Stadium's green grass and blue walls and dreamed about it? Striding out onto the pitcher's mound, blowing a fastball past Ruth, Aaron or McGwire? Or maybe coming to bat in the bottom of the ninth and taking a fastball from Whitey Ford or Jim Palmer, walloping it over the leftfield wall? How many of us have imagined ourselves trotting around the bases? No matter what position, or what era, always the backdrop was Tiger Stadium. Our field of dreams.

"No field like this one," mused Gates Brown of the 1968 championship team as he shook his head and smiled. "I remember the first day I got here. I took one look at that short rightfield fence and started smiling."

He smiled again. "Yep, no field like Tiger Stadium."

It wasn't always Tiger Stadium, of course. Back in 1896, they had a wooden structure called Bennett Park, built on the site of an old haymarket. Someone constructed illegal bleachers across the street, and people climbed up to peer in at the action.

In 1912, after razing Bennett Park, they built Navin Field, named after the owner, Frank Navin. The Tigers played their first game there the same week the Titanic sunk. Over the years, there were construction additions, and additions made to those additions. New owners took over from old owners, and new names were attached. New colors. New seats. New food plazas. Still the same old place. A century's worth of baseball at the intersection of two streets.

"You know the part I liked the most about this building?" Petry asked. "After I pitched a good game, I would walk to my car by cutting across the field. It would be an hour or so after the game, and the stadium would be completely empty. I would look up and say to myself, 'Just an hour ago, this place was filled, and there were so many people and they were all cheering.' And now it was so quiet. I never got over that. It was such a great feeling."

A church. A workplace.

The Ballpark of the Century.

As the final season goes on, more and more fans will come to say so long. They will point to a row of seats and tell of the day their dad took them out of school to see a game, or the day they sneaked in through the back gate, or the day they caught that foul ball. And, of course, it will build up to the day the Tigers leave for good, their final home game, Sept. 27, 1999. That will be the last good-bye.

April 12, 1999, was the last hello. And the building that has been called everything from heaven's playground to a rusty girder welcomed the snow-melted crowd on a sunny day, making everyone feel young again. No, the Tigers didn't win. They fell, 1-0, in 12 innings to the Minnesota Twins. But this day was less about the scorecard than the ticket.

"Do you still have that program, the one with the picture on it?" Petry was asked.

"Oh yeah, somewhere up in the attic," he said. "You would never throw away something like that."

The same goes for our memories. We will move on to a new Opening Day at a new stadium, at a new site. But we will never throw this away. It will always be with us, in our hearts, in our heads, in the ticket stubs we save in our scrapbooks.

The Ballpark of the Century. Detroit's field of dreams. ◆

Mitch Albom is a Free Press columnist.

Kirthmon F. Dozier / Detroit Free Press

IT WAS A DAY FOR FANS TO HAVE THEIR PICTURES TAKEN, TO TAKE PICTURES AND EVEN TO WAVE A PICTURE, THIS ONE OF LANCE PARRISH, A FAVORITE SINCE THE '80S AND A MEMBER OF THE TIGERS '99 COACHING STAFF.

All: Pauline Lubens / Detroit Free Press

THE FINAL OPENER

FROM DAWN TILL DUSK

By NICHOLAS J. COTSONIKA

7:17 a.m. Silence. Still early yet. Outside, the streets were mostly empty. Inside, leftfield was covered with a huge plastic tarp that had been dragged off the infield.

"All right!" yelled Ed Goward. "Bring it over!"

As Goward's voice echoed in the emptiness, the grounds crew pulled the tarp back over the infield, smoothing it out. That done, Goward yelled once again.

"All right! Bring it back!"

The workers folded the tarp in half, then walked over it to coax out the air. No one spoke but Goward, a 30-year veteran of the grounds crew. All that could be heard was a bird chirping in the rafters and the hum of electrical transformers.

"All right! All together! Let's roll it!"

The crew rolled the tarp in shallow leftfield like a big burrito, pushing it to the wall until nothing was left but the green grass and the brown dirt.

Near home plate, Heather Nabozny began pulling the stakes out of a smaller tarp. She had been waiting for this day. The field was hers. A Milford native and Michigan State grad, she is thought to be the first female head groundskeeper in the modern history of big-league baseball.

"This is very special," said Nabozny, who replaced Frank Feneck after the 1998 season, when he retired after 35 years with the Tigers. "A lot of hard work went into building up to this."

She looked around. "There's a buzz here," she said.

She looked up and laughed. "You know what the best part about this day is?" Nabozny said. "It's not raining."

7:34 a.m. The clubhouse was quiet. All the Tigers' white jerseys hung in their lockers, numbers facing out. All the shined shoes were in neat rows, as were the crisp, new home caps, lined up on a table in the middle of the room.

A phone rang, but no one answered.

"Anyone here?" a visitor asked.

"Yeah," someone said.

"Where are you?"

"Up here."

Jeremy Kelch, a 22-year-old clubhouse attendant from

Anticipation: Nine-year-old Chris Withorn waits for the gates to open on the final Opening Day; the uniforms are ready and, on the facing page, grounds crew member Gary DeMilde makes sure the field is ready too.

North Branch, poked his head out of the tiny attic where the Tigers store equipment. He threw a couple of bags to the floor, then climbed down the ladder.

About 11 the night before, the team's equipment had arrived from New York. Kelch helped unpack it, did laundry, then went to bed. In the clubhouse. He just rolled a cot into the middle of the room and crashed.

"Every boy's dream bedroom," he said. "It's like a big suite at a hotel."

Clubhouse manager Jim Schmakel slept there, too, with his 13-year-old son, Jay. He threw a mattress onto the floor in the clubhouse. Jay stayed in a storage room, snug in a sleeping bag, which he shoved underneath uniforms hanging on hooks and behind boxes of baseballs, T-shirts and shaving cream.

Both: Pauline Lubens / Detroit Free Press

"I LOVE THIS PLACE," SAYS BLANCHE HEIDER, REPORTING FOR WORK. AND FANS LOVE ALAN TRAMMELL, DOING HIS JOB BY OBLIGING COUNTLESS AUTOGRAPH SEEKERS.

Jim Schmakel looked around the room, then pointed to his locker. "That's my office," he said. Schmakel was the last clubhouse manager in baseball without a desk to call his own, and the Tigers were the last team to store stuff in an attic. After 22 years at Tiger Stadium, Schmakel won't miss it much.

"It's just time," he said.

8:26 a.m. A gray Grand Marquis stopped on Michigan Avenue, and out stepped Blanche Heider, reporting for work at Tiger Stadium for the 21st consecutive year. She sells hot dogs proudly; she wears makeup, complete with bright red lipstick. Her gray hair is permed.

"How old are you?" someone asked.

"I'm 77."

"You can't possibly be 77."

"Oh," she said after punching in, "when you work here, you look like this."

Heider loves baseball. Her husband, Joe, drops her off before every home game and picks her up afterward.

"I love this place," she said. "Why would I work anywhere else?"

8:38 a.m. Marvin Wells, 75, wiped off the counter of his souvenir stand, beneath the stands down the rightfield line. He began working at The Corner in 1970 and always made it a point to get there early.

"Got to," said Wells, a retired post office worker. "Fans'll be here soon. We start early. We leave late."

Wells, who grew up on the east side of Detroit, came to his first game in 1937 with his father. He had Lions season tickets when they played at The Corner.

He looked at the souvenir T-shirts hanging on his stand, the ones celebrating Tiger Stadium's final season, and he sighed. "It has a lot of history, this place," he said. "It's a nice place. These old ones, you hate to see 'em go. But then" – he tugged on his Tigers cap – "that's progress."

9:06 a.m. Alan Trammell came racing ahead, running in full uniform, with his jacket on his back and his glove on his hand. But he wasn't on the field. He was in the concourse.

Comerica, the bank that paid millions to have its name on the new park, wanted a picture with Trammell next to one of its ATMs. Trammell obliged, meeting a group of bank executives with a smile and the greeting, "Hi! I'm Alan Trammell!"

He had to be a good sport. A photographer asked him to pose in several silly ways. He held his glove under the machine, where the money would spurt out. He joined hands with the suits in a let's-go-team pose.

But he never frowned, never winced. And he always had his mind on business. After the photo-op, Trammell – once a star, now a hitting coach – turned to everyone and asked, "You guys staying for the game?"

9:51 a.m. Already, Kale Dipert had 35 autographs for the day. Bobby Higginson. Dean Palmer. Justin Thompson. Gabe Kapler. Others. But he wanted more. He doesn't have a collection 4,000 strong because he's timid.

Kale, 24, stood on the curb of Michigan Avenue near the visitors clubhouse entrance with his father, Dave, as they had for nearly 20 years. They don't have season tickets, and they live in Nashville, near Grand Rapids. Still, they come to about 40 games a season.

And they weren't going to miss this. "We go to every Opening Day," said Dave, 47. "It is emotional for me. We love Tiger Stadium. There are so many great memories here for us."

In 1997, Kale snagged Mark McGwire's bat. McGwire was appearing for the final time at The Corner with the Oakland Athletics, and as he left the on-deck circle during batting practice, he stuck his bat behind his back for a fan to grab. Kale was waiting.

"I got it autographed the next day," he said. "It's the prize of my collection. I don't sell anything I get. I just do it because I love the game of baseball."

Dave, wearing a Tigers cap like his son and holding two gloves and a radio, began telling more stories as Kale went off to chase arriving Minnesota Twins. After all these years, going to Tiger Stadium is still exciting, he said. Just then, his son came back, grinning and shouting.

"I got Marty Cordova!"

10:29 a.m. The stands were still empty, but the Tigers had emerged. Higginson, Palmer and Frank Catalanotto played catch in leftfield. Batting practice screens were in place. Kapler, a rookie, wandered wide-eyed through the media horde.

11:00 a.m. And the gates opened. Fans streamed in, screaming, lunging and trying to be first through the turnstiles.

At Gate 2, closest to Michigan and Trumbull, 63-year-old Ron Miller squeezed through the crowd. Though a lifelong Tigers fan, he was attending his first home opener. He car-

ried a handheld video recorder, pressed a button and scanned the stands. He was standing in the first row down the rightfield line.

"I want to get this," said Miller, a retired Detroit Edison worker from Warren. "You're so close. The players are right there. And memories. There are so many memories."

Miller played at Tiger Stadium once. In 1954, he was a second baseman for St. Joseph's High in Detroit when the school advanced to the Catholic League title game. Years later, his son, Michael, also played at The Corner for Harper Woods Notre Dame. In 1968, when the Tigers won the World Series in St. Louis, Ron Miller was watching on television when Bill Freehan ended Game 7 by catching a foul pop-up. Miller drove straight to The Corner, cruising around with his wife and infant son, enjoying the atmosphere.

Miller said he liked to think about those days while sitting in a reserved seat, away from the crowd. He said he liked it when the park wasn't crowded, when he could put his feet up. Miller put his camera down as he talked, then looked out at the field with soft eyes.

"My dad brought me here," he said.

11:36 a.m. Trammell stood on the steps of the dugout, having finished a barrage of interviews, when fans started yelling for him. They wanted his autograph.

"All right," he said. "Real quick."

Trammell grabbed a newspaper and signed it, but then he had to go. He apologized.

"I've got a job to do, guys," he said, as fans continued to beg. "We've got to have a meeting. We want to win for you."

In a flash, he was gone. But he was back later.

With a pen.

11:40 a.m. American League president Gene Budig stood on the grass near the Tigers' dugout and pointed toward the outfield. "Joe DiMaggio played here," he said. "Ted Williams played here. Hal Newhouser pitched out there."

Budig stared at the field. "It's a privilege to be here," he said. "Tiger Stadium is a historic facility. It has seen baseball's best over the years. It's hard to believe this facility opened in 1912 – the same year the Titanic went down. This, in many ways, is a monument. I hope this summer people can take special pride in what has transpired here. I would hope they would remember not only the very good people of the Detroit Tigers but also those of other American League clubs. The very best were here."

12:05 p.m. Mike Reilly of Battle Creek and Tim Welke of Coldwater stood outside the Tigers' clubhouse before the game. They are umpires. They can take booing and arguing and dirt-kicking. But when it comes to The Corner, they have feelings, too.

"I worked my first World Series here in 1984," Reilly said.

Pauline Lubens / Detroit Free Press

FANS, ONE BY ONE, ADDED UP TO 47,449 FOR THE FINAL OPENER.

FOR MANY, JUST ONE MORE AUTOGRAPH WOULD MAKE THE DAY COMPLETE.

Kirthmon F. Dozier / Detroit Free Press

"To have it in your home state, that was a big thrill for me because my parents could be here, and all my brothers. Tiger Stadium is a great ballpark."

Welke nodded knowingly.

"I can remember coming down once or twice a year on the Little League bus and sitting out in the leftfield stands," he said. "My mom always had the radio on growing up, and Ernie Harwell was always on the radio. When I think of Tiger Stadium, that's what I think of. It's a beautiful place. It's one of our favorite places to work."

12:40 p.m. The players were introduced to rousing ovations. Each stepped out of the dugout, jogged to the foul line and stood still. Only one wore a glove. As a tribute, reliever Todd Jones wore the one Al Kaline used in his final game in 1974. There were other festivities, too.

The 1984 World Series champions were honored. The Mosaic Youth Theatre, a nationally known troupe from Detroit, sang the national anthem. The state Senate made a presentation to Harwell, the Tigers' Hall of Fame broadcaster, The Voice. Mayor Dennis Archer and Gov. John Engler threw out the ceremonial first pitches. A thunderous threesome of military aircraft flew overhead. Only one thing remained: the game.

1:04 p.m. Tigers starter Willie Blair threw the first pitch to the Minnesota Twins' Torii Hunter. It was a ball. Outside.

2:58 p.m. In every crowd of 47,449 people, there are a few fools. With two out in the top of the eighth inning, a fan ran across the outfield and into the arms of security officers. Later, copycats appeared. One bare-chested individual even slid headfirst into second base and touched third with his foot before being apprehended. All were booed.

3:28 p.m. With the game scoreless, Damion Easley struck out, ending the ninth with a runner on third, wasting an opportunity for a dramatic finish. The crowd groaned.

4:17 p.m. The Twins' Todd Walker, who already had two doubles, hit a 3-2 pitch from Sean Runyan into the upper deck in rightfield with none out in the top of the 12th. The ball landed on the ramp leading to Section 437. It bounced around and fell into the lower deck, where John Poplawski, 60, of Grosse Pointe retrieved it from the seat in front of him.

"I looked down, and I saw red and white," said Poplawski, who got the ball signed by Walker. "Of course, I'll go across the street to the bar, and they won't believe me."

4:37 p.m. Tony Clark grounded out to shortstop, ending the game. The Tigers lost, 1-0. The fans shuffled out silently. The players, who lost their sixth straight, did the same.

5:15 p.m. The men who rolled out the tarp at daybreak were back on the field, raking the mound and the plate area, hosing down the dugout steps, carrying dirt in wheelbarrows. The clubhouse guys started the laundry.

Shadows crept across the grass. Trash sat still in the stands. Bunting hung limply on the overhangs. Reporters clicked away on computers in the press box and talked into cameras on the field. Music blared from postgame parties at Nemo's and Hoot's and Shelley's. Pigeons returned to roost in the rafters. Seagulls swirled.

Dusk was orange … like a tiger. ◆

Nicholas J. Cotsonika is a Free Press sports writer.

YEARBOOK

OPENING DAY FACES '99

PHOTOS BY
J. KYLE KEENER

STORIES BY
GEORGEA KOVANIS

The newcomer

JADE GREEN'S first Tigers game included popcorn, a hot dog and pink lemonade. His dad, Patrick, went to his first game when he was a Cub Scout and remembers how excited he felt. So when his boss gave him tickets to the opener, Patrick thought immediately of Jade. "I think he'll be a fan after he's got the first game under his belt," Dad said. For Jade, the only thing missing was Sidney, the family's golden retriever. Jade had hoped the dog would be able to attend the game, too.

MAGGIE BANTA made the vow from her bleacher seat: " 'The Farewell to Tiger Stadium Shrine' will go up in the basement." She plans to save her ticket stub and her program booklet from the game. She might also frame the Tigers jersey she customized with an iron-on reading, "Opening Day, April 12, 1999, The Farewell Season." She adjusted her sunglasses and said, "I can't imagine that next year we're not going to be here."

HELENE SMITH usually spends about 10 minutes applying her makeup – mascara, eye shadow, a little blush and, if she remembers, lipstick. But for the opener, as she has done for important games since 1980, she spent close to an hour doing her thing. And when she was finished, her face was covered in shiny gold paint and accented with black painted-on whiskers, a white mouth and tiger stripes. "I had to take my daughter into day care. The teacher said, 'Are you going anywhere special today?' " Smith assured the teacher she was indeed headed someplace special.

The legacy

DENNY KAPP'S mother, Joyce, started wearing the tiger suit in 1984. Twelve years later, she passed it down to Denny, who had finally grown tall enough to wear it well. As for giving it up, Joyce said, "It didn't bother me, as long as it stayed in the family." Denny only wears the suit for the opener. "You want to save it for special occasions," he said. "You don't want to wear out a good thing."

The old-timer

CURTIS COOPER has been to three straight openers – not bad for a 4-year-old. "He really started begging me when he saw the Tiger game on TV last week," said Curtis Cooper Sr., who works midnights and slept for only a couple hours before taking his son – who wore a brand new Tigers jersey – to the game. "He seemed excited."

The entrepreneur

HAROLD TROSPER said he should be resting because he's undergoing treatment for prostate cancer. But soon after 9 a.m on Opening Day, there he was, in the lots he owns near Tiger Stadium, parking cars as he has for 25 years. "After this season, it's all over with," he said. "I was ready to quit. I'm 79 years old. I'm going to take it easy." Then he hurried back to work. "I got to go over there – they park a mile away from each other."

The chaperone

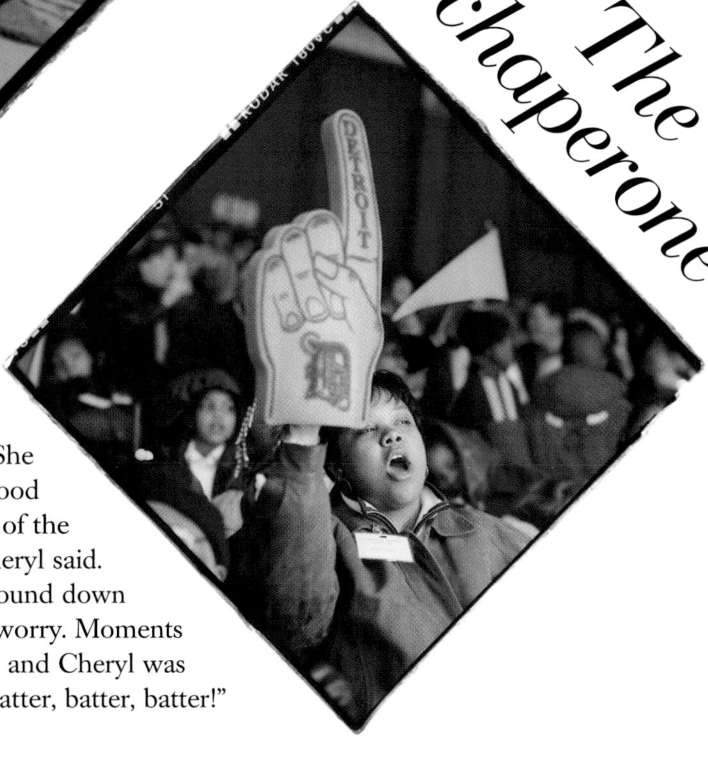

CHERYL SHORT was recruited to go along on her daughter's field trip. She and daughter Shana reported having a good time, but there was a crisis with another of the students. "One of my girls threw up," Cheryl said. "She had a hot dog. She was jumping around down here. I think she got shaken up." Not to worry. Moments later the stricken girl was asking for pop, and Cheryl was leading the students in chants of "Hey, batter, batter, batter!"

ROGER CROUSE said, "My whole thing in life is, I try to be a little bit different," which explains his choice of headgear – a blue balloon fashioned into a crown and topped with an orange balloon in the shape of a tiger. "The truth," a pal said, "is his friends bought it for him because they said, 'What will make Roger look the most ridiculous?' " Roger responded, triumphantly, "I can be a bigger fool than anyone!"

GLORIA GREGORY said she would feel odd if she didn't wear at least one piece of Tigers paraphernalia to the ballpark. So she sat in the upper deck wearing an orange and blue warm-up suit, a sweatshirt commemorating the old stadium, a blue turtleneck with an old English D on the neck and a hat festooned with commemorative Tigers pins. "I knew it was going to be cold," she said. "I layered up."

KEEPING SCORE ◆ HOME OPENERS SINCE 1896

DATE	RESULT	ATTENDANCE
1999 (April 12)	Minnesota 1, Detroit 0 (12 inn.)	47,449
1998 (April 7)	Detroit 3, Tampa Bay 1	45,768
1997 (April 7)	Detroit 10, Minnesota 4	42,749
1996 (April 9)	Detroit 10, Seattle 9	42,932
1995 (May 2)	Cleveland 11, Detroit 1	39,398
1994 (April 11)	Baltimore 7, Detroit 4	50,314
1993 (April 13)	Detroit 20, Oakland 4	49,674
1992 (April 6)	Toronto 4, Detroit 2	51,068
1991 (April 8)	Detroit 6, New York 4	47,382
1990 (April 12)	Detroit 11, Boston 7	44,906
1989 (April 7)	Detroit 10, Milwaukee 3	51,473
1988 (April 12)	Detroit 4, Texas 1	51,504
1987 (April 6)	New York 2, Detroit 1 (10 inn.)	51,315
1986 (April 7)	Detroit 6, Boston 5	51,437
1985 (April 8)	Detroit 5, Cleveland 4	51,180
1984 (April 10)	Detroit 5, Texas 1	51,238
1983 (April 8)	Chicago 6, Detroit 3	51,350
1982 (April 15)	Detroit 4, Toronto 2	51,038
1981 (April 9)	Detroit 6, Toronto 2	51,452
1980 (April 18)	Kansas City 9, Detroit 6 (11 inn.)	50,687
1979 (April 7)	Texas 8, Detroit 2	43,708
1978 (April 7)	Detroit 6, Toronto 2	52,528
1977 (April 7)	Kansas City 7, Detroit 4	46,807
1976 (April 13)	Milwaukee 1, Detroit 0	48,612
1975 (April 10)	Baltimore 10, Detroit 0	40,139
1974 (April 9)	New York 3, Detroit 0	44,047
1973 (April 11)	Baltimore 3, Detroit 1 (12 inn.)	46,389
1972 (April 15)	Detroit 3, Boston 2	31,510
1971 (April 6)	Detroit 8, Cleveland 2	54,089
1970 (April 14)	Detroit 12, Cleveland 4	46,819
1969 (April 8)	Detroit 6, Cleveland 2	53,572
1968 (April 10)	Boston 7, Detroit 3	41,429
1967 (April 18)	Detroit 4, California 1	33,211
1966 (April 15)	Detroit 8, Washington 3	36,674
1965 (April 21)	Detroit 1, Kansas City 0	32,658
1964 (April 14)	Detroit 7, Kansas City 3	35,733
1963 (April 10)	Chicago 7, Detroit 3	37,781
1962 (April 13)	Detroit 5, New York 3	29,411
1961 (April 11)	Cleveland 9, Detroit 5	41,643
1960 (April 22)	Detroit 6, Chicago 5	53,563
1959 (April 10)	Chicago 9, Detroit 7 (14 inn.)	38,322
1958 (April 18)	Cleveland 7, Detroit 5	46,698
1957 (April 18)	Cleveland 8, Detroit 3 (11 inn.)	31,227
1956 (April 18)	Kansas City 2, Detroit 1	40,037
1955 (April 14)	Cleveland 5, Detroit 3	42,684
1954 (April 13)	Detroit 3, Baltimore 0	46,994
1953 (April 16)	Cleveland 11, Detroit 8	25,253
1952 (April 15)	St. Louis 3, Detroit 0	43,112
1951 (April 17)	Cleveland 2, Detroit 1	43,470
1950 (April 21)	Detroit 4, Chicago 1	44,642
1949 (April 19)	Detroit 5, Chicago 1	53,485
1948 (April 23)	Cleveland 8, Detroit 2	45,233

DATE	RESULT	ATTENDANCE
1947 (April 18)	Detroit 2, Cleveland 0	46,111
1946 (April 16)	Detroit 2, St. Louis 1	52,118
1945 (April 20)	Cleveland 4, Detroit 1	28,357
1944 (April 18)	St. Louis 2, Detroit 1	26,034
1943 (April 28)	Detroit 4, St. Louis 2	17,943
1942 (April 14)	Cleveland 5, Detroit 2	39,267
1941 (April 18)	Detroit 4, Cleveland 2	42,165
1940 (April 16)	St. Louis 5, Detroit 1	49,417
1939 (April 18)	Detroit 6, Chicago 1	47,000
1938 (April 22)	Cleveland 4, Detroit 3	54,500
1937 (April 20)	Detroit 4, Cleveland 3	38,200
1936 (April 17)	Chicago 5, Detroit 3	32,175
1935 (April 17)	Chicago 7, Detroit 6	24,000
1934 (April 24)	Detroit 7, Chicago 3	24,000
1933 (April 12)	Cleveland 4, Detroit 1 (13 inn.)	19,000
1932 (April 13)	Cleveland 6, Detroit 5 (11 inn.)	10,000
1931 (April 23)	Detroit 1, St. Louis 0	20,520
1930 (April 15)	Detroit 6, St. Louis 3	26,125
1929 (April 24)	Detroit 7, Cleveland 6	30,000
1928 (April 11)	St. Louis 4, Detroit 1	33,000
1927 (April 20)	Detroit 7, St. Louis 0	33,971
1926 (April 13)	Cleveland 2, Detroit 1	36,565
1925 (April 14)	Detroit 4, Chicago 3	34,000
1924 (April 15)	Detroit 4, Cleveland 3	35,000
1923 (April 26)	St. Louis 4, Detroit 3	36,000
1922 (April 20)	Cleveland 5, Detroit 4	23,000
1921 (April 14)	Detroit 6, Chicago 5	23,000
1920 (April 22)	Chicago 8, Detroit 2	25,216
1919 (April 25)	Detroit 4, Cleveland 2	9,000
1918 (April 24)	Detroit 5, Cleveland 2	15,624
1917 (April 11)	Cleveland 6, Detroit 4	25,884
1916 (April 20)	Detroit 2, Chicago 1	20,760
1915 (April 14)	Cleveland 5, Detroit 1	19,893
1914 (April 14)	Detroit 3, St. Louis 2 (13 inn.)	20,143
1913 (April 17)	Detroit 4, St. Louis 3	16,579
1912 (April 20)	Detroit 6, Cleveland 5 (11 inn.)	24,384
1911 (April 13)	Detroit 4, Chicago 2	5,107
1910 (April 14)	Cleveland 9, Detroit 7 (10 inn.)	14,203
1909 (April 14)	Detroit 2, Cleveland 0	11,514
1908 (April 17)	Cleveland 12, Detroit 8 (12 inn.)	14,051
1907 (April 11)	Detroit 2, Cleveland 0	6,322
1906 (April 17)	Chicago 5, Detroit 3	13,875
1905 (April 19)	Detroit 3, Chicago 0	9,412
1904 (April 22)	Detroit 4, St. Louis 4 (12 inn.)	15,996
1903 (April 22)	Detroit 4, Cleveland 2	16,482
1902 (May 1)	Detroit 4, Cleveland 1	14,183
1901 (April 25)	Detroit 14, Milwaukee 13	10,023
1900 (April 19)	Buffalo 8, Detroit 0	5,000
1899 (April 27)	Columbus 4, Detroit 3	4,500
1898 (April 29)	Indianapolis 7, Detroit 6	2,700
1897 (May 3)	Indianapolis 5, Detroit 4 (10 inn.)	3,500
1896 (April 28)	Detroit 17, Columbus 2	6,000

CHAPTER 2

Charlie Bennett's park

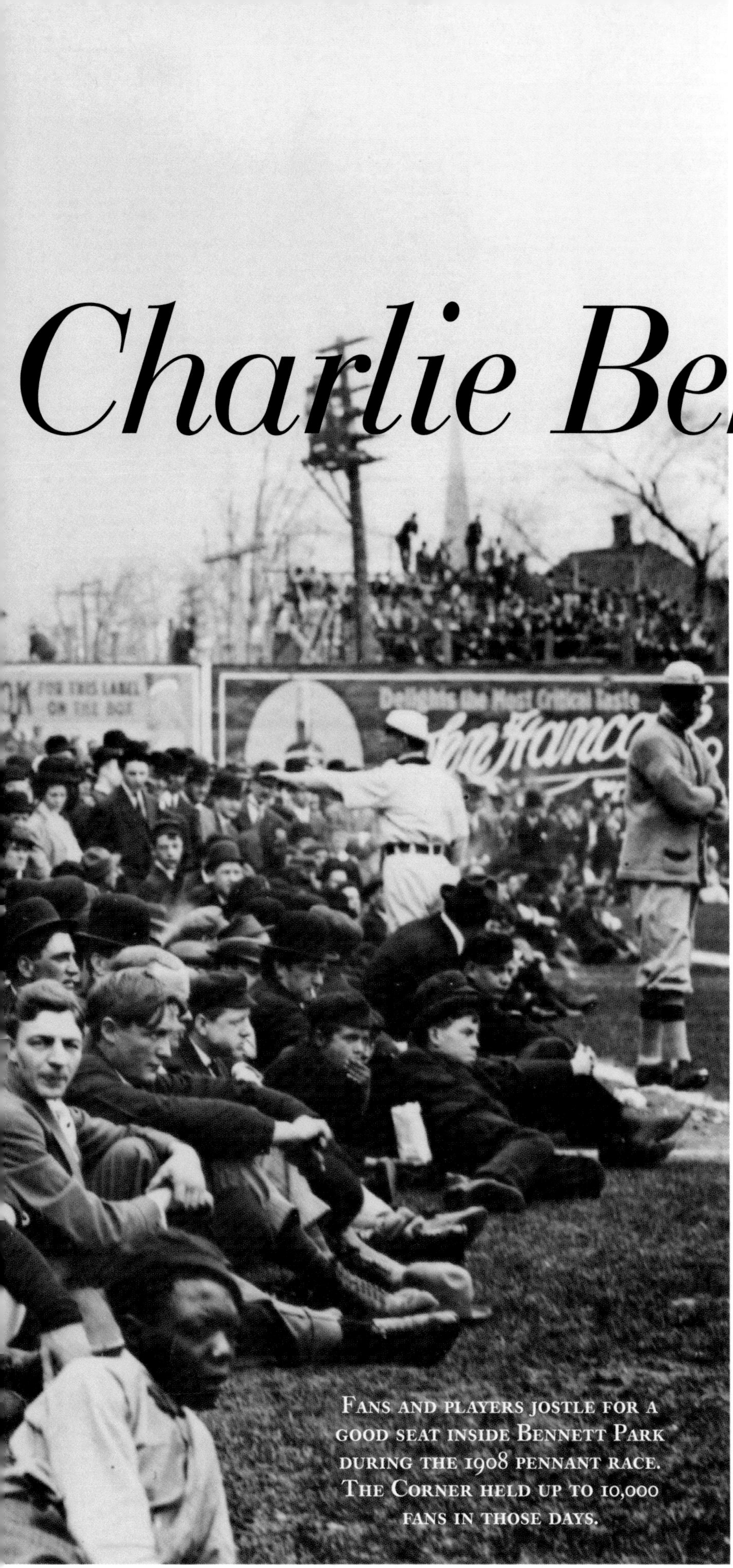

Fans and players jostle for a good seat inside Bennett Park during the 1908 pennant race. The Corner held up to 10,000 fans in those days.

Richard Bak Collection

Shaking hands with Charlie Bennett was like grabbing a fistful of pretzels. He had the mangled fingers of most 19th-Century catchers, handling fastballs, curves and other pitches with only thin, unpadded, fingerless gloves to cushion the impact. By the end of a game his hands were swollen from bruises and tiny fractures, and bleeding from dozens of cuts.

"If he felt the punishment," a reporter remarked upon Bennett's death in 1927 in Detroit, "he took it as stoically as an Indian warrior."

Bennett had played eight seasons with the Detroit Wolverines of the National League, backstopping the team to a world championship in 1887 that solidified his position as the fans' favorite. During this period, even a person without the slightest interest in what was making Recreation Park rock every afternoon could still pick out the local hero in a restaurant or hotel lobby. Bennett was the fellow who could barely lift a spoon of soup to his lips, the fellow who struggled to tie a loose shoelace.

On a spring day in 1896, Bennett's battered digits were not his only conspicuous physical deformity. There also were his legs, or what was left of them. Hushed accounts of the accident that had recently cost him his limbs, his career and nearly his life circulated through the crowd as the 41-year-old hobbled to home plate to catch the ceremonial first pitch from Wayne County treasurer Alex McLeod.

A year and a half earlier, in the fall of 1894, Bennett had slipped while boarding a train in Kansas. People watched in horror as the heavy wheels of the moving train sliced off his left foot and crushed his right leg, which later had to be amputated below the knee. Bennett, a Pennsylvania native who had first played ball in Detroit as a sprightly 21-year-old amateur shortstop, returned to the city with artificial legs. To support himself he ran a cigar stand and, in his later years, painted china dishes. Bennett's dignified response to his tragedy elevated him to near-sainthood status among his many friends, which included almost everyone in Detroit.

Although Bennett repeated the first-toss ritual every spring for the next 30 years, this particular Opening Day was the most noteworthy of the bunch – the first game at the new home of the Detroit Tigers.

It was April 28, 1896, a cool, wet Tuesday. The weather didn't dampen the enthusiasm of the overflow crowd of 6,000 on hand to watch the home team launch its third season in the Western League. Fans left happy, as following the usual pregame hoopla – a parade, brass bands, some speechifying and a cannon shot – the Tigers clobbered the visitors from Columbus, Ohio, 17-2.

Along with the outcome of the game, the issue of what to call the place also had been resolved. Owners normally didn't concern themselves, principally because the wooden parks of the era never were intended to be

Both: Burton Historical Collection

TOP: TIGERS OWNER GEORGE VANDERBECK SITS SECOND FROM THE RIGHT IN THIS 1899 PHOTOGRAPH OF WESTERN LEAGUE MAGNATES. ABOVE: THE 1899 TIGERS.

permanent structures. And nobody in 1896 dreamed of selling the park's name. (Who in the world would want to buy it? And what would they do with it?) So it was left to the public to decide informally.

The year before, fans and reporters had started calling the team the Tigers, a name borrowed from the Detroit Light Guard, a militia unit that had long been the city's pride and joy. Similarly, locals mulled what to call the Tigers' new home. Suggestions had been mailed to owner George Vanderbeck and discussed in the newspapers before the opening. They ranged from the prosaic (Michigan, Vanderbeck and League Park) to the more fanciful (American Beauty, Au Fait and Occidental Park).

Detroiters settled on a name. In conversation and in ink, the Tigers' lair habitually was referred to as "Charlie Bennett's park" – or Bennett Park, as it officially came to be known during its 16 summers of service. There was a purity to the process. There were no polls, no contests, no discussions of merchandising possibilities. It was simply a heartfelt, grassroots form of public applause for a favorite son who had long had trouble putting his hands together without wincing.

The Corner could boast an interesting past before it became Detroit's major sports venue. Long before the site welcomed such visitors as the Cleveland Indians and Washington Redskins, its woods sustained real Native American families, including the Potawatomi and Huron. Legend has it that Chief Pontiac held a war council there during the bloody uprising of 1763.

After an expedition of explorers led by nobleman Antoine de la Mothe Cadillac built the first permanent settlement in Detroit in 1701, a succession of French and English settlers held title to the property. The most famous was William Woodbridge, who served as governor and U.S. senator after Michigan joined the Union in 1837.

By then, intersecting roads had been carved out of the wilderness. The log road leading westward from downtown to Chicago opened in 1807 and was named Michigan

Both: Richard Bak Collection

Old reliable Charlie Bennett snares an Opening Day toss circa 1915, as former teammate Sam Thompson holds his cane. Bennett, whose legs had been shattered in a train mishap, was a fixture at openers for three decades. Donie Bush (below) was a mainstay at The Corner and at shortstop for 14 seasons, starting in 1908.

Richard Bak Collection

THE EARLIEST KNOWN PHOTOGRAPH OF A DETROIT BASEBALL TEAM DATES FROM ABOUT 1870.

BEFORE THEY WERE TIGERS

The evolution of organized baseball in Detroit, from a game played strictly by local amateurs to a business employing imported professionals, encompassed the second half of the 19th Century. Here are historic firsts reached along the way:

AUG. 15, 1857

FIRST RECORDED GAME

The Free Press reported on an intramural game played by members of the Franklin Baseball Club at the corner of Beaubien and Adams. No score was given. It's safe to assume Detroiters had been experimenting with various forms of baseball for several years. The likely reason for this particular contest making it into print was that the team (named after Ben Franklin) included Free Press employee Henry Starkey.

AUG. 8, 1859

FIRST GAME BETWEEN OPPOSING CLUBS

A form of class warfare was played out on the grounds of the Lewis Cass farm, roughly in the vicinity of Grand River and Cass. The Detroits, organized in 1858, were a group of well-heeled citizens who, bored with cricket, decided to give baseball a try. A second team of clerks and office workers was organized in 1859. Because of their long work hours, they practiced at sunrise and called themselves the Early Risers. In the first of several games involving the two amateur teams, the Detroits routed the Early Risers, 59-21.

MAY 12, 1879

FIRST PROFESSIONAL GAME

Hollinger's Nine was a house team of Eastern professionals, formed specifically as an attraction for Recreation Park. Although it was not affiliated with any league, Hollinger's Nine can be considered the first play-for-pay team to represent Detroit. As such, its 7-1 loss to the Troy, N.Y., Haymakers before 1,500 park patrons two days after the facility opened can be judged the first professional game in the city and Detroit's first Opening Day.

Detroit Free Press

MAY 2, 1881

First major league game

The Detroit Wolverines, newest member of the country's most powerful baseball circuit, the National League, inaugurated big-league ball in Detroit with a 6-4 loss to Buffalo before 1,265 at Recreation Park. The Wolverines lasted eight years, winning the National League pennant in 1887 and an unusual cross-country "world's series" against the St. Louis Browns of the American Association, before disbanding at the end of the 1888 season.

MAY 2, 1894

Tigers' first game

Detroit was awarded a franchise in Ban Johnson's reorganized Western League, a minor league circuit of eight Midwestern clubs. In its first game, Detroit lost to Toledo, 4-3, at Boulevard Park. The Detroit team was occasionally referred to in the press as the "Creams" and the "Wolverines." It wouldn't be until the following season that the home team would start being called the "Tigers," a name that stuck.

APRIL 28, 1896

Tigers' first game at Michigan and Trumbull

The Western League Tigers, after having spent their first two seasons at Boulevard Park, christened Bennett Park with a 17-2 drubbing of Columbus.

APRIL 19, 1900

Tigers' first game in the American League

The Tigers kicked off play in Ban Johnson's renamed American League with an 8-0 loss to Buffalo, as Doc Amole twirled a no-hitter. After operating for six seasons

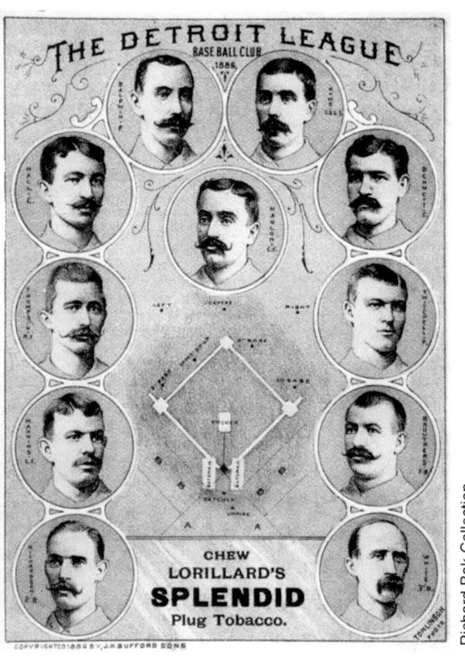

Richard Bak Collection

Detroit's first enclosed ballyard, Recreation Park, was home to the Detroit Wolverines from 1881 to 1888. Left: The 1886 edition of the Wolverines.

as the Western League, the name change signified little; the circuit was still a minor league and a signatory to the National Agreement, meaning its players were subject to being drafted by major league clubs.

APRIL 25, 1901

Tigers' first major league game

Before the season opened, American League owners voted to withdraw from the National Agreement and to declare themselves a major league. This launched a two-year war with the National League over players and territorial rights. At Bennett Park, the Tigers beat Milwaukee, 14-13, in the city's first big-league contest since 1888. For the purpose of recognizing records and anniversaries, the Tigers and the American League date the team's history to 1901. ◆

Avenue in 1837. The north-south dirt road that marked the Woodbridge farm's eastern boundary and the city's western limits was named Trumbull Avenue in 1858. Its namesake was Woodbridge's father-in-law, John Trumbull, who had distinguished himself during the American Revolution.

Before Woodbridge's death in 1860, he allowed the use of the northwest corner of Michigan and Trumbull as a public picnic grounds. Its magnificent shade trees and berry-laden shrubs made the bucolic spot – known as Woodbridge Grove – so popular that an overseer had to be hired. As Detroit continued to expand rapidly after the Civil War, Woodbridge's son took advantage of the growth by leasing most of the site for use as a municipal haymarket. In 1895 the city decided not to renew its lease, allowing Tigers owner Vanderbeck to sign a five-year agreement. Vanderbeck, disgusted with the sandlot dimensions of Boulevard Park, looked to build a more modern facility at The Corner.

The exact price for building Bennett Park is unknown, but judging by the cost of labor and materials in those days, it likely was no more than several thousand dollars.

The adjacent lumber mill, DeMan Brothers, got the contract to cut down and plane the many mature elm and oak trees on the site. Some of the forest giants were between 150 and 200 years old, creating a stir among preservationists. To placate them, Vanderbeck agreed to leave a few of them standing in deep left-centerfield and in the carriage area between the leftfield foul line and the grandstand. Those that toppled provided lumber for the L-shaped covered grandstand that ran from behind third base to home plate and for the attached bleacher section that stretched along the first-base line.

Bennett Park occupied roughly half the space of latter-day Tiger Stadium. A local bill-poster, Walker & Co., constructed the 12-foot fence surrounding the eight-acre site and sold advertising that appeared on both sides. The ticket office and main entrance were at the corner of Michigan and Trumbull, and home plate was in the vicinity of what became the rightfield corner. In the late innings, batters had to struggle with the blinding rays of the sun setting over the rooftops along National Avenue, the north-south street that ran parallel to the leftfield fence.

There were no dugouts as the modern fan knows them. Both teams had their own field-level bench, which backed against the grandstand wall and had a roof to protect the players from the sun. A clubhouse for the home team was built in deep centerfield. Visiting players dressed and showered at a down-

Both: Burton Historical Collection

THE CORNER HOUSED A HAYMARKET IN 1875, THE YEAR THE TOP PHOTOGRAPH WAS TAKEN. THIRTY YEARS LATER, THE VIEW FROM THE TRUMBULL AVENUE POLICE STATION SHOWED A QUIET NEIGHBORHOOD SURROUNDING BENNETT PARK.

Courtesy Bruce Kutney

FROM INFIELD TO ICE RINK: BENNETT PARK, CIRCA 1900, FLOODED AND FROZEN FOR A WINTER CARNIVAL.

town hotel (usually the Cadillac Hotel on Washington Boulevard, where the lobby floor was scarred by thousands of tiny spike marks) and took a horse-drawn bus to and from the park.

The playing field was primitive. "The field is a mass of mud and cobblestones," observed a Detroit daily as work continued during the winter of 1895-96, "and will require a vast amount of work to fit it for the game."

Vanderbeck, looking to shave costs, didn't remove the cobblestones but instead had a thin layer of loam laid over them. During the coming years, the stones regularly worked themselves to the surface. They were a hazard to fielders, who could do little but protect themselves from the resultant bad hop and weakly explain, "It hit a cobble." Despite a major resurfacing in 1903, Bennett Park's field always had a cow-pasture look.

The Tigers were a middle-of-the-pack team during their four Western League seasons (1896-99) at The Corner. At times the caliber of play was as uneven as the playing surface. By the end of their first summer at Bennett Park, one reporter accused them of performing "like men who had smoked opium."

This is an unfair assessment, for the Western League Tigers fielded several fine players.

Burton Historical Collection

Paying customers, including ladies, have a swell time in the grandstand at Bennett Park in 1909, while it's men only in the wildcat stands set up by entrepreneurs beyond the leftfield fence.

Richard Bak Collection

Catcher Frank Bowerman was destined to become Christy Mathewson's receiver in New York, and third baseman Harry Steinfeldt became the unheralded fourth member of the Chicago Cubs' famous Tinker-to-Evers-to-Chance infield of the early 1900s. Pitchers Rube Waddell and Frank (Noodles) Hahn became stars for the Philadelphia Athletics and Cincinnati Reds, respectively, after the turn of the century. Another hurler, Aloysius (Wish) Egan, later gained recognition as the Tigers' chief scout. Outfielder Sam Dungan never made much of an impact in the majors, but he was a perennial batting champion during his several seasons as a Western League Tiger.

In their first summer at Bennett Park, the Tigers drew twice as many fans as they had attracted to Boulevard Park. They scheduled morning-afternoon doubleheaders for holidays, emptying the park after the first game to welcome another full house for the second. In subsequent years, the support fell off as the novelty and the home nine faded, but it was still good enough to allow Vanderbeck to stay in business – not a small achievement, given the depression gripping America in the 1890s and the mayfly life spans of ballclubs in general.

Although the operating expenses were laughably small when compared with today, owning and running a ballclub was a risky economic venture. Selling tickets and the occasional ballplayer were the principal sources of income. A series of rainouts could determine whether an owner slapped a fresh coat of paint on the outfield fences, replaced a section of rotting bleachers or planted new sod in the off-season. Cash-strapped Vanderbeck regularly spoke of expanding and updating Bennett Park, but little work actually got done.

What he did do was successfully skirt the local ordinance outlawing Sunday baseball. Owners knew that games played on the Sabbath, the only day off for most workers, always drew the largest crowds outside of Opening Day. Ministers in communities across the country were effective in having Sunday amusements banned, though public support for the antiquated "blue laws" was beginning to wane. Nonetheless, as late as 1910, only three big-league cities (Chicago, Cincinnati and St. Louis) officially allowed Sunday ball.

Between 1896 and 1899, Vanderbeck scheduled a dozen games in Mt. Clemens and River Rouge, where enforcement of the local blue laws was more lax. The crowds were respectable, though getting hauled off to jail remained a possibility for fans and players alike. Before Vanderbeck could work up the courage to test Detroit's ordinance with a Sunday game at Bennett Park, a divorce settlement forced him to sell the Tigers for $12,000 to Jim Burns in early 1900.

Burns, a popular saloon owner, booked as

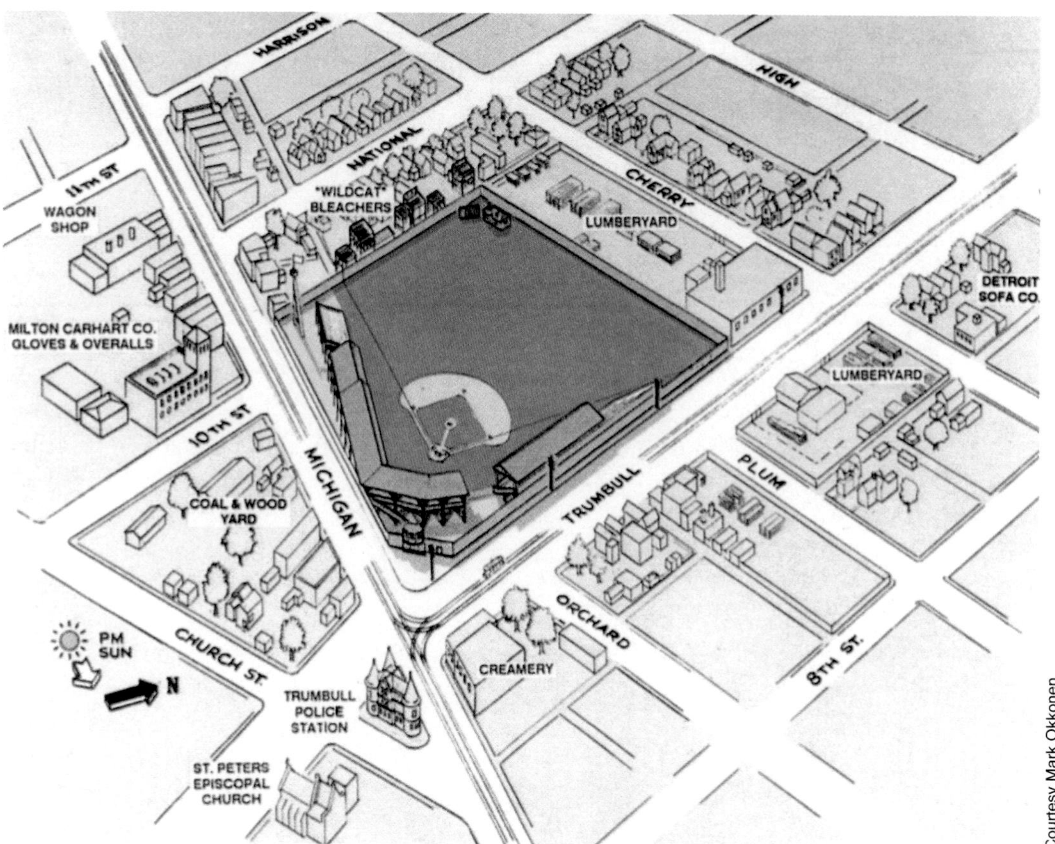

Courtesy Mark Okkonen

Bennett Park was well integrated into the surrounding neighborhood. In deep centerfield can be seen the home team's clubhouse and groundskeeper's shed.

Burton Historical Collection

TETE-A-TETE: MILLIONAIRE BILL YAWKEY (LEFT), WHO OWNED THE BALLCLUB, AND FRANK NAVIN, WHO RAN IT. BELOW: TY COBB CHOOSES A WEAPON.

many of the profitable Sunday games as he could at a ramshackle park built on his family's property in neighboring Springwells Township. Burns was politically well-connected (he later was elected Wayne County sheriff), so he didn't have to worry about raids disrupting the games.

Drunken fans were another matter, however. The park was next to the Garvey Hotel, whose bar was jammed with fans getting a snootful before games. By the late innings, the crowd could be more accurately described as a howling mob. Fistfights, bottle showers and assaults on visiting players and umpires were regular features of a Sunday afternoon at Burns Park.

This kind of behavior was guaranteed to offend league president Ban Johnson, who was promoting the American League as the better-behaved alternative to the rowdy National League. Johnson also noted the poor upkeep of Bennett Park. Burns ran the Tigers during their first two American League seasons before Johnson, weary of dealing with the franchise's many problems, forced its sale to local insurance man Samuel Angus in 1902.

At the time, the upstart American League was going hammer-and-tongs with the established National League over territory and player contracts. Most observers correctly assumed that Angus was "Johnson's man," ready to move the Tigers to another city when Johnson gave the word. The most likely destination was Pittsburgh, where Johnson eyed placing an American League team to compete with the Pirates.

The Pittsburgh Tigers? It almost happened. What kept the Tigers at The Corner and Bennett Park from being turned into kindling was the 1903 peace accord between the leagues. The agreement recognized the American as a second major league, created the modern World Series between the circuits, and specified that the American League stay out of the Steel City. Reflecting Bennett Park's new status as a legitimate major league venue, its deteriorating grandstand was repaired and expanded and the entire field leveled and fitted with new sod.

Meanwhile, Johnson searched for a new, financially sound owner for the Tigers. Frank Navin, then a clerk in Angus' office, suggested Bill Yawkey, whose family had made its fortune in lumber. From 1904 until the playboy millionaire's death in 1919, Navin bought stock in the team and ran its operations with little interference from Yawkey. Navin sold quarter shares in the club for $250,000 each to industrialists John Kelsey

and Walter O. Briggs in 1920. But he remained the Tigers' principal owner until dying of a heart attack shortly after the team won its first World Series in 1935.

Under Navin's stewardship, the once unsteady franchise became one of the most stable in baseball, thanks mainly to two factors: the rise of the auto industry and the arrival of Ty Cobb.

Two local tinkerers, Charles Brady King and Henry Ford, had driven the first automobiles through Detroit's streets within weeks of Bennett Park's opening. By 1910, the city had 23 companies manufacturing cars and was established as the motor car capital of the world. The need for unskilled labor to man the assembly lines created a boom in which the city's population leaped from 286,000 in 1900 to 466,000 a decade later. By 1920, one million people called "Dynamic Detroit" home; the rest of the world called it the Motor City.

Cobb's ascent as the greatest name in baseball paralleled Detroit's emergence as an industrial goliath. In 24 contentiously brilliant seasons, all but the last two spent at The Corner, Cobb established a standard of excellence that generations of observers have tried to capture in words.

"Good as I was, I never was close to Cobb, and neither was Babe Ruth or anybody else," said Hall of Famer Tris Speaker, the only man to beat Cobb for the batting championship between 1907 and 1919. "The Babe was a great ballplayer, sure. But Cobb was even greater. Babe could knock your brains out, but Cobb would drive you crazy."

Cobb and his teammates made rooters out of the growing ranks of newcomers to the Motor City, many of whom were foreign-born and viewed a passionate understanding of the national pastime as another step on the road to becoming a true American.

Sam Crawford, a slope-shouldered former barbering student from Wahoo, Neb., joined the team in 1903, two years before Cobb. Nobody will break Crawford's major league records of 309 triples and 51 inside-the-park home runs, the product of a dead ball being smacked to the outer reaches of prairie-sized outfields.

"I have seen rightfielders, playing against the fence, catch five fly balls off Crawford's bat in one game," marveled a sports writer of the time, "five fly balls that would have cleared the fence anytime after the … jackrabbit ball was introduced."

Bennett Park's chief vaudevillian was Herman (Germany) Schaefer, a pockmarked infielder whose ad-libs, comical gestures and colorful high jinks entertained Tigers fans from his arrival in 1905 until a mid-season trade in 1909. He is justifiably famous for stealing first base one afternoon, but he also got the grandstands in an uproar by trotting to his position in a raincoat when it was raining, or with a lit lantern when dusk was gathering. He tiptoed foul lines like a high-wire performer, jawed constantly with players, fans and umpires, and he was up to any gag

Both: Richard Bak Collection

TWO GLOVES ARE BETTER THAN ONE, SAYS GERMANY SCHAEFER, THE TIGERS' PRANKSTER DURING THEIR PENNANT-WINNING SEASONS AT BENNETT PARK.

"And along about 10 o'clock every evening I want one of my pals to say to the bartender on duty, 'Where's old Schaef tonight?' And I want my bartender to be able to say, 'He's upstairs, drunk.' "

GERMANY SCHAEFER

LET THERE BE LIGHT

The Tigers played their first home game under the lights June 15, 1948, a 4-1 victory over Philadelphia, right? Wrong.

The 1948 game was the first league game played at night at The Corner. But 52 years earlier, the club had a similarly illuminating experience, though the result never made it into the books as an official game.

On the evening of Sept. 24, 1896, George Vanderbeck's Tigers concluded their first season at Bennett Park with a send-off doubleheader against the Cincinnati Reds of the National League. These benefit exhibitions were designed to give fans a last glimpse of their heroes and to provide a little pocket money for the players before they left town for the off-season. They were rarely taken seriously, with the program usually including such activities as foot races, ball tosses, boxing exhibitions and players made up "in fantastic costumes." Anything to draw a crowd.

After Detroit scored four runs in the eighth, stretching its lead to 13-4 in the opener, the "other half was rattled off quickly and Umpire Campau called the game to allow the linemen to put up the electric lights for the night game," reported the Free Press.

By 1896 a baseball game played under portable lights was considered a novelty, not a historic first. At least seven other such games had been played since 1880. These included an attempt three months earlier in Wilmington, Del. The manager of the Wilmington team was Ed Barrow, later an executive with the Tigers and Yankees. "You could hardly see the outfielders," he remembered. "For improved visibility, we used (a softball)."

The number of arc lights strung around Bennett Park that September evening is uncertain; one paper reported 75, another said 54. The lights' power is unknown, though it's safe to assume that they provided about the same illumination as in previous attempts – which is to say, not nearly enough to make a batter step into a fastball with confidence.

No score or other details of the game were given for this first stab at night baseball in Detroit, though one daily termed it "an amusing and financial success." Players from both teams probably groped around in the semi-darkness for a couple of innings or so, giving the 1,200 fans a few laughs before leaving town with "a tidy little sum" and no sense of the history they had just made. ◆

---

that a teammate or photographer could dream up.

Schaefer's aspirations were simple: a few laughs, a few beers. Asked what he intended to do after he left baseball, Schaefer replied that he'd like to buy a little corner saloon.

"Not a big, gaudy place," he explained, "but a cozy spot where my friends can enjoy a glass of beer and a sociable evening. And along about 10 o'clock every evening I want one of my pals to say to the bartender on duty, 'Where's old Schaef tonight?' And I want my bartender to be able to say, 'He's upstairs, drunk.' "

Hughie Jennings was hired to manage the Tigers in 1907 and stayed through 1920. The generously freckled Jennings was a graduate of the coal mines of Pennsylvania, the famously bawdy Baltimore Orioles of the late 1890s and Cornell's law school, a range of experience that came in handy when dealing with the many disparate personalities on the Tigers' roster. He was a piece of work himself, using a whistle, war whoops and a variety of jigs to encourage his boys from the third base coach's box. He even contributed to the American lexicon, his favorite encouragement of "That's the old boy!" shortened over the years to the familiar "Attaboy!"

Behind the hitting and base-running theatrics of Cobb, Crawford and Schaefer, and a pitching staff built around Bill Donovan and George Mullin, Jennings' squad became the first to win three consecutive American League pennants. The excitement surrounding the team was reflected in attendance, which nearly tripled from 174,000 in 1906 to 490,000 in 1909.

Detroit hadn't produced a pennant winner since the Wolverines in 1887, but now "the boys and girls were parading the streets with torches," Cobb recalled. "A Hughie Jennings Club was organized, buttons were struck off for all to wear, and banners decorated the streets. Extra newspaper editions heralded every game. Everyone in town seemed to

Richard Bak Collection

WILD BILL DONOVAN SPENT 10 SEASONS WITH THE TIGERS AND WAS AT HIS BEST IN 1907, WHEN HE WAS 25-4.

own a tin whistle, using them to imitate Jennings' piercing sound effects from the coaching box."

Community support was so rabid and widespread that Navin felt safe in scheduling the first Sunday game at The Corner. On Aug. 18, 1907, the Tigers whipped the New York Highlanders, 13-6, before a record crowd that included the mayor and police chief. This was a watershed event. Although the ordinance wouldn't be struck from the books for several years, it was clear that authorities would not interfere with future Sunday dates. Within two years, Bennett Park was hosting 10 Sunday games, one drawing an unprecedented 18,478 to The Corner.

Unfortunately for their followers, the Tigers were a flop in the postseason. They lost the 1907 and 1908 World Series badly to the Cubs and were demolished by Pittsburgh in Game 7 of the 1909 Series. To make the embarrassment complete, all three series ended with shutout losses at Bennett Park.

The upside was that the money that flowed into Navin's coffers allowed him to expand Bennett Park's capacity, though he quickly ran out of space. Frustrated by the refusal of a handful of property owners on bordering Cherry and National streets to sell, he abandoned plans to build a covered outfield grandstand – a rarity for the time. Instead, before the 1908 season, he shrank the playing surface by extending the front of the main grandstand 40 feet. This and a new permanent bleacher section raised seating capacity to 10,000.

Two years later, it climbed to 13,000 with two small additions to the main grandstand. When Navin opened the 1911 season with new permanent bleacher sections in left and rightfield, The Corner could squeeze in as many as 18,000 fans, including a few thousand shoehorned behind ropes in the outfield.

During this period, Navin continued his losing battle with the operators of "wildcat stands," the jerry-built structures along National Street that towered over the leftfield fence. Similar structures had first appeared in the neighborhood surrounding Recreation Park, robbing the team of precious revenue.

For important games, several hundred hardy souls – mostly young, working-class males – paid a dime each for the privilege of clambering up the shaky bleachers, which typically used a barn as their foundation. Navin's only recourse was to try to obstruct the freeloaders' view by stretching a wire along the fence and hanging strips of canvas. The response was a barrage of rotten fruit and vegetables from the wildcatters and another story added to the slightly swaying stands.

Richard Bak Collection

HUGHIE JENNINGS WAS A LIVE WIRE IN THE COACHING BOX, COMPILING A 1,131-972 RECORD DURING HIS 14 SEASONS AT THE TIGERS' HELM.

With the end of the 1911 season, Bennett Park had faithfully served the community for 16 summers. It also had outlived its usefulness by several years. The era of wooden parks was passing – the wobbly, rotting fire hazards of the 19th Century replaced by more sturdy and comfortable facilities of concrete and steel. Navin was adamant that Detroit would have such a place. Only the capitulation of the last of the holdout property owners prevented him from looking elsewhere in the city to build it.

In the fall of 1911, Bennett Park went down as easily as if it had been made of Lincoln Logs. In its place a modern facility, one keeping with Detroit's stature as a big-league city, was erected. There was no communal outpouring of nostalgia, no baseball Jeremiahs warning of dire tomorrows spent inside the 23,000-seat structure rising at The Corner, just excitement about the future. When Charlie Bennett, the embodiment of Detroit's baseball past, took his familiar position at home plate the following Opening Day, the issue of what to call it had already been settled. Frank Navin had resisted, but not too strenuously, when city fathers suggested that he name the new park after himself. ◆

The Venues

Richard Bak Collection

Mack Park ▲

Opened in 1910, the wooden 5,000-seat park at Mack and Fairview is best remembered as being the home of the Detroit Stars of the Negro National League from 1919 to 1929. In 1914, there was serious talk of a third major league, the Federal League, installing a team at Mack Park. The facility hosted numerous sporting events until falling to the wrecking ball in the early 1960s. An apartment complex occupies the site.

Tiger Stadium ▶

The Tigers moved into Bennett Park (right) at the northwest corner of Michigan and Trumbull in 1896. Bennett Park was demolished after the 1911 season to make room for Navin Field, a modern facility whose concrete-and-steel "horseshoe," stretching from first to third, provided the base for several stages of expansion in the 1920s and '30s. The enlarged park underwent two name changes: Briggs Stadium in 1938 and Tiger Stadium in 1961.

Burton Historical Collection

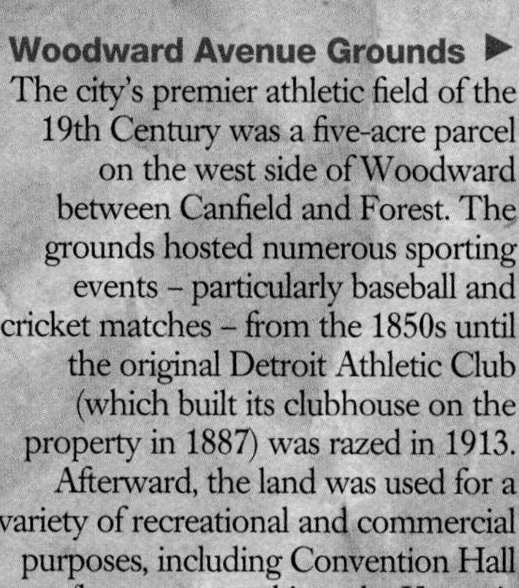

Woodward Avenue Grounds ▶
The city's premier athletic field of the 19th Century was a five-acre parcel on the west side of Woodward between Canfield and Forest. The grounds hosted numerous sporting events – particularly baseball and cricket matches – from the 1850s until the original Detroit Athletic Club (which built its clubhouse on the property in 1887) was razed in 1913. Afterward, the land was used for a variety of recreational and commercial purposes, including Convention Hall (later converted into the Vernor's bottling plant). A gas station and parking lot occupy the site today.

Richard Bak Collection

Recreation Park
Opened in 1879, this multi-use recreational facility extended along Brush between Brady and Willis, in the heart of today's Medical Center. When it wasn't hosting bicycle races, cricket matches and other amusements, it served as Detroit's first enclosed ballyard. The city's first professional baseball teams – Hollinger's Nine and the Detroit Wolverines of the National League – called the place home between 1879 and 1888. The park closed in 1894 and its 18 valuable acres subdivided into residential lots. ▼

Burns Park
No pictures exist of Burns Park, which was on Dix between Livernois and Waterman, in Springwells Township. Also known as West End Park, the slapdash, wooden facility was the principal venue for the Tigers' bootleg Sunday games in the early days of the American League. Between 1900 and 1902, the Tigers played 34 times there, regularly outdrawing weekday crowds at Bennett Park. Today the area is a weed-choked industrial site.

Boulevard Park
The Tigers' first home was a wobbly, 3,500-seat structure at Helen and Champlain (later Lafayette), near the Belle Isle bridge. The Western League Tigers played for two seasons (1894-95) before owner George Vanderbeck decided to build Bennett Park. Like all wooden neighborhood parks of the period, it had a short life, either being demolished or burning down not long after the Tigers left.

Burton Historical Collection

Graphic by Rick Nease

YEARBOOK

By Bill McGraw

1901

No one knew the horseless carriage was on the verge of transforming the city and the world

Detroit was known as "City Beautiful" at the turn of the century because of its shaded streets and gracious homes. An old city even then, Detroit celebrated its bicentennial in 1901. It was already a busy city, the 13th-largest in the country, with a population of 285,704 living within a 3½-mile radius of city hall.

Despite urban trappings such as factories, streetcars, immigrants and a crowded skyline of chimneys, buildings and steeples, Detroit had not developed the overwhelming industrial feel for which it would become famous in the next 20 years. Most manufacturing plants were in three areas: along the Detroit River, on the west side and on the northeastern edge of the city near what is today the intersection of Milwaukee and the Chrysler Freeway.

Detroit in 1901 possessed a remarkably balanced economy, with foundries, machine shops and small factories specializing in making stoves, pharmaceuticals, tobacco products, clothing, railroad cars, marine engines and ships, iron, steel and lumber products.

Oh, and automobiles.

No one knew in 1901 that the horseless carriage was on the verge of transforming the city and the world. Detroit was to cars then what Silicon Valley was to computers in about 1978: The brains, capital and tools were converging on one place to create a business that would change the way people lived. The auto industry in 1901 employed only 2,500 people who produced 4,192 vehicles. Cars were a rich man's toy; the average price was $1,000. A horse and buggy cost $400.

Ransom Olds was producing cars at a factory on E. Jefferson and Concord, but his factory burned to the ground in 1901. Henry Ford sold some cars and incorporated the Ford Motor Co. in 1903. Detroit's largest company in 1901 was American Car and Foundry, which manufactured railroad cars and employed 2,200.

Detroit was an ethnic city and a Catholic city. Historian Olivier Zunz estimated that more than seven in 10 Detroiters were either foreign-born, had at least one foreign-born parent or belonged to the small black community. The largest immigrant groups were English Canadians, Germans, British and Irish, but Poles, Russians and Hungarians were arriving in increasing numbers.

Nearly four in 10 Detroiters were Roman Catholic. Detroit was a city of single-family dwellings, and many immigrants managed to buy their own homes.

The city in 1901 held an elaborate celebration of the city's founding 200 years earlier, though lack of funds prevented the construction of a riverfront tower to commemorate founder Antoine de la Mothe Cadillac.

On July 24, citizens paddling canoes and dressed in 18th-Century French clothing reenacted the arrival of Cadillac and the 100 soldiers and settlers who accompanied him.

In self-congratulatory language typical of the day, the official celebration booklet proclaimed: "Certainly, if any city on the American continent deserved an elaborate memorial on reaching its Bi-centennial, Detroit is that city.

"Its history in many particulars is so unique and peculiar, its age for an American city so remarkable, and its natural and artificial attractions so numerous and universally pleasing, that as was well said, Detroit is worthy of the best." ◆

Detroit Public Library / Automotive History Collection

Postcards: Richard Bak Collection

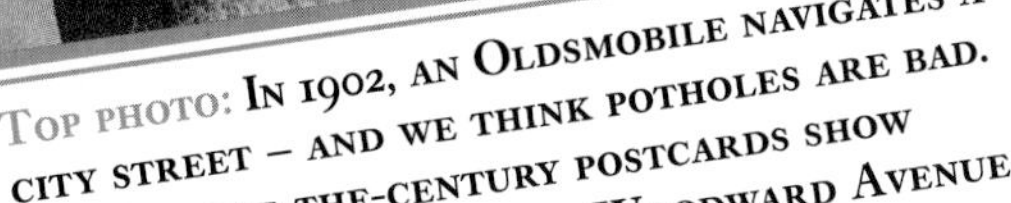

TOP PHOTO: IN 1902, AN OLDSMOBILE NAVIGATES A CITY STREET – AND WE THINK POTHOLES ARE BAD. TURN-OF-THE-CENTURY POSTCARDS SHOW BELLE ISLE'S GRAND CANAL, WOODWARD AVENUE LOOKING NORTH AND THE SIDEWALKS OF DETROIT.

CHAPTER 3

Cobb's corner

The plaque on the outside wall of Tiger Stadium calls Ty Cobb a genius in spikes. To Fred Collins, he was a bigot in asphalt-covered shoes.

The confrontation between the black laborer and the greatest name in baseball occurred one day in 1908 when the young Tigers star accidentally stepped into some freshly poured asphalt outside the original Pontchartrain Hotel at Michigan and Woodward. A word-fest ensued, with Cobb yelling several choice racial epithets before punching Collins to the ground.

"Collins demanded $100, or court action," was Cobb's recollection of the event.

"I was inclined to let it go to court, since Collins had started it, but finally paid $75 to be rid of the nuisance."

If only the rest of the world could have gotten rid of Cobb that easily. His exhaustive history of run-ins included knifing a night watchman in Cleveland, pummeling a disabled fan in New York and pistol-whipping a man and leaving him for dead in a Detroit alley.

Baseball's scoundrel later offered a defense of his often abysmal behavior. "If I'd been meek and submissive, instead of fighting back," he wrote in his autobiography, "the world would never have heard of me."

Three-quarters of a century after he last played, Cobb remained

Burton Historical Collection

Ty Cobb – the most ferocious Tiger – appears uncharacteristically serene in this photograph from 1907, the year he won his first of 12 batting titles. Said Cobb: "My idea was to go on the attack and never relax it."

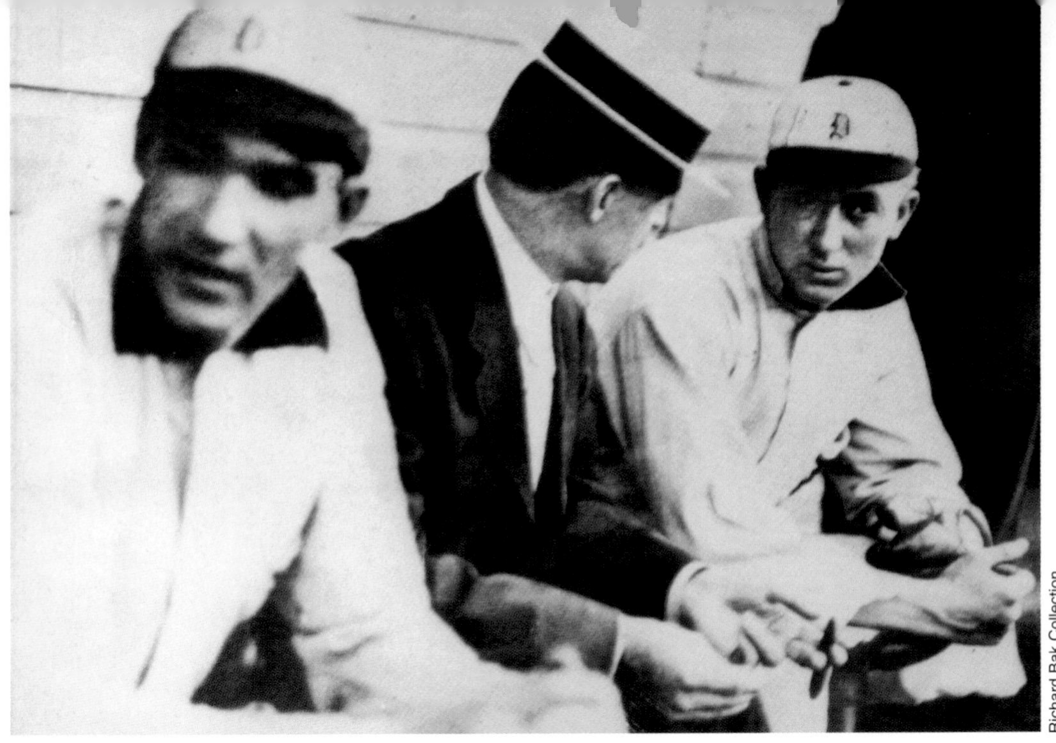

Richard Bak Collection

baseball's most compelling figure. He was a penny-pincher with a short fuse but also was a sentimental man capable of remarkable generosity. He is legitimately remembered as being a rolling ball of hell on the field, yet his reputation for foul play has been greatly exaggerated.

"Despite what has been said, Cobb never went out of his way to spike people," insisted former Tiger Billy Rogell, who broke in with the Boston Red Sox in 1925.

"Since I was a shortstop, he slid into me quite a few times, but he never tried to spike me. Others would come in with their damn feet in your face. They always made a big deal out of him sharpening his spikes. You had to sharpen your spikes with those infields or else you couldn't dig in."

Cobb played 22 seasons in Detroit, a transitional period that bridged dead-ball days at cramped Bennett Park with fence-rattling afternoons at Navin Field. He played two more seasons with the Philadelphia Athletics before retiring in 1928 with more than 70 records. Eight years later, he was the first man elected to the Hall of Fame. Some of Cobb's most notable records have since been eclipsed, though his .367 career batting average and 12 batting titles are unassailable.

Cobb made his first appearance at The Corner on Aug. 30, 1905. The 1,200 fans at Bennett Park that Wednesday afternoon curiously looked over the 18-year-old newcomer who had just been acquired from the Class C club in Augusta, Ga. News of the minor leaguer's purchase, made necessary by a rash of injuries to Tigers outfielders, made little impression on local papers, one of which reported the arrival of "Cyrus" Cobb.

Nobody knew what was percolating inside the high-strung youngster. A few days earlier he had buried his father, the victim of a dark family tragedy whose particulars would be hushed up for years.

COBB EXPECTED TO MAKE HIS LOCAL DEBUT TODAY

Georgian in Town Anxious to Start Work in Tiger Outfield.

Detroit probably will present a new face in the outfield this afternoon, Tyrus Cobb, the speedy youngster from the Augusta South Atlantic league club, having arrived in the city last evening, ready to go in as soon as called on. Cooley is out of the game for a time, and Bob Lowe is willing to surrender an outfield job to anybody that wishes it. Accordingly, it is likely that Tyrus will get his chance in a hurry. The Georgian was a little fatigued last evening, having been on the way since Saturday. Ordinarily the trip is one of about thirty hours, but missed connections at Atlanta and Cincinnati set back the tourist. He thought, however, that one night's rest would put him on his feet.

TYRUS COBB.

Cobb played on Thursday and Friday with Augusta, and in those two games hit a batting clip that regained for him the leadership of his league, which he had lost for a time to Sentell, of the Macon club. He quit the South Atlantic with a hitting batting average of .328. He won't pile up anything like that in this league, and he doesn't expect to. If he gets away with a .275 mark he will be satisfying everybody.

The local players had opportunity to watch Cobb last spring, when training in Augusta, and were impressed with his speed. Bill Byron, who umpired in the South Atlantic, says the youngster is one of the fastest men getting away he has ever seen.

Herschel Cobb had been a well-respected man in Royston, the small Georgia community that he served at various times as schoolteacher, businessman, mayor and newspaper publisher. In 1905, he was a state senator and was often mentioned as a possible future

TOP: COBB, AS AN 18-YEAR-OLD ROOKIE, DISCUSSES STRATEGY WITH MANAGER BILL ARMOUR IN 1905. THE FREE PRESS REPORTED COBB'S ARRIVAL IN ITS AUG. 30 EDITION.

Both: Richard Bak Collection

SAM CRAWFORD HAILED FROM WAHOO, NEB., ACCOUNTING FOR HIS NICKNAME. THE SLOPE-SHOULDERED SLUGGER BATTED .308 AS A TIGER BETWEEN 1903 AND 1917 AND AT VARIOUS TIMES LED THE LEAGUE IN DOUBLES, TRIPLES, HOME RUNS AND RBIs.

governor. Although he had opposed his son's choice of careers, he finally relented. "Don't come home a failure," had been his only instruction.

Herschel's wife, Amanda, was a shapely woman and the subject of local gossip. On Aug. 8, 1905, the senior Cobb announced to his family that he was leaving on one of his frequent overnight trips. But he doubled back that evening, intent on seeing for himself whether his wife was cheating on him. Revolver in hand, he climbed to the landing outside their second-story bedroom.

Amanda would later testify that she heard somebody trying to open the locked window. Fearing a break-in, she unloaded both barrels of a shotgun at the shadowy figure.

Ty, who had always desperately sought his father's approval, remained devastated by his death for the rest of his life. The circumstances surrounding it battered his psyche. To this day, nobody knows for sure who pulled the trigger. However, the smart money in Royston always has been on the presence of a paramour. In any event, three weeks after the shooting, Amanda Cobb was awaiting trial for manslaughter while her emotionally wrung-out son dug in for his first big-league at-bat.

On the mound was New York Highlanders right-hander Jack Chesbro. Swinging from the left side of the plate, Cobb spotted Chesbro two strikes before ripping a run-scoring double. At the time, nobody could have predicted that another 4,190 base hits ultimately would fly off his bat.

Cobb did not have an auspicious debut, batting .240 in the last weeks of the 1905 season. The following year, his first full campaign, he batted .320. He also suffered a nervous breakdown as he sweated out his mother's acquittal and contended with several veterans who made his life miserable. By now, Joe S. Jackson of the Free Press had dubbed Cobb "the Georgia Peach," but the environment was far from peachy. Nearly everything about him rubbed his crusty teammates the wrong way: his youth, his confidence, his Southern accent. They openly ignored him and sawed his homemade bats into pieces.

Cobb, a big man for his time (he'd eventually top out at 6-1, 190 pounds), fought back. One day at batting practice, he confronted the team's biggest star and highest-paid player, Sam Crawford. Crawford, who was envious of the newcomer, backed down. On another occasion, Cobb beat the living daylights out of Ed Siever, a veteran pitcher who was orchestrating some of the abuse.

In 1907, Cobb had matured physically and toughened emotionally. A new manager, Hughie Jennings, turned him loose at bat and on the base paths. Cobb responded with his first batting (.350) and base-stealing (49) championships and led the Tigers to their first pennant. Most of his teammates still didn't associate with him away from the park, but for two hours every afternoon they worked toward a common goal.

Davy Jones shared the outfield with Cobb and Crawford between 1906 and 1912.

"Of course, playing by the side of two fellows like that was a good deal like being a member of the chorus in a grand opera where there are two prima donnas," Jones told Larry Ritter in "The Glory of Their Times."

"I always got along with Sam just wonderfully. ... Cobb, though – he was a very complex person – never did have many friends. Trouble was, he had such a rotten disposition that it was damn hard to be his friend. I was probably the best friend he had on the club. I used to stick up for him, sit and talk with him on the long train trips, try to understand

"Of course, playing by the side of two fellows like that was a good deal like being a member of the chorus in a grand opera where there are two prima donnas."

DAVY JONES,
who shared the outfield with Cobb and Wahoo Sam Crawford between 1906 and 1912.

the man. He antagonized so many people that hardly anyone would speak to him, even among his own teammates.

"Ty didn't have a sense of humor, see. Especially, he could never laugh at himself. Consequently, he took a lot of things the wrong way. What would usually be an innocent-enough wisecrack would become cause for a fistfight if Ty was involved. It was too bad. He was one of the greatest players who ever lived, and yet he had so few friends. I always felt sorry for him."

The pity was misplaced. It should have been reserved for the infielders and catchers who routinely felt the sting of Cobb's spirited play as he maneuvered around the bases.

Many adjectives have been used to describe Cobb's baserunning exploits. Audacious. Foolhardy. Suicidal. Improbable. If you were a Tigers rooter or simply a purist who loved scientific baseball, he was a joy to watch. If you were an opponent about to be embarrassed in front of thousands of fans, including possibly your girlfriend or parents, you were understandably nervous.

Branch Rickey, a catcher with the St. Louis Browns, recalled a signature play at The Corner. Cobb had reached first base and coaxed a throw from the pitcher.

"But as the first baseman lobbed the ball back to the pitcher, Cobb was off in a flash, streaking for second. The pitcher hurried his throw, and it went into centerfield. Cobb popped to his feet and headed for third. The throw had him beaten, but the third baseman dropped the ball. Cobb slid for the ball and kicked it into the dugout, then got up and jogged home with the winning run."

It was an obvious case of interference, Rickey said, "but the umpires said it must have been an accident. They could not believe that any player could perform such a stunt on purpose."

"My idea was to go on the attack and never relax it," was Cobb's explanation. "An offensive attitude is the key to making any play, and if it meant gambling and getting tough, I was willing. If they roughed me up, I knocked them kicking with my spikes. I used my legs like an octopus when I was thrown out."

It was standing room only on April 20, 1912, the very first Opening Day at Navin Field.

A favorite partner was Donie Bush, whose 400 stolen bases between 1908 and 1921 trail only Cobb's 865 on the Tigers' all-time list. The diminutive, switch-hitting shortstop was the ideal leadoff man. He led the league in walks five times and exhibited the kind of heads-up baserunning that usually made the difference in the low-scoring games of the dead-ball era.

"With Bush the runner on first and me at bat, I'd signal for the hit-and-run, then drag the ball through the infield for a single," Cobb said.

"Second base would be impossible to reach, but I'd make the dash anyway, which drew the play away from Bush, now approaching third base. As Bush kept going for the plate, I'd slide and scissor my legs around the second baseman who'd tagged me out, wrapping him up so tightly he

Osborn Engineering Co.

couldn't make any sort of throw. It looked accidental, was anything but. I'm out, but Bush had scored."

Another of Cobb's signature plays was stealing home. He did it far more often (50 times, plus another in the 1909 World Series) than any other player in history. In 1912, he stole home a record eight times, all at Navin Field. The first one was particularly memorable, for it occurred during Navin Field's dedication game April 20, 1912, the same day Boston was inaugurating Fenway Park.

The Tigers' new home at The Corner had been reconfigured and covered an area almost twice the size of Bennett Park. No longer was the afternoon sun in the batters' eyes; now the rightfielder had to fight off the glare. The outfield dimensions were 365 feet down

Courtesy Bil Dow

The Corner in 1912, shortly before Navin Field's grand opening. The Tigers' new lair cost $300,000 to build.

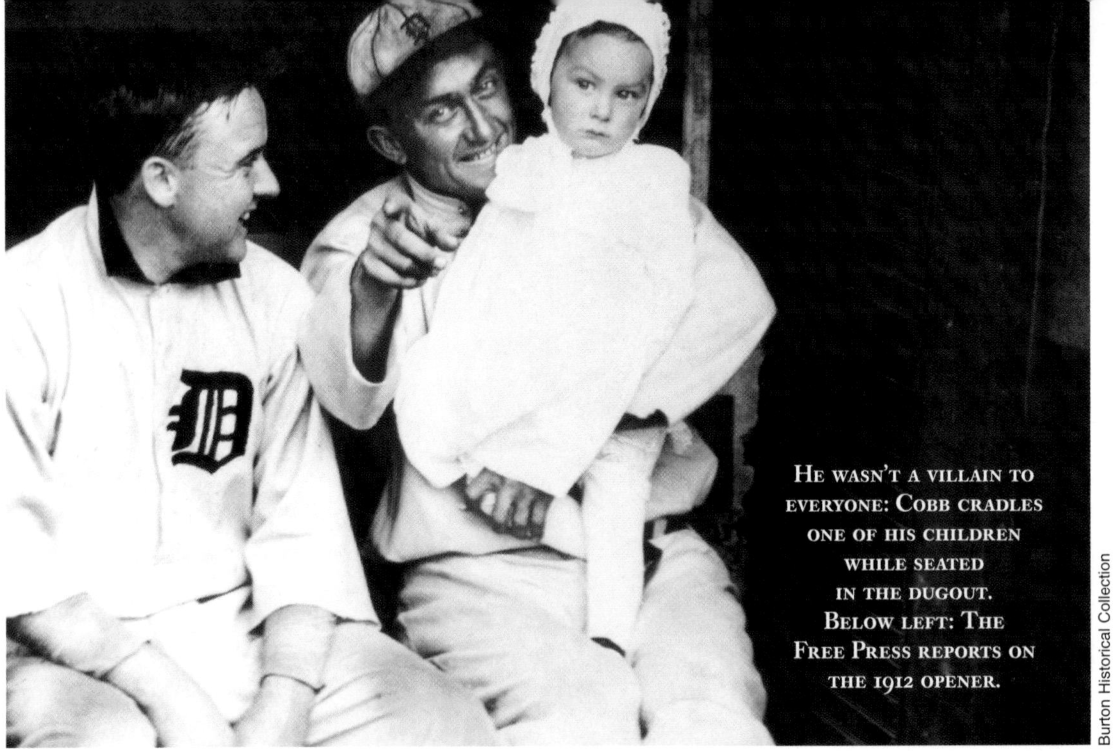

He wasn't a villain to everyone: Cobb cradles one of his children while seated in the dugout. Below left: The *Free Press* reports on the 1912 opener.

Burton Historical Collection

The Detroit Free Press
SPORTING SECTION

VOL. 77. NO. 209. DETROIT, MICHIGAN, SUNDAY, APRIL 21, 1912. PRICE: FIVE CENTS.

Immense Throng Sees Tigers Win Opening Battle

PANORAMIC VIEW OF THE FLAG RAISING THAT PRECEDED THE OPENING GAME ON NAVIN FIELD YESTERDAY

MICHIGAN TOYS WITH BUCKEYES

Wolverines Open Their Batteries Up in the First and Thereafter Never Are Headed—Score is 7 to 2.

"SMI" SMITH IS AT BEST FORM

Mossie is Declared Eligible and Holds Down the Third Sack Job—Mechling and Rogers Best at Bat.

Masons Suspended for Refusal to Take Johnson In

ATHLETES BY THE SCORE WILL RUN

Seventy Colleges Enter Teams in the Penn Relay Races Saturday.

CROWD ESTIMATED AT 26,000 PARTICIPATES IN DEDICATION OF NAVIN FIELD STADIUM; JUNGALEERS BEAT CLEVELAND IN 11 INNINGS

Mullin's Great Work in Pinches Enables Him to Stave Off Defeat. His Single Sends Winning Run Across After Bush and Stanage Have Hit Safely in Final Round.

BY E. A. BATCHELOR.

Ty Cobb, Sam Crawford and Oscar Vitt Are Detroit's Stars With the Stick—Georgia Peach Makes Two Great Catches and Steals Third and Home.

Michigan Relay Men Trying for Places on Team

'RASLIN' FEST AT 'Y' MONDAY NIGH

For Our Amateur Tourney Will Be Decided—Big Entry List.

STATE FAIR ENTRY LIST A CORKER

Michigan Stake of $10,000 is Leader With 42 Horses and Several More Are to Come From California Stables.

PACING CLASSIC ALSO DOES WELL

STANDINGS OF THE VARIOUS LEAGUES.

JACK COOMBS INJURED BADLY; OUT MAJOR PORTION OF SEASON

the rightfield line, 340 feet down the leftfield line and 400 feet to center. The walls were painted gray; a large green panel in centerfield provided a splendid backdrop for hitters. A 125-foot flagpole, still the tallest obstacle built in fair territory inside a big-league park, loomed in centerfield.

It was a sunny but chilly Saturday in Detroit. More than 24,000 filled a park designed to accommodate 23,000 in its yellow slat seats. Those not already standing in the roped-off outfield got on their feet in the bottom of the first inning when Cobb, timing the Cleveland pitcher's delivery perfectly, took off from third base and hook-slid around the lunging catcher to register the first Tigers run at Navin Field. Cobb later added another stolen base and a couple of nifty catches as the Tigers won, 6-5, in 11 innings.

Strictly speaking, Navin Field was designed by the Osborn Engineering Co. and built by Hunkin & Conkey, both Cleveland contractors. But the man who was truly responsible for the $300,000 park was Cobb, whose brilliant play had kept the turnstiles spinning for years. In recognition of this reality, the normally penurious owner, Frank Navin, eventually gave his franchise player a contract calling for him to receive 10 cents for every ticket sold over a certain figure.

Curiously, attendance during Navin Field's inaugural season fell by more than 82,000 from the previous summer at Bennett

THE OTHER COBB

BY REID CREAGER

This is a story about a boy and his dog.

And Ty Cobb.

William McBrearty had heard how the Tigers' Hall of Famer was a borderline psychotic – a ruthless, violent, paranoid, walking time bomb. But in a 1994 Free Press interview, McBrearty, then 93, remembered Cobb differently.

"When I was 12, when we were living on the corner of Canfield and Lincoln, our family had an Irish setter named Jessie," said McBrearty, a former lawyer for the City of Detroit. "Cobb lived just a few blocks away from me, and he craved that dog.

"I'd be walking the dog that spring, and Cobb would come down Trumbull in his Stanley Steamer and ask me how much I wanted for him. Of course, I wouldn't sell that dog for anything.

"After awhile, it was like a routine: 'Going to the park, Sonny?' he'd ask. I'd say, 'Yes, Mr. Cobb.' And he'd say, 'Ready to sell that dog, Sonny?' "

Soon, Cobb was picking up his newfound friends at the corner of Grand River and Trumbull on Saturday mornings.

"I'd wait on the west side of Trumbull, right by Scripps Park," McBrearty said. "I can't remember how many times, or how long it went on before the season started, but Jessie and I would get into his car, and Cobb would take us to Navin Field, just after Bennett Park had been torn down.

"He and some other Tigers – oh, Hookie Dauss, Donie Bush, Oscar Stanage, George Moriarty – would hit fungoes in the outfield, and Jessie would run 'em down. Afterward, he'd drop me off at Canfield and Trumbull, not far from my house.

"He was a delight, and he was so nice to me. Here I was, 12 years old, practicing with Ty Cobb.

"It was just so comfortable being around a ballpark in those days," McBrearty said. "For a while I worked as a stile boy – they're better known as turnstiles now, I guess. It was my job to turn the stile when each person came through. I got two bits (25 cents) for it and got to see the game free.

"I'm not sure exactly where Cobb lived; think it was Commonwealth. Bobby Veach lived right around the corner on Spruce. They named all the streets after orchards – Plum, Cherry and like that."

McBrearty, who closely followed baseball and Cobb's career, was aware of Cobb's dark side. But the Georgia Peach, it should be noted, gave millions to charity and had a soft spot for dogs. He was a regular at shows across the country.

"It was just a very pleasant experience with this fearsome guy who loved dogs," said McBrearty, whose father manufactured DAC cigars in a factory on Cadillac Square. "He was just a guy who loved dogs.

Richard Bak Collection

FONDLY REMEMBERED: COBB AT THE WHEEL OF HIS 1910 OWEN.

"I think without question he was the greatest hitter who ever lived. Here's a guy with a .367 lifetime average who played in a dead-ball era. He did it all – the Gretzky of baseball, in my book."

Just before Cobb died a recluse in 1961 in Atlanta, he confessed that if he had his life to live over again, "I would have been nicer to people."

"I can believe that, from all we know about him," McBrearty said. "I realize he wasn't exactly the fourth person of the Blessed Trinity, but he did right by me. He couldn't have been all bad." ◆

Reid Creager is a Free Press copy editor.

BREAKING THE COLOR BARRIER, FINALLY

BY JODIE VALADE

Ozzie Virgil doesn't think of himself in terms of black and white. What makes that so notable is Virgil's legacy in Detroit: On June 6, 1958, he became the Tigers' first black player.

In his nine-season major league career, Virgil hit .231 – and his highest average was .265 with Pittsburgh. Not exactly the kind of numbers that make a player memorable.

But when he joined the Tigers, they became the next-to-last team with a black player – 11 years after Jackie Robinson broke the color barrier with the Brooklyn Dodgers. Only the Boston Red Sox took longer; they waited until 1959.

Virgil said he received a warm welcome in Detroit from most fans but thought he was not regarded as a "true representative" by African Americans.

He was born in the Dominican Republic to Puerto Rican parents and grew up in the Bronx. Virgil said he thought of himself as a baseball player, not a black player or a Latin American player.

"The only thing I didn't like was that the black people in Detroit didn't accept me," he said. "They thought of me more as a Dominican Republic player instead of a Negro.

"If they called me black, fine. If they called me white, fine. If they called me Latino, fine. I didn't care what they called me – I just wanted to play."

In 1997, Virgil was honored at Tiger Stadium for his role in breaking the color barrier as part of the team's third annual Negro leagues celebration. At the time, he was managing the San Francisco Giants' team in the Dominican Republic.

Virgil said he's surprised when he hears younger players say they don't know who Robinson was.

"He gave me the opportunity to make a living in baseball. If these kids don't know Jackie Robinson, they're crazy. He opened the game to all of us.

"There were many Negro players before I was in baseball who deserved to be up there. They were cheated."

Virgil enjoyed his most success as a Tiger right after he was brought up from the minors to replace Reno Bertoia at third base. Virgil had an eight-game hitting streak, including 5-for-5 in his first game at Briggs Stadium on June 17, 1958. That game was capped by his first standing ovation from the crowd of 29,794.

Detroit Free Press

ELEVEN YEARS AFTER JACKIE ROBINSON JOINED THE DODGERS, OZZIE VIRGIL BECAME DETROIT'S FIRST BLACK PLAYER. "I JUST WANTED TO PLAY," HE SAID.

After that performance, Virgil's Tigers career didn't work out quite as planned. He was traded to Kansas City in 1961, bounced around until his playing days ended in 1969, and didn't return to Detroit until the 1984 World Series, when he was a third-base coach for the San Diego Padres.

For Virgil, though, his career in baseball and his games in Detroit will never be just about color. "I don't believe the Tigers called me up because I was black," he said. "They called me up because I was a player." ◆

Jodie Valade was a Free Press reporter.

MEMORIES DREW SHARP

Detroit's African Americans have long felt unwelcome at The Corner

Sorry, but there won't be any tears streaming down these cheeks when the last out comes in the last game at Tiger Stadium. Did you cry when you got rid of that broken-down jalopy?

If there's a lottery to award the prize of swinging the first wrecking ball, I'd buy $100 worth. The stadium has outlived its usefulness.

During the 1998 Stanley Cup finals, there was a Washington, D.C., sportscaster who bubbled with excitement during his stay in Detroit. He would finally get to see a game at Tiger Stadium, which he glowingly referred to as "a great old park."

Have I been missing something?

Perhaps you occasionally take for granted blessings that have been under your nose all along. Personally, seeing Tiger Stadium never provided the jolt that comes from taking an el train through north Chicago and suddenly seeing a majestic ballpark emerge amid homes and apartment buildings. Or walking through the bustle of Boston's Kenmore Square and approaching the red-bricked cathedral called Fenway.

Detroit Free Press

EVEN AS LATE AS 1968, GATES BROWN – BEING CONGRATULATED BY TEAMMATES FOR LATE-INNING HEROICS – WAS ONE OF FEW BLACK PLAYERS ON THE TIGERS.

Maybe I'd feel differently had Tiger Stadium maintained its original green decor, or if they hadn't stapled the tacky aluminum siding around the exterior. Even so, there's nothing terribly distinctive about The Corner.

Fenway has the Green Monster. Wrigley has the outfield ivy. Tiger Stadium has the – wait, don't tell me.

"It has history," Mark Grace told me in '98 when his Chicago Cubs visited Tiger Stadium for the first time since the 1945 World Series. As we stood behind the batting cage, Grace gazed around the park, looking like someone revisiting his youth, reacquainting himself with what made him love the game.

"You have no idea how exciting it is to know that you're walking on the same field that Ruth and Gehrig walked on. Ty Cobb played here during the park's early days. He probably stood at this same spot at some point. Places like this and Wrigley and Fenway Park connect you to the game's history."

Unfortunately, it didn't connect to a large segment of the city.

Detroit's African Americans have long felt unwelcome at The Corner because the organization lagged far behind others in making a commitment to scouting and attracting black players.

Tiger Stadium became a symbol of exclusion.

My father says that attitude prevailed until the mid-'60s, when native Detroiter Willie Horton and crowd favorite Gates Brown finally gave the team a local identity. Even then, some would say it was a token effort.

For many Detroiters, Tiger Stadium was merely the place where the local team played ball. We'll all say good-bye soon, and more than a few will say good riddance as well. ◆

Drew Sharp is a Free Press sports columnist.

Burton Historical Collection

Cobb, who played his final two seasons with the Athletics, is flanked by Philly teammates Eddie Collins (left) and Tris Speaker at Navin Field in 1928.

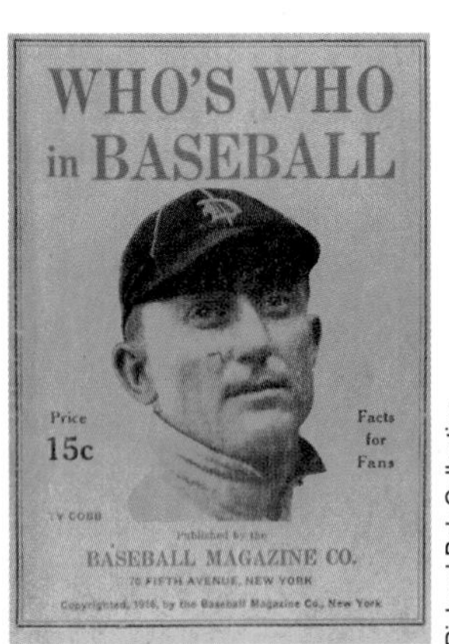

Richard Bak Collection

Cover boy Ty Cobb.

Park. Of course, the club's sixth-place finish factored in the decline, but the notion of a ballgame as being more of a social event than an athletic competition had not yet taken hold.

Attendance picked up in 1915 as the Tigers finished second to the Red Sox. In 1919, the Tigers led the league in attendance for the first time, drawing 643,805. Before the 1923 season, Navin had the grandstand double-decked between first and third base. This increased capacity to 30,000 and in 1924 allowed the Tigers to become only the second team to top 1 million admissions in a season.

Cobb replaced Hughie Jennings as manager before the start of the 1921 season. He spent six summers at the helm of one of the finest offensive machines assembled at The Corner. His 1921 squad hit an eye-popping .316, as safe a record as there is in the book.

"It was murder," Yankees pitcher Waite Hoyt lamented. "You'd go into Detroit for a series and find the entire Tiger outfield was hitting .400."

The new manager had his faults. He was impatient with less-gifted players. In the new age of home runs ushered in by Babe Ruth, he continued to play for one base at a time. And the only thing he knew about pitching was how to teach others to hit it. In this he was remarkably successful.

Harry Heilmann, the plodding rightfielder, turned Cobb's instruction into a batting title in 1921, when he hit .394, five points higher than the master himself. The big right-handed batter followed that with batting titles in 1923 (.403), 1925 (.393) and 1927 (.398).

Another future batting champion, second baseman Charlie Gehringer, came under Cobb's wing in 1924. The quiet "Mechanical Man" from Fowlerville, Mich., had so impressed Cobb during an informal late-season tryout at Navin Field that he rushed into Frank Navin's office and demanded that he come out and take a look.

"Cobb was jealous of everybody and a strict disciplinarian," Gehringer remembered some 60 years later. "All players shrunk away from him, especially the pitchers. Golly, he wore a path from centerfield to the pitcher's mound. When he'd relieve a pitcher, he'd just grab that ball away from him.

"But he was super for the first couple of years I was up. Golly, he was like a father to me. He took care of me, coached me, rode with me on the train and all that. He even made me use his own bat, which was kind of a thin little thing. I said, 'Gee, I'd like a little more batting space,' but I didn't dare use another one. He would've shipped me to Siberia.

"Then all of a sudden he got upset with me about something. To this day I don't know what it was. He would hardly speak to me. He wouldn't even tell me what signs I was going to get from the coaches. Weird. But he kept playing me, so it didn't really matter whether he talked to me or not."

With some pupils, a simple whistle sufficed. Cobb noticed that Heinie Manush, an Alabaman who was being groomed as his successor in centerfield, had a bad habit of holding his bat below the waist, a position that caused him to uppercut the ball. Whenever he saw Manush's arms dropping, Cobb

NAVIN PARK, DETROIT, MICH.

Both: Richard Bak Collection

would let loose with a whistle and Manush would adjust his stance. On the last day of the 1926 season, Manush banged out six hits in a doubleheader against the Red Sox to edge Ruth for the batting title, .378 to .372.

That September Sunday at Navin Field also was Cobb's last day in a Tigers uniform. That fall he announced his retirement, though he changed his mind and played two more seasons with Connie Mack's Athletics.

Cobb had taken his share of abuse as manager, but all was forgiven as Detroiters planned a rousing tribute for his return to The Corner as a member of the opposition. Fittingly, Cobb was under suspension for bumping an umpire when Philadelphia made its first visit of 1927 to Navin Field on May 10. The suspension was lifted at the last minute, allowing the festivities to proceed as scheduled.

A turnout of 27,410 paid homage on Ty Cobb Day. Friends and fans presented him with a new automobile, a silver service and a floral horseshoe. The guest of honor responded with a double his first time up. After taking his position in the bottom of the inning, the game had to be held up as "the friendly enemy" was mobbed by autograph hounds.

Later that summer, on July 19, Cobb collected a milestone hit at The Corner. It was another first-inning double, this time the ball sliding off Heilmann's stone glove. The fixation on records was decades away, so it took five paragraphs for the next day's Free Press to get around to mentioning the feat.

"When Cobb made his fluke double in the first inning, it was his 4,000th major league safety," Henry Bullion wrote. "He's so far

The Corner, pretty as a postcard in 1913, and a tobacco card of Harry Heilmann, who won four batting titles playing there.

TWO CUPS OF COFFEE

About 1,200 men have played for the Tigers during their tenure at The Corner. Some, such as Ty Cobb, Al Kaline and Alan Trammell, spent 20 or more seasons in a Tigers uniform. Others have worn the home whites for one major league game – the proverbial cup of coffee.

Of the latter, two stand out: Robert Troy and Bill Moore. Both were pitchers whose single day under the big-league sun occurred at Navin Field. And each has a twist to his story that lifts him from the agate anonymity of the Baseball Encyclopedia.

Robert Troy was born in Germany in 1888 and died in France 30 years later. For several years in between, he managed to make a living playing America's national pastime in the high minors. The 6-foot-4, 195-pounder was a stud in Adrian, leading the team to the Southern Michigan League pennant in 1912 with a lively mix of fastballs and forkballs. Tigers owner Frank Navin, who hailed from Adrian, kept an eye on Troy. When Adrian's season was over, he bought Troy's contract and called him to Detroit.

Troy made his major league debut Sept. 15, 1912, before a middling Sunday crowd that was more interested in seeing Senators great Walter Johnson, whose record 16-game winning streak had been snapped a few days earlier.

Despite his nervousness, the 24-year-old rookie matched Johnson pitch for pitch until the seventh inning, when his wildness and some sloppy fielding by his teammates –

Both: Richard Bak Collection

including an error by Cobb – rubbed out a 3-0 Detroit lead. Washington won, 6-3, but the losing pitcher's final line was commendable: nine hits, three walks and a strikeout in 6⅓ innings. He also hit a batter and was charged with four earned runs.

During the next few minor league seasons, however, Troy never was able to rein in his scattershot right arm, a problem that prevented him from returning to Navin Field.

His death became his distinction. He was one of hundreds of professional ballplayers to serve during World War I, though one of only a handful to see heavy action. On Oct. 7, 1918, the infantry sergeant was shot in the chest by German gunfire during the Meuse offensive. The war ended five weeks later.

Troy's remains laid in a hastily dug grave in the French countryside for several years until being shipped to his mother in Pennsylvania. Where he rests today is unclear. But statistics buffs know where to find his name and numbers. And trivia experts recognize him as one of three former big-leaguers to die in the war.

By the time Bill Moore made his cameo appearance in the bigs, Cobb was managing the team – and not very well, according to Moore.

A fastball pitcher for the Rochester Red Wings, Moore was invited to spring training in 1925. There, he made the mistake of dusting off his manager in batting practice. In the word-fest that followed, Moore told Cobb that he could perform an anatomically painful act with the ball. Then he stomped off the mound and into the clubhouse.

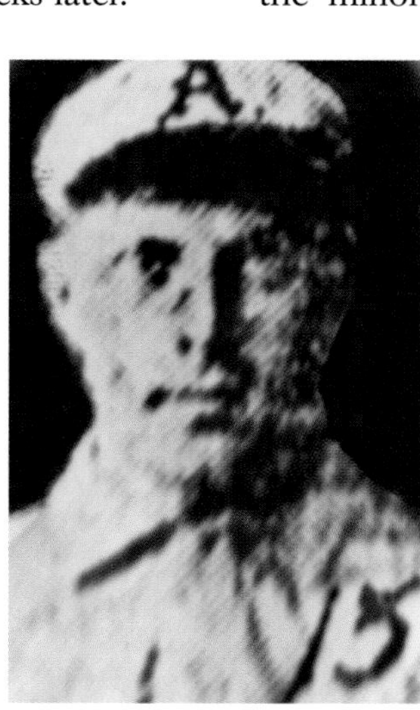

Minutemen: Pitchers Bill Moore (facing page) and Robert Troy each played but a single major league game, both their cameo appearances occurring at The Corner. Moore believed Cobb had a vendetta against him. Troy, who was born in Germany, was killed during World War I.

Despite the ruckus, Moore was the last man on a woefully thin pitching staff when Detroit opened the season with a victory over Chicago. The next day, April 15, 1925, the 21-year-old right-hander was called to the mound in the sixth inning of a losing battle with the White Sox.

It was a wet and rainy Wednesday, the Navin Field crowd was restless, and Cobb was irritated by the blowout. The nervous rookie's performance did nothing to improve his mood. Of Moore's 14 pitches, one found the strike zone. Cobb never left the dugout. He simply waved him off the mound. The crowd jeered the dejected pitcher.

"Bill Moore had a terrible time while making his major league debut," the Free Press reported. "He walked the first three men to face him, then was yanked after pitching another ball to the next man."

Moore was immediately shipped back to the minors, where he spent another eight seasons hoping for a chance to redeem himself. It never arrived. Moore came to believe that Cobb had a vendetta against him, one that he somehow passed on to management after leaving the club the following season. Irrational, perhaps, but that's what Moore thought. It was too painful to contemplate that maybe he didn't have major league stuff.

Two runners Moore put on base eventually scored. Because he never got anybody out, his ERA is impossible to calculate – thus the quirky symbol indicating infinity in his record. As far as the Baseball Encyclopedia is concerned, runners will be circling the bases against Moore for eternity until he can somehow get into another major league game and retire at least one batter.

Which will be difficult. Moore died in 1984, having spent his post-baseball days as a police officer in his native Corning, N.Y. He often mused about his blown chance.

"From the day I told Cobb to stick that ball up his ass," he reflected in his old age, "I think I was cooked." ◆

Bill Moore told Cobb that he could perform an anatomically painful act with the ball. Then he stomped off the mound and into the clubhouse.

ahead of all records of other batsmen that he will never be beaten or tied."

Pete Rose would prove Bullion wrong, but most observers understood that such a force of nature could never be adequately measured in mere numbers. It was the passion, the unpredictability, the blowtorch intensity that Cobb brought to the diamond for so long that made The Corner slightly less interesting after he left. Simply put, Detroiters had been spoiled by watching the best.

"I must admit that, having watched this piece of greased lightning in human form ever since that first day he joined the Tigers in August 1905 until after he had hung up his spiked shoes for good, the game was never the same for me," Free Press editor Malcolm Bingay – the original Iffy the Dopester – confessed many years after Cobb's retirement.

"I never see a runner rounding second now, hesitating and dancing back to the bag like a frightened bird whose mother is trying to push him out of the nest, that I don't recall what Cobb would have done in the same situation."

Cobb returned to Michigan and Trumbull several times as a spectator and to participate in old-timers events. Depending on the amount of alcohol and medication in his system, he could be mellow or crotchety. His last appearances were in the late 1950s, by which time he was battling cancer, diabetes and cardiac problems. He was a millionaire several times over, having shrewdly invested in Coca-Cola and automotive stock, but money never could buy him peace of mind. He was divorced twice, estranged from his five children and restlessly moved around the country.

Cobb died in an Atlanta hospital on the afternoon of July 17, 1961. He was 74. Before that evening's game at Tiger Stadium, Ernie Harwell read a tribute over the public address system.

"And now," he concluded, "here in this baseball stadium where the cheers were the loudest and longest for this greatest of Tigers, let us stand and pay final tribute to him in a moment of respectful silence."

Tiger Stadium was mute for several moments. Then it jumped back to life with the two words the Georgia Peach had heard more often than any other player in the long history of The Corner:

"Play ball!" ◆

Richard Bak Collection

FORMER TEAMMATE AND THEN TIGERS MANAGER GEORGE MORIARTY (RIGHT) GREETS THE RETURNING HERO ON TY COBB DAY AT NAVIN FIELD IN 1927. BELOW: EVEN IN RETIREMENT, THE GREATEST TIGER OF THEM ALL OCCASIONALLY RETURNED TO THE CORNER.

Burton Historical Collection

YEARBOOK

BY BILL McGRAW

1935

The labor movement grew, the UAW came of age, and sitdown strikes spread across the city

Detroit by the 1930s had become famous as the center of the most important industry in the world's most industrialized nation. Awed visitors from overseas flocked to this blue-collar metropolis to watch the complex process that combined workers and technology. "Detroit's brooding horizon of factories and its masses of industrial laborers became icons of modernity," wrote historian Thomas Sugrue.

The number of car companies had shrunk from about 230 in 1908 to 44 in 1927. By 1937, the Big Three had cornered 85 percent of vehicle sales, according to University of Michigan researcher Thomas Ticknor. The auto industry provided more than 500,000 jobs in Detroit. Ford employed 101,000 workers at the Rouge plant alone in 1929.

That's the year the world plunged into the Depression, an era that had a searing effect on Detroit as auto production plummeted and, by conservative estimates in 1931, nearly 225,000 auto workers were unemployed.

By the mid-1930s, though, factories were beginning to hum again. Car production, while still down from pre-Depression levels, increased by 30 percent between 1934 and 1935.

These were years of widespread worker unrest. The labor movement grew, the UAW came of age, and sitdown strikes spread across the city from auto plants to department stores to hotels. In March 1937, Detroit workers conducted 78 sitdowns.

Richard Bak Collection

THOUSANDS OF WORKERS ASSEMBLE OUTSIDE THE FORD PLANT.

The Battle of the Overpass, the famous incident in which Ford Motor Co. goons beat UAW organizers outside the Rouge plant, took place in 1937, as did the historic, 44-day sitdown strike at the General Motors Corp. plant in Flint. Conservative commentators warned of a worker-led revolution. Michigan Gov. Frank Murphy, a labor ally, said he would join a union if he could.

Detroit was constantly in the national news in the mid-1930s, and three of the best-known people in America lived in the city. Henry Ford, the auto pioneer, had lost some glamour because of his strident anti-Semitism, but he remained a legendary industrialist.

The Rev. Charles Coughlin, the radio priest who broadcast from Shrine of the Little Flower parish in Royal Oak, mesmerized audiences across America, though he, too, eventually received criticism for his anti-Semitic views.

In sports, Joe Louis was one of the nation's most famous athletes, dominating the ring and winning the heavyweight boxing crown in 1937.

Detroit, in fact, became known as the city of champions after the Tigers (1935), Lions ('35) and Red Wings ('36) won their respective titles. ◆

CHAPTER 4

Growing the legend

For nearly one-half century, from Navin Field's opening in 1912 until Briggs Stadium officially became Tiger Stadium for the 1961 season, the ballyard at Michigan and Trumbull sported the names of its two principal caretakers.

Although their personalities and business practices differed, Frank Navin and Walter O. Briggs shared the vision of making Detroit the best baseball town in America. Collectively, the owners shepherded the franchise from its formative years before World War I through the economic roller-coaster ride of the 1920s and '30s and into the age of electronic media and night ball. In the process, they expanded and improved Navin's original ball orchard into a modern sports showplace.

Navin's poker face suggested that he could squeeze a nickel until the silver turned to powder. His tight-

ROLE PLAYERS (FROM LEFT) FLEA CLIFTON AND RAY HAYWORTH, ALONG WITH FRANK DOLJACK (FAR RIGHT), FLANK THE HEART OF THE ORDER IN THE HEART OF THE CENTURY, 1934: SECOND BASEMAN CHARLIE GEHRINGER, FIRST BASEMAN HANK GREENBERG AND CATCHER/MANAGER MICKEY COCHRANE. GEHRINGER AND GREENBERG COMBINED FOR 266 RBIS THAT YEAR.

Detroit Free Press

Burton Historical Collection

Frank Navin – a spendthrift in personal life, a miser as an owner – ran the club for nearly 30 years. He died a few weeks after the Tigers won the World Series for the first time, in 1935.

State Archives of Michigan

Walter O. Briggs puffs on a cigar during a rain delay at the stadium he named for himself. The industrialist was meticulous about the ballpark's upkeep during his 17 years as owner.

fistedness at contract time was perfectly reasonable to fellow club owners. But it galled those players who were aware of his propensity for wagering – and often losing – several thousand dollars in one day at the racetrack.

"Mr. Navin was like all the owners then," said Charlie Gehringer, the Tigers' second baseman in 1924-42. "He was in it to make a living. He was hard to deal with. In those days an owner didn't need millions, but it took some money to move ballplayers around and whatnot. I remember one year during the Depression he had to borrow money from the bank to take us to spring training." Gehringer eventually made as much as $40,000 a season with Detroit, but during his first couple of years, he worked off-seasons at Hudson's to make ends meet.

Navin occasionally turned to his silent partner, who had made his fortune manufacturing car bodies. At the same time that Briggs was buying yachts and estates and pampering players, he was under siege by the underpaid workingmen who toiled inside his unsafe factories. His stone-age labor policies during the 1920s and '30s made him the most hated industrialist in Detroit.

Whatever one thought of Briggs personally,

For Mickey Cochrane, bubble gum cards and gifts of livestock were among the fringe benefits of being a local hero.

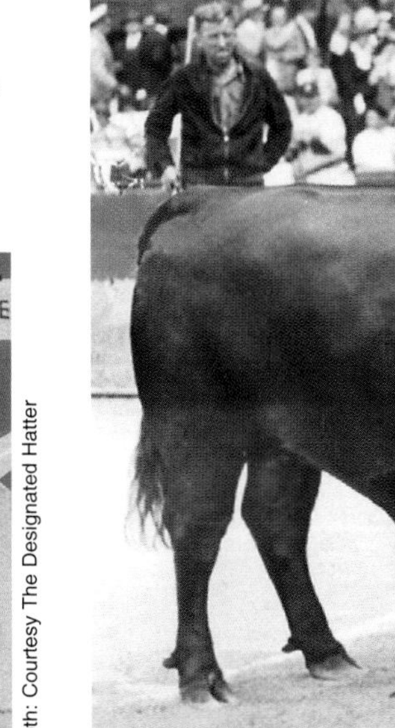

Both: Courtesy The Designated Hatter

Burton Historical Collection

Schoolboy Rowe often suffered from a sore arm during his 10 seasons at The Corner but still racked up records of 24-8 in 1934 and 16-3 in 1940.

Burton Historical Collection

Tommy Bridges was no bigger than a paperboy, but the curveball specialist stood eight feet tall on the mound. He spent his entire 16-year career at The Corner, winning 194 games and compiling a sparkling 4-1 record in World Series play.

there's no denying that his checkbook changed the course of Tigers history. In the fall of 1933, the team was coming off its sixth losing season in a row. The team's sad-sack performance, combined with a crippling economic depression, had produced the lowest attendance for a full season since Bennett Park days.

Navin shopped for a new manager to right the Tigers' listless ship and found the perfect pilot in Mickey Cochrane. The jug-eared catcher had been a dynamo on three pennant winners in Philadelphia, but cash-strapped owner Connie Mack was willing to sell him to keep creditors at bay.

The asking price was $100,000. Navin went to Briggs for the money. "If Cochrane's a success here," Briggs said, "he may be a bargain at that price."

Was he ever.

"He was simply one of the greatest," Eldon Auker said. "He was the reason we won in '34 and '35. Cochrane formed a relationship between himself and us. We were like a family. We followed him around like kids, and we would do anything Mike wanted us to do. He was very inspirational. There wasn't anything we felt we couldn't do. He really handled our pitching staff."

Besides Auker, the young staff included little Tommy Bridges and towering Lynwood (Schoolboy) Rowe. All benefited from Cochrane's steady, expert guidance from

Burton Historical Collection

Burton Historical Collection

Richard Bak Collection

From open space to a double deck, the look of The Corner changed dramatically in an eight-year span. For important games like Opening Day 1930 (top left), temporary bleachers were erected in the outfield at Navin Field. A new grandstand in rightfield was ready for the 1937 opener (above), but it wasn't until after the season that work on the centerfield bleachers began (left). The expansion, completed in 1938, made Detroit's ballpark, renamed Briggs Stadium, the first in the country to be completely double-decked.

Female admirers considered Charlie Gehringer a matinee idol, but the bashful second baseman remained a bachelor until after his mother's death. Mother and son are pictured at The Corner in 1940.

Into the 1950s, streetcars carried fans – and more than a few cost-conscious players – to and from the ballpark. "If you had a bad day, though, you had to put some plugs in your ears," Gehringer said. "The fans were getting on the same car and you'd hear about it. They'd say, 'Who was that turkey playing out there today?' "

Both: Richard Bak Collection

behind the plate. Bridges won 22 games in 1934, the first of three straight 20-win seasons, and finished second in strikeouts. The next two seasons he became the first Tiger to lead the league in K's.

"I was always glad he was on our side," Gehringer said of Bridges. "A super little pitcher. In fact, I'd have to say he was as good as Hal Newhouser. Maybe his record wasn't as good, but he had some great years. He had probably the best curveball I ever stood behind. I've seen him throw that curveball at a guy's head, and the batter would fall flat on his rear end thinking it was going to hit him, and then the ball would go over the plate for a strike. You think he didn't make the batter look silly?"

The rawboned Rowe was the pitching sensation of 1934. The 6-foot-4, 210-pounder from Waco, Texas, finished 24-8 and tied a league mark with 16 straight victories.

"He was so tall," Gehringer said, "that when he'd stand on that mound and start his delivery from way up here, from second base you'd swear that the ball was going to hit the ground before it reached the plate. Just sizzle."

Cochrane's impact as a teacher, field leader and inspirational force can be gauged by the voting for the 1934 Most Valuable

Player award. Although Lou Gehrig won the Triple Crown and several other players put up numbers that dwarfed Cochrane's statistics, it was "Black Mike" who walked off with the honor.

The Tigers, picked for fourth or fifth place by most observers, beat out the Yankees for the pennant, then lost a hard-fought World Series to St. Louis' "Gas House Gang" of Dizzy Dean and Ducky Medwick. But the city, down for so long, rediscovered the joys of an afternoon at the ballpark. Attendance tripled to 919,161, the best in the majors. The following season, when the Tigers won a second flag and their first World Series, more than 1 million visited The Corner. Again, the turnout was tops in the majors.

"I believe we helped bring Detroit out of the Depression," Auker said. "We helped change the attitude of the state. We gave people hope, and they became proud of Detroit and their Tigers. They were crazy for us. Even when we played in other cities, it was usually in front of a packed house."

One of the draws was the lanky first baseman, Hank Greenberg, a New York native who formed one-third of the "G-Men" trio that included Gehringer and leftfielder Goose Goslin. All were heavy hitters. But only Greenberg carried the baggage of being Jewish in a largely gentile sport.

Greenberg's ethnicity appealed to a generation of Jewish youngsters tired of being stereotyped as unathletic and brainy.

"I don't think anybody can imagine the terrific importance of Hank Greenberg to the Jewish community," said Bert Gordon, a Navin Field regular. "He was a god, a true folk hero. That made baseball acceptable to our parents, so for once they didn't mind if we took a little time off from the big process of getting into college."

Greenberg was a special mark for every bench jockey in the league, recalled Billy Werber, an American League infielder during the '30s.

Detroit Free Press

Burton Historical Collection

Dizzy Trout (above) and Birdie Tebbetts were batterymates for six seasons. Trout – putting on a clinic for kids in 1953 in the photo – won 27 games in 1944. Tebbetts, who died in 1999, put on baseball clown Al Schacht's glove for a gag shot at Briggs Stadium.

"Of all the ballplayers I played with and against, nobody took the abuse that Greenberg took. The ballplayers would call him every name you can think of: 'You Jew son of a bitch!' 'You kike!' All manner of things. He wasn't married at the time, so they used to accuse him of everything along those lines.

"The language can be pretty rough coming out of that dugout. I remember when I was with the Red Sox that Doc Cramer was a great needler. He was always after him. First base was almost in the visitors dugout in Detroit, so you could see the color rise in

GEHRIG SITS DOWN

Art Hill, a college student playing hooky from class, hadn't noticed anything unusual as the public address announcer at Briggs Stadium announced the starting lineups for the first meeting of the season between the Yankees and Tigers. Then it dawned on him: He hadn't heard Lou Gehrig's name.

This was startling news, even if it took a few moments for its impact to soak in. After 2,130 consecutive games spanning 14 seasons, baseball's fabled Iron Horse had pulled himself out of the lineup. As Gehrig walked stiffly out to home plate bearing the official lineup card for May 2, 1939, the 11,379 people on hand that afternoon rose in a spontaneous gesture of admiration.

"There was no shouting, just sustained vigorous applause," Hill remembered. "But they were on their feet, which meant something in those days." In an era where standing ovations were rarely given, Detroiters applauded for two minutes before finally sitting.

"He worked hard. Then when the batting practice period was over, he went to the clubhouse, and that's the last we saw of him."

HANK GREENBERG

The Corner had never been a particularly favorite stop for the Yankees' captain. He hit for a higher average there (.381 in 155 games) than at any other ballpark. But his home run production – a mere 22 taters, including only one of his record 23 grand slams – was at its lowest in Detroit. He also knocked in fewer runs at The Corner than at any other park, save Washington's cavernous Griffith Stadium. Unlike teammate Babe Ruth, a pull hitter who loved Navin Field, the left-handed-batting Gehrig was a spray hitter whose mighty smashes typically translated into screaming drives to the power alleys.

The Corner also had been the scene of a gimmick that tarnished his streak. On July 14, 1934, the Yankees played the Tigers for first place. Although ailing from lumbago, a form of rheumatism that afflicted him in the later part of his career, he convinced manager Joe McCarthy to pencil him in at shortstop and let him bat leadoff.

"I don't think I can go nine today," he said. "But I'd like to keep the streak alive, Joe, because I'm sure I can play tomorrow."

Bent over from pain, Gehrig hobbled to the plate and swung at the first pitch. Amazingly, he hit it to right for a single. After dragging himself to first base, he was replaced by a pinch-runner, having played – if barely – in his 1,427th straight game. The following day his lumbago disappeared and he belted three doubles off Schoolboy Rowe.

Going to such lengths to keep a record alive didn't set well with local reporters. "Instead of enhancing his reputation for durability," one sniped, "he sullied it."

Gehrig never maintained that his record was pure. In fact, in only one season – 1931 – did he play every inning of every game. During the course of building his streak, he was substituted for on more than 70 occasions, sometimes after only a couple of at-bats. It's interesting to compare these early absences with the you'll-have-to-carry-me-out-on-my-shield attitude of Cal Ripken Jr. In the process of shattering Gehrig's record, the Baltimore shortstop/third baseman prided himself on never being taken out of a game for any reason.

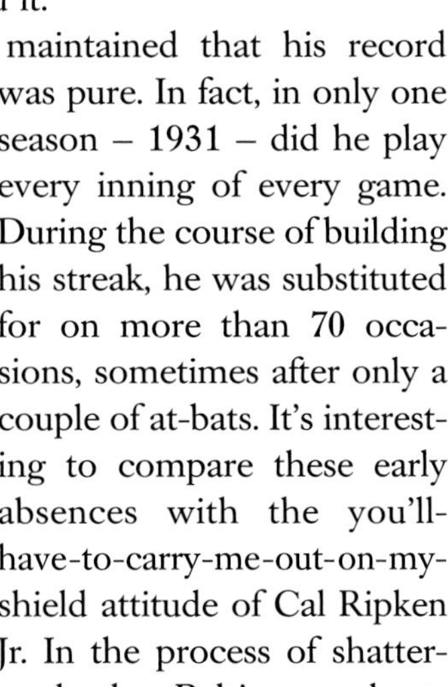

All of this is not to say Gehrig didn't frequently play injured. Jammed fingers, sprained ankles, beanings and a chronic bad back never kept him from suiting up. One day he was knocked cold by a fastball. The following afternoon he banged out three triples, presumably one for each pitcher the still-woozy Iron Horse saw on the mound.

Throughout the spring of 1939, it looked as if the 35-year-old first baseman was slowing down from age, not withering away from a rare, unpronounceable disease.

National Baseball Library

Lou Gehrig on the dugout steps at Briggs Stadium, May 2, 1939, the afternoon his iron-man streak ended. Two months later he would remark, "I consider myself the luckiest man on the face of the Earth."

His counterpart on the Tigers, Hank Greenberg, later recorded his impressions of the day on which the streak ended.

"It was customary for the visiting team to have 20 minutes to a half-hour of batting practice and 10 minutes of fielding practice before the game. …

"I was very curious about what happened to Gehrig, and I noticed that he went out to the outfield with the pitchers to chase fungoes from the rightfield foul line to the centerfield flagpole, back and forth for half an hour. He had quite a workout; it looked like he was trying to shake himself out of some sort of physical lethargy and get loose. He worked hard. Then when the batting practice period was over, he went to the clubhouse, and that's the last we saw of him."

Gehrig was diagnosed with amyotrophic lateral sclerosis, a degenerative nerve disease that quickly reduced him to a wasted, bedridden shell. He died June 2, 1941, 16 years to the day that he had started his streak by replacing Wally Pipp in the lineup. ◆

MEMORIES HAL NEWHOUSER

Tiger Stadium has charm. ... To me, she's a woman with a lot of grace

HANK GREENBERG PLANTS A WET ONE ON HAL NEWHOUSER'S CHEEK. THE PAIR SHARED A WORLD SERIES TITLE IN 1945.

In 1937, I was playing for the Roose Vanker Legion Post and was pitching on the sandlots at Northwestern Field. One day the Tigers' chief scout watched me strike out 24 of 27 batters. When the game ended he walked over to me and said, "My name is Wish Egan. Can I have your name and address and telephone number? And congratulations on what you did. Would you like to come down to the ballpark and pitch batting practice?"

Well, your stomach kind of churns a little bit, but I think the No. 1 thing was I didn't want to show him I was so excited. I tried to play it in a casual way. My folks were from the old country, and they didn't know anything about baseball. They'd ask me how the game went and I told them fine, but that was about it.

So on the day I went to the ballpark, I walked in and didn't know where to go. I was only 16 years old. I told the guy at the gate that I was there to throw batting practice, and he let me in and pointed me toward the locker room. Wish Egan came along and said, "I see you made it. I want to introduce you to some guys."

He introduced me to Hank Greenberg, Charlie Gehringer, Gee Walker, Jo-Jo White and some others. Then he sat me down next to Gehringer and told me to put on my uniform.

Well, Gehringer never said a word to me. He just sat there. Pretty soon Walker walked by and said, "This is only for players in here," and it was pretty clear that he considered me an outsider. But Wish came back and told me not to mind them, to finish getting dressed and come with him. And he took me over to Greenberg.

Hank was simply great. After he had finished putting on his uniform, he said, "Come on with me," and that's the first time I went through the tunnel to the field. Me and Greenberg.

I got up those steps and into the dugout and saw the field and I thought, "Boy, oh boy, this is really something. If I ever become good enough to pitch in the majors, this is where I want to pitch." It turned out that I had a great career pitching at Briggs Stadium.

Some of my fondest memories were the Ladies Day games. My mother would always come with a bunch of women. They'd sit at the 325-foot mark in rightfield, and she'd always wear the same hat. It was her lucky hat. Dad never got into it because we played all day games back then, at 3 o'clock, and he had to work. We were the next-to-last team to put up lights, and I was fortunate enough to pitch the first night game (June 15, 1948) and win it.

Lots of memories. … I remember Gehringer never said much more than he had that first day. He just went about his business. He would come to the ballpark, walk in, put his uniform on and go out on the playing field. That was the extent of it. When we won a ballgame, whether it was important or not, there was no razzamatazz. He took his uniform off, went to the shower, came back, dressed and went home.

Back when the stadium was called Navin Field, there used to be a wall that ran from the leftfield foul line to centerfield. Cherry Street was behind the wall. When Ty Tyson was broadcasting and someone hit a ball over the wall, he'd say, "That's another one out on Cherry Street." But then they put bleachers in back of that wall.

You know, some of the old parks were bad stadiums, like Cleveland's old stadium. It was so mammoth. But Tiger Stadium has charm. What I feel about the stadium is this: To me, she's a woman with a lot of grace, a lot of charm and a lot of pride. And she's given so much pleasure to the people who have been there all of these years. ◆

Hal Newhouser moved from Detroit's sandlots to the mound at Briggs Stadium, to a berth in the Hall of Fame in 1992. He died in 1998.

Detroit Free Press

Richard Bak Collection

EMILIE NEWHOUSER WAS SON HAL'S BIGGEST FAN. "SHE'D GO TO THE STADIUM AND ROOT LIKE THE DICKENS FOR ME," HE ONCE SAID. WHEN EMILIE DIED IN 1997, AT AGE 99, HAL REMEMBERED THAT SHE GOT THE LOUDEST APPLAUSE OF ANYONE WHEN INTRODUCED DURING NEWHOUSER'S INDUCTION INTO THE BASEBALL HALL OF FAME. "I WISH PEOPLE ALL OVER THE WORLD COULD HAVE A MOTHER AND FATHER LIKE I HAD," HE SAID. EMILIE WAS A REGULAR ON LADIES DAY, LIKE THE ONE ON THE LEFT IN THE 1930S.

Richard Bak Collection

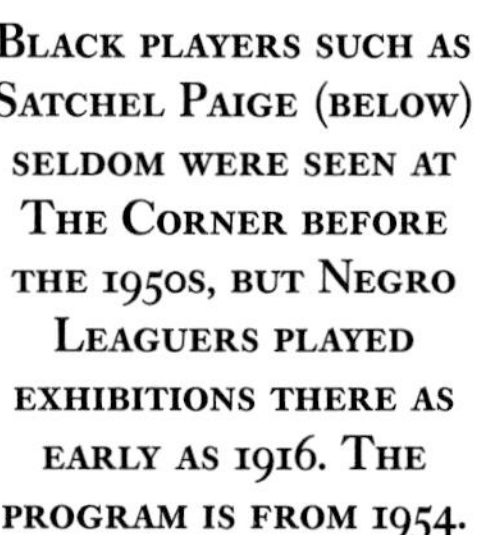

Black players such as Satchel Paige (below) seldom were seen at The Corner before the 1950s, but Negro Leaguers played exhibitions there as early as 1916. The program is from 1954.

National Baseball Library

Burton Historical Collection

Not a bad year at The Corner, 1937: Automobiles were stylish; Hank Greenberg led the majors with 183 RBIs, and Charlie Gehringer led the league with a .371 average.

Hank's neck. But I admired the guy. He was a great fighter. He didn't have much to say. He was there to beat you. He was intense."

In 1934, Greenberg, in his second full season, set club records with 26 home runs and a league-high 63 doubles. The following summer he topped the majors with 36 home runs and 170 RBIs, a performance that earned him the MVP award.

Nothing came easy to Greenberg. Werber remembered his lunch-bucket work ethic.

"He didn't look too good when he first came up. But he made himself into a hell of a ballplayer through intelligence, determination and hustle. You could walk from the Book-Cadillac Hotel to Navin Field, and I don't care how early you got to the park, you'd see Greenberg out there already. I'd just go out there and sit in the stands and watch. You'd see him in the batting box with a bunch of kids in the outfield, shagging balls."

Greenberg suffered a broken wrist early in the 1935 World Series against the Cubs, a mishap that had Navin and the rest of Detroit wondering whether the team would ever be anything but snake-bit. But the Tigers, after four failures, finally won one. On Oct. 7, 1935, Goslin's ninth-inning single beat the Cubs, 4-3, in the sixth game at Navin Field. Cochrane had barely touched the plate with the winning run before the populace launched into an all-night revelry that surpassed anything the city had ever seen.

Navin walked around with a smile creasing his normally placid face. "I have waited 30 years for this day," he said over and over.

Making life even sweeter was the $150,000 he had made in profits. He announced that he would put the money into improving the park. Navin meant to keep pace with the growing fan base by installing more permanent seating. He wanted to replace the "circus" bleachers, the temporary outfield stands built to accommodate big gates, with a roofed grandstand in left and right.

This was smart business, for The Corner had become common ground for countless Detroiters. Through the years the site had hosted amateur and professional sports of all types: wrestling, boxing and hurling matches, not to mention a couple of early attempts to establish a National Football League franchise. The House of David played donkey baseball there, and Negro leagues contests occasionally were booked. In 1935 Navin introduced a summer-long series of open-air operas to the park. Even pickets from the United Auto Workers assembled at The Corner when they had a beef against the Briggs Manufacturing Co.

Navin never got the chance to realize his plans. Five weeks after celebrating his first world championship, the 64-year-old owner suffered a fatal heart attack while horseback riding on Belle Isle. Briggs bought the club from his widow for $1 million, then set about expanding on his late partner's dreams.

"Navin Field was nice," responded Auker, asked to compare it with its remodeled successor, Briggs Stadium. "But when the stadium was remodeled in '38, it was more like the major leagues."

That sort of judgment was exactly what Briggs sought as he carried out an ambitious expansion program between 1936 and 1938. The $1-million investment boosted seating capacity to more than 53,000 as the Tigers' park became the first in the majors to be enclosed and completely double-decked.

The first stage of renovation involved replacing the single-decked first-base pavilion with a two-story grandstand that extended into rightfield. The problem was that Trumbull Avenue ran directly behind the rightfield wall, eliminating any hopes of expanding backward. Briggs was not opposed to bringing in the rightfield wall, but he didn't want to cheapen the home run by making the new grandstand too close to the plate.

The solution was to shorten rightfield from 367 to 325 feet to accommodate a narrow lower deck with a larger upper deck that overhung the playing field by 10 feet. This quirk added an interesting dimension to the game: an arching 315-foot fly ball would plop into the seats, while a screaming 325-foot line drive got caught at the fence.

The short porch has vexed pitchers and outfielders since, turning hundreds of ordinary fly balls into mighty home runs. Tiger Stadium's overhang has become so much a part of baseball lore that in the mid-1990s, builders of the Texas Rangers' neoclassic sta-

MEMORIES EARL KENDLER

The third baseman, Jim Tabor, yelled, 'Hey, kid, want a bat?'

It was the summer of 1943. I was 11 years old, and World War II was on. My cousin, Jack Kendler, had come to visit us from Toronto and was wearing his Royal Canadian Air Force uniform. He was due to ship out shortly for England and an uncertain future.

I wanted to take him someplace special and decided we could go to Briggs Stadium and see my beloved Tigers play the Boston Red Sox. We took the Trumbull streetcar, and I found out you have to ask for change before putting money in the fare box.

I expected to pay for him, but since he was in uniform, we were given free seats in the area for servicemen and women in the lower rightfield deck, next to the foul line. That year, the Tigers had a screen that went all the way up that section with only a six-inch gap to the second deck. Some of the GIs started yelling at the Tiger outfielders during the warm-ups to throw a ball through the little gap. After numerous tries, a ball did get through and everyone dove for it. Being the smallest person there, I got the ball.

When the game was over in those days, you could walk across the infield to the other side of the stadium. As we passed the Boston dugout, the third baseman, Jim Tabor, yelled, "Hey, kid, want a bat?" And with that he threw me a signature bat with a slight crack in it.

On the streetcar ride home, I felt 10 feet tall as the bat and ball made the rounds of the passengers. I taped the bat and used it for years, even though it was too long and too heavy for me. The ball was lost in a game at Northwestern Field. ◆

Earl Kendler is a retired engineer living in Troy.

Courtesy Earl Kendler

YOUNG EARL KENDLER POSES WITH AN UNCLE AND A BAT, BUT NOT JIM TABOR'S BAT. NOT YET.

MEMORIES KEN FIREMAN

For Jews like my father ... Greenberg was a figure of empowerment and self-validation

"Son, it's way past your bedtime. Why are you still awake?"

"Dad, I can't sleep. Can you tell me about the team again?"

"OK, son, OK. On first base was Hank Greenberg. He was a power hitter, a really great one, best in the league for my money. On second base was Charlie Gehringer, the Fowlerville Flash. He was as smooth as they come in the field, and a great hitter, too, for average. The shortstop was Billy Rogell."

Some children have lullabies and fairy tales to put them to sleep. I had the Tigers of the mid-1930s. They were the team of my father's youth and a great civic unifier that pulled together a Depression-battered city riven by bitter divisions over politics, religion and unionism. They came from nowhere to vanquish the lordly Yankees two years in a row and, in 1935, brought Detroit its first World Series championship.

Courtesy Ken Fireman

KEN FIREMAN AND HIS FATHER, CARL, TOGETHER IN 1985, JOINED FOREVER BY THE LONG RIVER OF BASEBALL.

And on sleepless nights two decades later, my father would perch on the side of my bed and fill me with tales about the boys of his summer: Black Mike Cochrane, the iron-willed catcher-manager; Schoolboy Rowe and Tommy Bridges, the strong arms of the pitching staff; Marv Owen, the feisty third baseman whose fight with Ducky Medwick in the 1934 World Series precipitated a near-riot in the stands.

But mostly he would talk of Greenberg, the powerful Jewish kid from the Bronx, who arrived in Detroit for good in 1933 and quickly became the hero of a city where hatred of the Jews was flourishing under the venomous tutelage of Father Coughlin and Henry Ford. For Jews like my father, who grew up in the shadow of such anti-Semitism, Greenberg was a figure of empowerment and self-validation, much as Jackie Robinson would become for African Americans a decade later.

My father was an austere and distant figure to me as a child, and sports was one of the few bridges to his world. The Tigers of the '50s were modestly endowed (there was the great Al Kaline and precious little else), but a trip with my dad to the ballpark – all green and wooden in those days and still known as Briggs Stadium – held the promise of something more than just a game. It was a chance to bond, to root together (mostly in vain) and get my father talking about his memories of Greenberg's rockets and Gehringer's graceful footwork around second base. Even if the players in front of us fell far short of such artistry, they were painting their mediocre pictures on the same emerald canvas.

My parents eventually moved to Florida, but in the spring of 1983, just as a new generation of Tigers was beginning to flower, they returned to Detroit for a visit.

It was the year before the Great Roar; this club of Trammell, Whitaker, Parrish, Gibson and Morris was just beginning to jell into a contender. I was all hope and optimism; my father, true to form, was wary. But I convinced him to take in a game, and on a warm Sunday in June – Father's Day – we headed to the ballyard for a doubleheader with the Indians.

From an upper-deck perch behind third, we watched the Tigers take the Tribe apart in the first game. Then, as the players retreated to their clubhouses between games, a spacious convertible emerged from under the centerfield stands and began circling the warning track.

In the back seat were Hank and Charlie, the Bronx Bomber and the Fowlerville Flash, old men now, returning to the park to have their jersey numbers retired. As fans began to recognize them, a ripple of applause rose

Mary Schroeder / Detroit Free Press

No. 2 Charlie Gehringer, No. 5 Hank Greenberg, honored in 1983.

up, reaching a crescendo as the car pulled behind home plate.

My father sat up and a smile played upon his face. "Oh, man, they were something," he said. "You should've seen Gehringer turn a double play. And you should've seen Hank hit. He was a dead-pull hitter, but he could go the other way when he had to. Once, I saw him get fooled by an outside pitch and just fight it off with a weak swing, and he was so strong that it wound up in the rightfield seats. He had so much power."

His voice was drowned out by the PA announcer, who began reciting the honorees' accomplishments: Gehringer, a lifetime .320 average with 13 seasons above .300; Greenberg, a .313 career average, 331 lifetime home runs, 58 of them in one season, and in another season, 1937, 183 RBIs. That last number provoked an audible gasp from the fans.

The two old stars collected their framed jerseys – No. 2 for Gehringer, No. 5 for Greenberg – briefly expressed their thanks, then departed. The current generation took the field again, and the Tigers completed a sweep of the Indians.

Later, over dinner, I was full of enthusiasm about the Tigers' playoff chances, and my father listened indulgently. Finally, he put down his fork and said, "Well, I just hope they have a good season, and I think they will. But you should've seen Hank Greenberg hit. You just should've seen him."

Greenberg died three years later; the following year my dad passed away. That Father's Day doubleheader proved to be our last game together. I moved away from Detroit. Today, my 8-year-old daughter and I do our rooting at Camden Yards in Baltimore. Her favorite player is Cal Ripken. But a few years ago, on a family visit to Michigan, I took her to the old park to watch the Tigers.

The game was a poor one, blown open early by the visiting Oakland Athletics, and there was little to hold my daughter's interest as the innings went by. I tried to explain to her that when she looked out into rightfield and saw Bobby Higginson battling the sun to catch a fly, I could see in my mind's eye Kaline climbing the screen to rob Mickey Mantle – and my father, if he were still here, Greenberg going the opposite way on an outside pitch and still reaching the seats.

I don't think she really understood. Perhaps she will, later, just as I was able to tap into my dad's stretch of the long river of baseball, with its tribal loyalties and lore. But I guess she'll have to do it somewhere else. ◆

Ken Fireman, a former Free Press reporter, covers the White House for New York Newsday.

dium incorporated it into their design.

"As a pitcher, my most vivid memory of the stadium will always be that facing in rightfield," Dave Rozema said. "You'd see Kirk Gibson underneath it, ready to catch the ball, and you'd take a big breath and think, 'Oh, good, he's got it.' "

Instead, moaned Rozema, "it ticks the upper deck and falls on the grass in front of him and it kind of drove you crazy, you know? You didn't know whether it was going to be a home run or an out."

The final phase of construction involved replacing the third-base pavilion with a double-decked grandstand that extended into leftfield. The two new outfield wings were then connected by a two-story bleacher section that was topped by a giant hand-operated scoreboard. The 10,000 bleacher seats closed the circle of concrete and steel and gave The Corner the largest number of cheap seats in the majors.

ON OPENING DAY 1938, RESTRUCTURED AND NEWLY NAMED BRIGGS STADIUM IS ENCIRCLED BY TWO DECKS FOR THE FIRST TIME, A BANNER DAY INDEED.

Burton Historical Collection

The radically made-over park was officially christened Briggs Stadium on April 22, 1938, before a record Opening Day crowd of 54,500. Cleveland spoiled the fun, winning 4-3, but players, fans and writers walked away singing the praises of the most modern sports arena in America.

The new outfield dimensions were set for the duration: 340 feet to the foul pole in left, 365 to left-center, 440 to center, 370 to right-center and 325 to the rightfield corner. Hitters liked the reconfigured field. In the first summer at Briggs Stadium, Greenberg hit 39 home runs there, part of a season's total of 58, as he futilely chased Babe Ruth's record of 60. No major-leaguer had ever hit more round-trippers at his own park.

The Tigers won two pennants at Briggs Stadium and also hosted two All-Star Games. All came between the years of 1940 and 1951, a period that saw the population swell because of the manufacturing boom during and after World War II. The Tigers had a star-studded lineup. In addition to old standbys such as Greenberg and Rudy York, the roster at one time or another featured slick-fielding third baseman George Kell, slugging outfielders Vic Wertz, Hoot Evers and Johnny Groth, and pitchers Hal Newhouser, Dizzy Trout and Virgil Trucks.

This was an exciting time in Detroit, Evers recalled. "The war was over, and everyone was getting back on their feet and they were getting into recreation. There was a kind of general craziness about baseball in the city."

So much so that all but one of the 20 biggest crowds in team history occurred during this period. This included the largest congregation ever assembled at The Corner. On July 20, 1947, a Sunday twin bill with the Yankees attracted 58,369, a crowd so large that the club revived the abandoned practice of putting the overflow behind ropes in the outfield. In 1950, the Tigers drew more than 1.9 million for the season, an attendance record that would stand nearly two decades.

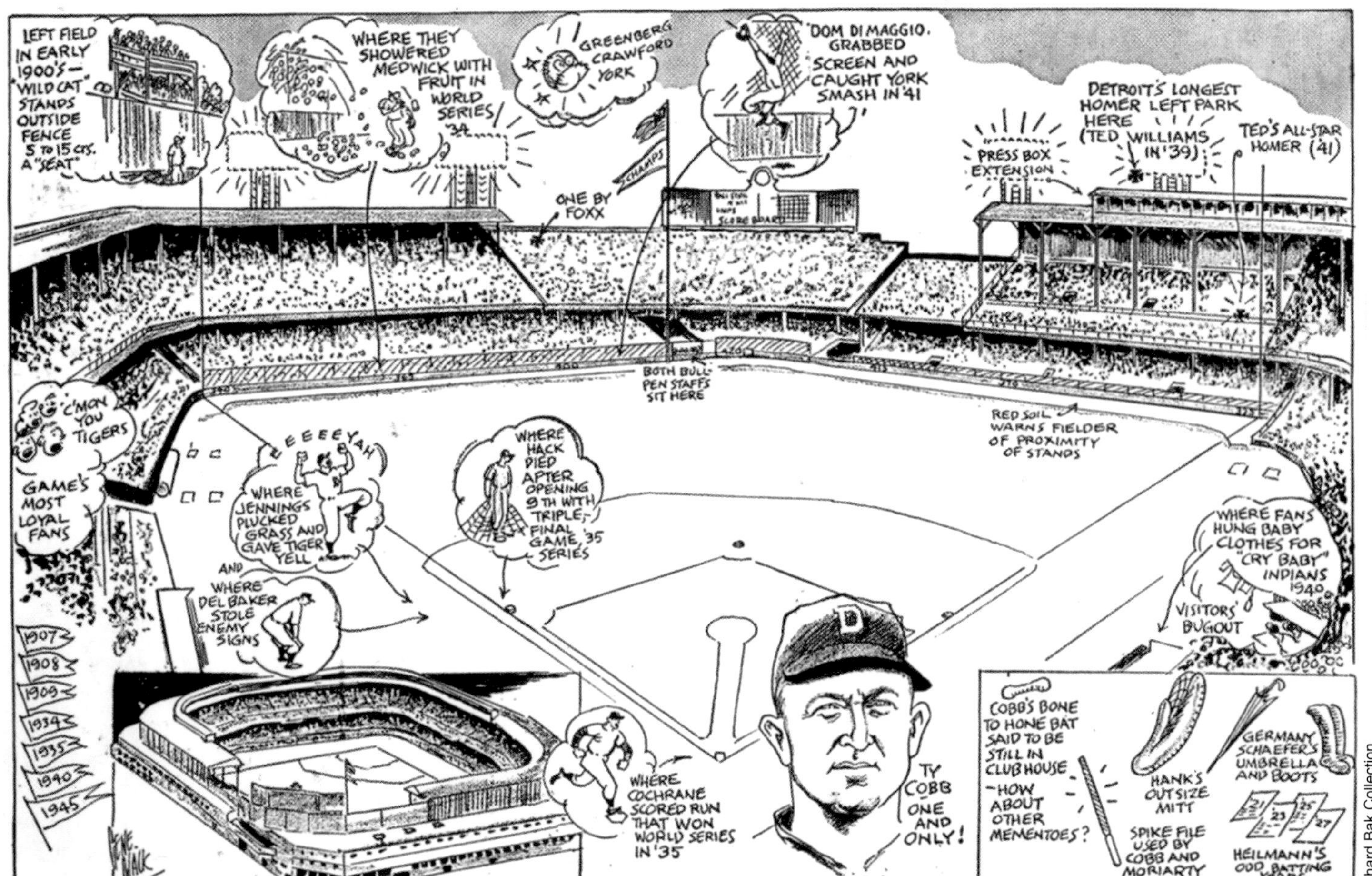

Richard Bak Collection

Gene Mack's 1947 cartoon celebrates seven pennant-winning teams and illustrates great moments and characters from The Corner's past.

Detroit was such a baseball hotbed that two years later the Tigers became the first last-place club to draw 1 million customers. Baseball people who eyed expansion regularly spoke of placing a National League team in the city, figuring it would support two big-league teams.

Boosting attendance was the introduction of night ball. On June 15, 1948, the Tigers became the second-from-last big-league club to host a game under the lights. Newhouser was selected to start the historic game.

"Mr. Briggs was a staunch believer that baseball was meant to be played in daylight," Newhouser told the Free Press in 1988, the year the last holdout, the Chicago Cubs, put lights in Wrigley Field. "But he was always thinking about the fans. He realized how difficult it was for the workingman to go to the stadium during the week. When he decided to do it, I think everyone held their breath waiting to see how the fans would react."

The start of a new era was welcomed by a crowd of 54,480, who watched in chilly good cheer as the Tigers, behind Newhouser's two-hitter, spanked Philadelphia, 4-1. The Free Press described the $400,000 state-of-the-art lighting system as "stretching 150 feet up into the skies, 1,386 mammoth bulbs played their radiance on the gleaming green playing field. … Then a thunderous cry of acceptance."

Briggs thought night baseball would be nothing more than a novelty in Detroit, but the original slate of 14 night games in 1948 steadily grew to the point where, by the 1960s, the majority of the schedule was played under the lights.

The lighting system Briggs installed was emblematic of his style. Everything at The Corner was first-cabin, from the underground sprinkler system (the majors' first) and spotless rest rooms to the spacious press facilities that wrapped around the third deck. Every year the stadium's gray exterior walls and canoe green seats got a fresh coat of

Tony Spina / Detroit Free Press

THE CORNER IS AGLOW FOR ONE OF THE FIRST NIGHT GAMES AT BRIGGS STADIUM, THIS ONE IN 1949. THROUGH THE LATE 1950S, NIGHT GAMES WERE CONSIDERED SPECIAL EVENTS – THE CLUB SCHEDULED NO MORE THAN 14 A SEASON.

paint. According to Briggs' grandson, by the early '50s the maintenance budget approached $1 million annually.

Publicly, the credit for the velvet-like quality of Briggs Stadium's grass went to head groundskeeper Neal Conway, which was perfectly all right to the fellow who actually did the work – Jim Conway, his older brother.

The pair had come to Detroit in 1923 from St. Louis, where Jim had performed his magic at Sportsman's Park. Neal, who at the time was working as a floorwalker at a department store, came along for the ride. A gregarious ham bone, he was the complete opposite of his quiet, publicity-shy brother.

"Neal was the front man," said Ted Colias, a member of the grounds crew in the '40s. "He was the personality guy. He was always the guy out there with the hose watering the infield just before the game started, when everybody could see. He was always in the spotlight."

Meanwhile, Jim Conway quietly tended Walter Briggs' lawn to perfection. There was nary a weed, thanks to his policy of watering in the morning and again at night. Fertilizer and weed-killer were not used. Instead, he had the grounds crew pull weeds by hand – an especially onerous chore that usually was reserved for those who'd had too many beers at lunch. Any bad patches were replaced with sections of sod cut from 100 acres of lush grass grown on a special site in Oakland County. This reserve came in handy after the turf was torn up after a football game or boxing match.

Jim Conway died a few days before the 1949 home opener. His passing exposed the shortcomings of Neal, who unsuccessfully tried to duplicate his brother's green thumb until his death three years later.

That was in 1952, the same year Briggs died at his Florida home. The aging industrialist, confined to a wheelchair for the last

KEEPING SCORE ◆ NOTHING DOING

Ten players have pitched no-hitters on the Tigers' home turf. These include Charlie Robertson of the Chicago White Sox, who recorded that rarest of gems — a perfect game — in 1922, and Cleveland's Bob Lemon, who in 1948 pitched the American League's first no-hitter under the lights.

DATE	PITCHER	SCORE
July 15, 1973	Nolan Ryan, California	6-0
April 27, 1973	Steve Busby, Kansas City	3-0
May 15, 1952	Virgil Trucks, Detroit vs. Washington	1-0
June 30, 1948	Bob Lemon, Cleveland	2-0
April 30, 1922	Charlie Robertson, Chicago	2-0
June 3, 1918	Hub Leonard, Boston	5-0
Aug. 30, 1912	Earl Hamilton, St. Louis	5-1
July 4, 1912	George Mullin, Detroit vs. St. Louis	7-0
Sept. 6, 1905	Frank Smith, Chicago	15-0
April 19, 1900	Doc Amole, Buffalo	8-0

NOLAN RYAN

Detroit Free Press

MEMORIES KEN KRAEMER

Lemon pitched a no-hitter that night, and I lost a hot dog

Lee Kraemer, a dad of undefined patience, loved the Tigers. His son inherited the love, but not the patience. When they won, my world was secure. When they lost, which would be so terribly often in the 1950s, my life was fractured – at least until the next game. But still we returned.

In 1948, the sun went down on Briggs Stadium, but the games went on: The yard was illuminated for night games. To see this dazzling sight for ourselves, the family got bleacher tickets for the night of June 30, 1948, against the Cleveland Indians and right-hander Bob Lemon, who won 20 games that season.

He was up to the challenge. Lemon pitched a no-hitter that night, and I lost a hot dog. In the late innings, Tigers third baseman George Kell – my mother once stood in a blocks-long line for hours at the downtown Kinsel's to get his autograph because she wouldn't let me skip school to talk to him myself – roped a line drive that shadowed the leftfield line into the corner, against the fence.

Leftfielder Dale Mitchell, a left-hander who averaged fewer than three errors a season for his major league career, hurled his 6-foot-1 body against the fence and put to death what would have been a double, preserving the no-hitter.

Courtesy Kraemer family

Hot dog in sweaty fist, I stood as tall as possible against the barricade separating the bleachers from the upper deck in left. When Mitchell plucked that ball with his gloved hand – a right-hander never would have had it – I squeezed my hot dog bun so hard that the dog popped out, slipped through the chain-link fence and plopped to its final resting place, as unreachable as Lemon.

Indians 2, Tigers 0.

Just another loss. However, in 1950, a wondrous thing happened: The Tigers were in a pennant race.

The Boston Red Sox and Cleveland Indians also were in it, but they were spear-carriers. My real scorn was reserved for the New York Yankees, who had won the World Series the previous season after finishing 10 games ahead of the fourth-place Tigers.

Late in the season, my dad and I were at The Corner when the pinstripers came to town. The Tigers were still in the race. But that day, disaster! The Detroiters took a lead into the late innings. Then, a throw from third base got away from the Tigers' first baseman, and the Yankees plunged the dagger deep. They scored and scored again and won the game – but I didn't see it.

Courtesy The Designated Hatter

INDIANS PITCHER BOB LEMON GAVE 12-YEAR-OLD KEN KRAEMER – PICTURED IN HIS BACKYARD ON SEYBURN STREET IN DETROIT – A NIGHT TO REMEMBER IN 1948.

I dashed from my seat to the left of home plate and stood in the concourse with my back to the field, never moving until my dad fetched me when the game was over. It was only one game, but it was the beginning of the end for the Tigers, who finished second, three games back, while the Yankees won another World Series.

Dad said little on the ride home that afternoon, but he didn't have to. His silent disapproval was punishment enough.

We went to many games in later years, but I never embarrassed him that way again. And we laughed about that day at The Corner, as dads and sons do.

How many times have I wished that he and I could go to just one more game together. ◆

Ken Kraemer is an assistant sports editor of the Free Press.

several years by a late attack of polio, had been an enigma. He was a ruthless labor boss who let 100,000 kids each year see games for free. As a baseball owner he was alternately paternalistic and petty, getting rid of fan favorites like Cochrane and Greenberg while making bonus babies out of outfielder Dick Wakefield and catcher Frank House, two of many failed phenoms to wear the Olde English D during the Briggs era.

However, every move he made was with the goal of making The Corner the center of the baseball universe. For this he was widely admired. Briggs "was, in the narrowest and best and most exacting sense of the term, a big-leaguer," Red Smith eulogized in the New York Herald.

Burton Historical Collection

"Mr. Briggs was a sportsman, one of the very few in a game that has become, over the years, more and more a business and less and less a sport. He was not in baseball to make money, which he didn't need. He wasn't in it for personal publicity, which he didn't want.

"He did not look upon Briggs Stadium as a monument to himself. He considered it a place to play baseball, a place where fans like him could watch baseball, and because he was a fan and a big-leaguer, he wanted it to be the best possible setting for the best possible baseball."

After Briggs' death, the franchise spent the rest of the decade in a competitive funk. Although the team was never a contender, and managers and front-office personnel came and went with alarming frequency, it fielded several solid performers, including two batting champions.

"Other than Mickey Mantle and Ted Williams, the best hitters in the American League were Al Kaline and Harvey Kuenn,"

Detroit Free Press

IT'S BEEN SAID THE CORNER HAD MORE OBSTRUCTED-VIEW SEATS THAN ANY OTHER PARK – A CHARMING DISTINCTION AS LONG AS YOU WEREN'T STUCK BEHIND A POST LIKE THIS LAD IN 1945. LEFT: SITTING BEHIND THE SCREEN PRESENTED ANOTHER OBSTRUCTION BUT ALSO PROTECTION FROM HARD FOUL BALLS. THE PHOTOGRAPH WAS TAKEN IN 1955, THE YEAR AL KALINE WON THE BATTING TITLE.

PUT UP YOUR DUKES

Walter O. Briggs envisioned Briggs Stadium as a multi-use sports palace along the lines of Yankee Stadium. To that end, he periodically rented his park for prizefights, including the only two title bouts staged at The Corner.

On Sept. 20, 1939, native son Joe Louis met Bob Pastor in a scheduled 20-rounder. It was the Brown Bomber's eighth defense of his heavyweight title but the first held in Detroit, an occasion that drew 33,868 to The Corner on a misty Wednesday night. They saw the 25-year-old champion floor his challenger six times, the last in the 11th round, en route to his 36th professional knockout.

"Bob didn't quite follow our plan," Pastor's disconsolate trainer told reporters afterward.

For his night's work Louis won $118,000 – three times what his favorite Tiger, Hank Greenberg, made that summer as baseball's best-paid player.

Ten years later, Louis had retired from the ring and was promoting bouts with the International Boxing Club. He and James Norris arranged for the second title fight at The Corner.

On the rainy evening of June 16, 1949, a bull-nosed brawler from the Bronx named Jake LaMotta squared off against middleweight champion Marcel Cerdan at brightly lit Briggs Stadium. A disappointing crowd of 22,183 saw LaMotta mash the face of the 32-year-old Algerian, who gamely fought the last several rounds with a left hand that was useless because of a shoulder injury.

"I'll kill myself first," Cerdan told his handlers as they repeatedly urged him to quit. Finally, before the start of the 10th round, they asked the referee to stop the fight. The technical knockout was the first time in 100 fights that Cerdan had been KO'd.

"It was the worst break a champion could have," Louis told Cerdan in the dressing room.

A close second was the gate flop, which cost promoters and fighters tens of thousands of dollars. Despite poor advance sales, the IBC had spurned radio, TV and newsreel films in anticipation of packing Briggs Stadium and drawing $350,000 in receipts. The 5,000 ringside seats, priced at $20, sold out. But the $15 and $10 grandstand seats remained half-filled. Cerdan, who reportedly rejected a $100,000 guarantee in favor of 40 percent of the net, wound up getting half that for losing his crown.

Bad luck soon gave way to tragedy. While LaMotta went on to forge a national reputation as boxing's "Raging Bull," Cerdan died in a plane crash in the Azores during a flight back to the States for a rematch with LaMotta.

Outdoor boxing never caught on in Detroit. Most bouts continued to be held at Olympia Stadium, a venue controlled by the Norris family, which was OK with Briggs.

Detroit Free Press

JOE LOUIS POUNCES ON BOB PASTOR IN THEIR 1939 FIGHT AT THE CORNER.

"My grandfather looked at the fights as being more of a civic obligation than a way to make money," said local attorney Walter (Mickey) Briggs III. "He always hated what it did to his grass." ◆

said Joe DeMaestri, who played shortstop for several teams during the '50s. "Kaline was probably one of the best of all time. He could do it all."

Kaline came to Detroit in 1953, a skinny 18-year-old straight from Baltimore's sandlots. He matured rapidly. One spring Sunday in 1955, he hit three home runs against Kansas City at Briggs Stadium, including two in one inning. He finished the season with a .340 average, making the 20-year-old rightfielder the youngest batting champion ever. Kuenn, unlike the abstemious Kaline, liked his chewing tobacco and beer. The Milwaukee native broke in at shortstop in 1952, then moved to centerfield in 1958.

Gus Zernial, who played the 1958 and '59 seasons at Briggs Stadium, discussed the Tigers' "K-K Kids" in Danny Peary's book, "We Played the Game."

Kaline "wasn't as dynamic a hitter as Mantle, but he was on that level. He led the league in hitting only once and never led in homers or RBIs, but he batted .300 with a lot of extra-base hits, was a tremendous clutch hitter, and was the best rightfielder in baseball. In those years, Kaline was as complete a player as Joe DiMaggio. I really admired his consistency. Although he wasn't a take-charge guy, he led just by the way he played the game.

"Harvey Kuenn also was a super player," Zernial continued, "though a completely different type than Kaline. Like Kaline, he was a lock to hit .300, but he didn't have as much power. He hit line drives into the gaps and led the league in doubles in both years I was with the Tigers. As was the case with Kaline, he led, but not verbally."

Kuenn batted a league-high .353 in 1959, then the following spring was swapped even-up for the defending home run champ, Cleveland's Rocky Colavito. Observers typically described the controversial trade as exchanging 135 singles for 42 home runs. The Tigers got the better of the deal, as Colavito went on to average 35 homers and 107 RBIs during his four seasons at The Corner.

While Detroit fans occupied themselves with these stars, ownership of the team passed to a syndicate of investors who paid the Briggs estate $5.5 million in 1956. By 1961, radio-TV magnate John Fetzer had bought out his fellow investors to become sole owner of the Tigers.

Fetzer was the original man in the gray flannel suit. At no time was his understated nature more evident than when he renamed the stadium. Unlike Briggs, whose byline had been writ large on his factories and the ballpark, Fetzer deflected the spotlight from himself by choosing the generic Tiger Stadium over something more personal, like Fetzer Field. The switch, effective the first day of 1961, signified nothing but a change in ownership. Everything else about The Corner remained the same, particularly the intimacy of the surroundings.

George Kell liked to tell of one postwar afternoon when Newhouser was getting rocked by the Red Sox. As the Tigers pitcher backed up third base on yet another Boston hit, a fan started getting on him.

"Hang in there, Hal," Kell said. "Don't worry about that guy."

Kell was walking back to his position when he heard the fan add, "You're not doing too good yourself, Kell." ◆

Burton Historical Collection

A winning trio: Cobb, Kuenn and Kaline. Together they won 14 batting titles – 12 for Ty, one each for Harvey and Al.

Courtesy Bill Dow

"The Rock" socked 45 homers in 1961 and led the Tigers in RBIs his first three seasons at The Corner.

MEMORIES GEORGE KELL

I tell you, I threw my bat 15 feet into the air

Even when I played with the Philadelphia A's – before I was traded to Detroit – Briggs Stadium was my favorite ballpark, along with Fenway Park. So when I was traded to Detroit in 1946, I was real glad about it.

A lot of folks from Arkansas were up there, people who had come up during the war to work in the plants. I had a lot of friends there. The day I was traded, probably 40 or 50 people came down to the dugout to say hello to me. I just liked it there. I really liked it. I had not hit .300 in Philadelphia, but after I got to Detroit I hit .300 six straight years. People just opened up to me.

I remember the first game I played there as a Tiger. It was a doubleheader against the Red Sox. They had more than 50,000 there, and I wasn't used to seeing that kind of crowd. Needless to say, I was a little bit jittery. But in the first inning, Johnny Pesky hit a line shot two hops just to my right. I speared it and threw him out, and after that I felt relaxed and comfortable.

Courtesy The Designated Hatter

In 1949, I beat Ted Williams for the batting championship on the last day of the season at Briggs Stadium. Williams was one point ahead of me going into the last day, and Hoot Evers told me, "If you get two hits, you'll catch him."

I doubled the first time up off Bob Lemon. Now normally, at that time of year you're pitching rookies, but Cleveland was trying to finish third. They had to win. I had a single in my second at-bat against Lemon. I looked up around the fifth inning, and here out of the bullpen comes Bob Feller. I'm thinking: "My God, is this the World Series?"

Well, Feller walked me the first time I faced him, so I'm still 2-for-2. But in the seventh inning Feller struck me out. Hoot said, "You've got it won – 2-for-3 will do." But in the ninth inning I'm the fourth batter due up and Hoot said, "God, you don't want to bat again." I said, "There's nothing I can do."

I found out later that our manager, Red Rolfe, had planned to have Joe Ginsberg pinch-hit for me because our PR man, Lyall Smith, had called from the press box to say that Williams had gone hitless in his game. But I learned all that after the game. At the time, I was doggoned if I was going to sit on the bench and win the championship. I always remembered Williams playing a doubleheader the last day of the '41 season when he topped .400.

Well, Dick Wakefield singles, and that means I'm going to bat. The next man went out and I'm in the on-deck circle when Eddie Lake hit a two-hopper to Ray Boone, who was playing shortstop for Cleveland that day. Boone stepped on second and threw to first for the game-ending double play, and, I tell you, I threw my bat 15 feet into the air. I wound up beating Williams by two ten-thousandths of a point: .3429 to .3427.

My whole time around that stadium was good – the broadcasting days, too. But in the end I just had to get home. I was having health problems, and I just couldn't deal with the travel. The club had been so good to me, allowing me to fly from Little Rock to games wherever the Tigers were playing.

I remember the last night I worked at Tiger Stadium, the last game I did in 1996, after 35 years of broadcasting on radio and television. There had been a long rain delay before the game and another one during the game, so I didn't walk out of the park until about quarter to 12 at night. When I walked out, I thought: "My Lord, this is the last time I'm ever going to do this."

I didn't want to quit, but I knew I had to. I was hurting all over. My back was hurting. My legs were hurting. But it was kind of like leaving home. ◆

George Kell spent half a century at The Corner as a Hall of Fame third baseman and longtime broadcaster.

TIGER STADIUM
OPENING DAY TUESDAY 1.30 P.M
CLEVELAND APRIL 11 & 13
CHICAGO 14 15 & 16
LOS ANGELES 21 22 &
FIRST NITE GAME

CHAPTER 5

Ray Glonka / Detroit Free Press

Ballpark people

Back in the days when every man sported a hat, the economic vagaries of operating a ballclub forced Frank Navin to wear several at once. For years the Tigers' owner and president ran practically every aspect of the front office, from signing paychecks and negotiating contracts to handling advertising, publicity and ticket sales. The supporting cast on game day was thin, particularly at Bennett Park, where ushers were unheard of and a full-time grounds crew was considered a luxury.

How times have changed.

Never mind the front office, where a squad of executives separately handle functions that Navin used to juggle daily. Today, according to Tom Folk, senior director of stadium operations, a small army of 700 to 800 people is needed to work a full house at Tiger Stadium.

Call them ballpark people. Roughly half are vendors and concession stand workers. The number also includes about 130 ushers, 100 security personnel and scores of ticket sellers, rest room and press box attendants, and the grounds crew.

HATS OFF TO TIGER STADIUM! AN ARMY OF USHERS SALUTES THE NAME CHANGE BEFORE THE 1961 OPENER.

The size of the work force is determined by the anticipated size of the crowd. Estimating how many employees should report to the stadium is more art than science, with department supervisors weighing various factors – ticket sales, meteorological reports, the attractiveness of the opponent, the starting pitchers, competing events, expected walk-up sales – before arriving at a figure a few hours before game time.

"Then the calls go out," Folk said. "Hopefully, we've got the right-sized crew."

Most of the folks who keep the park running smoothly and looking good are anonymous, although a handful of longtime employees have been seen by more Tigers fans than Cecil Fielder or Justin Thompson.

Bill Fundaro? You don't recognize the name, but if you sat anywhere near either dugout you'd probably know the face. He's the fellow who between 1976 and 1996 was stationed on a small chair near the visitors' dugout and kept the umpires supplied with balls.

"I'd take the balls that the umpires had rubbed down before the game and make sure the home plate ump didn't run low and have to slow down the game," Fundaro said. "From where I was, I got to know fans as well as players. Anybody who'll talk with me, I'll talk with."

It was a small but important job for Fundaro, a public school counselor who first started working at The Corner as an usher in 1968. Three decades later, he was put in charge of security on the field, deciding who belongs and who doesn't before and after games.

"During all of that time, Tiger Stadium was my place, after teaching," he said. "I could walk into a different world 80 days a year. It's been beautiful."

Not surprisingly, many stadium employees have been drawn from the surrounding neighborhood. Perhaps the ultimate ballpark person is Frank Feneck, the head groundskeeper from 1974 until his retirement after the 1998 season.

"Our house was so close to the stadium that I could look at a comic book in my bed using the lights from the stadium roof," said Feneck, who grew up on Plum and Sixth Street, behind the Checker Cab Co.

Courtesy Stanley Roginski

DETROIT'S LITTLEST BOY OF SUMMER IN THE 1930S WAS BATBOY JOE ROGGINS, A PRODUCT OF THE POLISH NEIGHBORHOOD JUST WEST OF THE PARK.

Briggs Stadium was only a block away, so he and his pals regularly used its smooth walls for games of strikeout. "We pretended to be the different Tiger players," he said. "My favorites were Eddie Mayo, George Kell and Hank Greenberg."

Feneck used to accompany Greenberg on

Patricia Beck / Detroit Free Press

ART WITKOSKY, A VENDOR AT THE CORNER FOR A QUARTER OF A CENTURY, DISPENSES ONE OF THE MILLION-PLUS RED HOTS SOLD IN 1999.

A FRANK HISTORY

As any baseball fan can tell you, a hot dog is more than a blend of meats stuffed inside a casing. It's a gastrointestinal institution, a staple of ballparks in Detroit and other cities since being introduced at New York's Polo Grounds in 1901.

The Tigers used a number of food suppliers through the years, but by 1958 had grown dissatisfied with their vendor. That year Gus Hauf, a sausage superintendent at Hygrade Food Corp., invented the company's famous Ballpark Franks. His special formula remains a secret.

In 1959, Ballpark Franks became the official Briggs Stadium hot dog. Later they went on sale commercially, rising to become the country's No. 2 best-selling red hot. As general manager Jim Campbell once claimed, "They're not eating hot dogs; they're eating tube steaks."

It didn't take long for the humble Ballpark Franks to become a part of Tigers lore. One day in the 1960s, Gates Brown was on the bench, surreptitiously munching on a red hot, when he suddenly was called upon to pinch-hit. He stuffed his hot dog under his shirt, hustled to the plate and promptly slapped the ball to the outfield.

As fate would have it, the Gator had to belly slide into second base. He emerged from the swirling dust with a yellow stain across his uniform shirt.

By the way, the reason vendors slather only mustard on the dogs is because ketchup, which contains sugar, spoils quickly in the heat and attracts flies.

In 1985, Cincinnati schoolteacher Bob Wood visited every major league park, grading each on, among other things, the quality of its hot dogs. He rated Tiger Stadium's dogs No. 1.

"A Ballpark Frank with a little mustard on the side is a dream fulfilled," Wood wrote in his book, "Dodger Dogs to Fenway Franks." "And proof that worthy experiences never die in the tradition of a fine baseball park."

Much to the dismay of fans who grew up on the flavorful franks, they were replaced in 1992 by Thorn Apple Valley's "sausage in a bun." A public backlash, however, forced the Mike Ilitch regime to reconsider its hasty dismissal of the famous dog. It was brought back a couple of years later.

Today, Tigers fans consume a couple million Ballpark Franks a season, with obvious relish – or not. ◆

MEMORIES JOE LAPOINTE

Detroit Free Press

USHERING IN THE '60S: JOE LAPOINTE OFTEN HAD THIS VIEW.

Usually you got a quarter or 50 cents, sometimes just a dime

When I was 17, it was a very good year for the Tigers. This was 1968, the summer before my senior year at St. Martin's High and my second season as an assistant usher at Tiger Stadium. We "badge boys" worked for free: No salary, just tips. On chilly spring nights and sultry summer days, with rags in hand, we ran up steep steps to wipe grime and pigeon droppings from green wooden chairs.

Aside from tips, the job's biggest perk was to see the games for free. When the Tigers won the World Series that fall against St. Louis, I watched from a dirty concrete step in the aisle of my upper-deck station, between posts 24 and 25, along the first-base line. From my vantage point, even early in the play, I realized Tiger leftfielder Willie Horton would throw out Lou Brock at home plate in Game 5. It was the pivotal moment of that game, that Series, that season and that era, and I had a perfect perch.

About half the customers tipped. Usually you got a quarter or 50 cents, sometimes just a dime. A sold-out game might yield $15 to $20. A bad night might mean $3 to $5, still more than enough for bus fare and a couple of Coneys while waiting to transfer outside Kinsel's drugstore on Michigan Avenue.

The senior ushers, older men on small salaries, wore green uniforms and worked the box seats in the low levels. There sat the swells, tipping well. We badge boys wore jeans and T-shirts and worked higher up in the reserved seats. Friday nights were best because people stopped at bars after work and entered the ballpark in a happy and generous mood. Saturday afternoons were the worst because it was Ladies Day with lots of mothers and kids. On Sundays we used to grumble about day-tripping farmers from outstate who would rather give you an ear of corn than a quarter.

We were city-slick, feeling worldly beyond our years. The previous season, the summer of '67, we worked a Sunday game while smoke from the nascent riot rose behind the grandstands. A rookie that year, I'd learned the fundamental hustle from the older kids. Grab the ticket stubs at the bottom of the aisle, run fast to the chairs, clean them briskly, smile and stand there waiting with one hand in your pocket, gently jingling loose change in a heavy-handed hint. Some of the guys, when stiffed out of a tip, would accidentally step on the shoes of the customers while walking back down the row. The innocently ignorant got a mere brush of the sole. The savvy cheapskates got the full heel.

The men who supervised us were colorful curs, always eyeballing each other suspiciously to guard their turf. My guy used to run a skid-row bar near the ballpark. In the long hours before first pitch, he enjoyed enlightening his youthful assistants about human frailty and vice in the big city. In those years, downtown Detroit seemed to be a vibrant place, and there was much for a teenager to see and learn about baseball and life on hot summer nights. ◆

Joe Lapointe, a former Free Press reporter, is a sports writer for the New York Times.

MEMORIES FRED RICE

The fans were not too generous with tips in those days

In the Depression years, pleasures were simple and my intense love for sports kept me out of trouble. My heroes were, to name a few: Charlie Gehringer, Hank Greenberg, Schoolboy Rowe and two Yankees, Lou Gehrig and Babe Ruth. I lived for the game of baseball.

My greatest thrill was a day's trip to old Navin Field at The Corner. I would hop on a Trumbull streetcar for six cents, plop down on the old wicker seats and head for my utopia. As we clattered toward the ballpark, the conductor, with his monotonous voice, would announce each stop. At last I could spot the old ballpark and my young heart would beat wildly with the expectation of seeing my heroes, the Tigers, playing a real major league game.

I never paid to see a game because I was tall enough to be picked to usher (no pay, of course) by the head honcho – Chic, a happy-go-lucky, rotund gentleman. A large group of boys lined up on Michigan Avenue at 11 a.m., four hours before the game, and waited for the big steel door to roll up. Finally, Chic would emerge and begin selecting from among us for the privilege of being an usher. With my fingers crossed, my eyes were fixed on Chic's face. When he spotted me, he would smile and beckon me inside. The fans were not too generous with tips in those days. But if I totaled a quarter for the day, I could buy a hot dog and a Coke and have a nickel left over. Life could not have been any sweeter.

The two G-men were my outstanding heroes: Greenberg, who thrilled fans with prodigious clouts over the wall and onto Cherry Street (before upper-deck seats were installed at the refurbished Briggs Stadium), and Gehringer, Mr. Smoothie. Every play he made at second base and every swing of his bat were effortless and as graceful as a ballet dancer.

On May 2, 1939, my station to usher was right behind the visitors' dugout. The Yankees were taking infield practice before the game, and first baseman Gehrig, the Iron Horse, was at his usual position.

I watched as he took a ground ball, scooped it up and tossed it weakly to Bill Dickey, the Yankees catcher. Gehrig turned around and walked off the field. Our eyes met. I waved at him and said, "Hi, Lou." He smiled, waved back and disappeared into the end of his career. Shortly thereafter came the end of his days on Earth – the saddest day of my young life was when that happened, June 2, 1941. It was the culmination of a sweet, memorable era. ◆

Fred Rice is a retired plumber living in Livonia.

Courtesy Fred Rice

USHERING IN THE '30S: FRED RICE SAW LOU GEHRIG'S STREAK END.

MEMORIES HERBIE REDMOND

'Come on and do it, Herbie!'

First you strut to third ... then you wave your cap ... next you shake those hips ... and jump for joy ... then kiss that cap ... and salute the team. ... In 1986, Herbie Redmond, the longtime Tiger Stadium groundskeeper, described for the Free Press the one dance Arthur Murray can't teach.

When it started, I was just looking at Jim Northrup when he knocked the ball out of the ballpark (Aug. 28, 1969, against Oakland). We were sitting on the bench, and the grounds crew jumped up, and I started doing it. The next day, they called me in the front office. I thought they were going to fire me, but they said, "Herbie, just keep doing what you want to do."

I was just out there dancing and twisting. I was trying to make my people happy. I love the ballplayers. They love me, too. They call me Shorty or Short Dog. The kids in the neighborhood call me Short Dog because when I get home, I look short. I look bigger on TV.

I go in the clubhouse after the game. The ballplayers like to see me talk. I don't beat around the bush. I tell it like it is. Kaline and them call it "Herbie Redmond's Show." They say: "Here comes Redmond and his show." Some folks call it the Herbie Shuffle. People like it and all the kids go nuts. The guys on the grounds crew all kid me. They say, "Get out of here, Herbie."

Before the games I go to the Stadium Bar, and all the people who come into the bar know I'm Herbie Redmond. I say, "Did you come to the stadium to see the game or to see me?" They say, "We came to see you, Herbie, so you better do good."

I watch kids playing softball right up the street from where I live. The kids ask me to umpire. When the Tigers are out of town for eight, nine, 10 days, I get out there and play with the kids.

In the bottom of the fifth, I wait till the first, the second and the third men go out. I'm the fourth. I start from third base. I start twisting my cap and wave at the bleachers. I come all the way around to first base, and that's when I cut up, picking on the out-of-town team. Then the people are going wild. Even the ballplayers come out of the dugout, and they all laugh. They'll yell, "Come on and do it, Herbie!" Then I come back around second base and throw my cap off. Sometimes I do kind of a polka dance, and they love that. As we're coming back around, we really get down.

It started that way, and that's what the people want. When the Tigers are in the lead, I do everything. I do a kind of limbo, too.

There's six of us on the field with the broom. We go back into the room after that and they say, "Oh, Herbie did it this time!" ◆

Craig Porter / Detroit Free Press

THE HERBIE REDMOND SHOW ENJOYED A LONG RUN AT THE CORNER.

his walks to a bathhouse on Vernor, where he got his legs and feet massaged. Feneck and his friends also got the chance to shag balls on those days when Greenberg, recently returned from the Army, took extra batting practice to get into shape.

With money tight in the 1940s, Feneck mastered various ways of sneaking into the stadium, including crawling under gates or racing past startled guards.

"I can honestly say that I never paid for a baseball or football game in my life. They would never chase me because I would run up the ramps, and they were afraid of having a heart attack," he said.

Feneck saw the 1945 World Series that way. He was only 9, but several years wiser in understanding the ins and outs of the stadium.

"At that time, the Tigers' bullpen was stuck behind the centerfield wall near the flagpole," he said. "There was a high bench for the players, and we used to beg them for balls. Sometimes, we would get lucky.

"One time, I climbed over the fence into the bullpen when the players were watching the game. I grabbed Paul Richards' mitt, stuck it in my mouth and climbed back up and over the screen. I was so scared, I saved it for about a month before using it. I ended up taking the padding out of this catcher's mitt and made it into a first baseman's glove. Years later, when Paul Richards was managing the White Sox, I told him I was the one who stole his glove. He got the biggest kick out of it but told me he didn't remember losing it."

Feneck's mildly criminal ways continued when he returned to The Corner in the 1950s after serving in the Navy.

"I even sneaked into the stadium as an adult," he admitted. "I remember seeing how my dad would operate. After he retired from Ford, he would go down there every Saturday when the buses were pulling up with all the kids. He would put his arms around a couple of kids, acting like he was their counselor, and walk right in. He loved to sit in the lower-deck bleachers in right to watch Kaline. Believe me, there were a lot of people from around the neighborhood who knew how to get into the park."

Mary Schroeder / Detroit Free Press

Groundskeeper Frank Feneck (left) dishes the dirt with Tigers manager Buddy Bell at the 1997 groundbreaking of Comerica Park in downtown Detroit. Bell's tenure at The Corner ended in 1998.

Feneck began working at The Corner in 1958, helping the cleanup crew. Five years later, he was a full-time employee of the grounds crew. One of his first assignments was handling the visiting team's telephone line during football season.

"I'll never forget standing next to Ray Nitschke of the Packers when they were getting beat up by the Lions. The Lions were just across from a table on the same sideline. Players from both teams would always be yelling at each other. They would sound so rough, it scared the hell out of you. But let me tell you, in general, the football players were a lot friendlier than baseball players.

"Even though our work was doubled for football, we really enjoyed being out there with the Lions. There was a lot of measuring

> *"Let me tell you, in general, the football players were a lot friendlier than baseball players."*
>
> Frank Feneck,
> *head groundskeeper at The Corner from 1974 through 1998*

MEMORIES RICHARD BAK

'STRAWBERRY SHORTCAKE! GOOSEBERRY PIE! V-I-C-T-O-R-Y!'

News of Joe Diroff's passing in early 1997 raised more than a few eyebrows around town – not so much in alarm, perhaps, as in a reflexive salute to a Detroit original. With his heavily forested forehead, homemade signs and cornball cheers, "The Brow" had long been a fixture at Tiger Stadium and other area sporting events, as recognizable as any of the athletes he supported to the absolute limit of his aerobic capability.

In a world of Type A personalities, the hyperactive Brow was Type AAA. Despite suffering from a bad ticker, every day and night he roamed the stands at will, incessantly imploring the crowd to get behind the home team.

"LET'S GO BANANAS!" he'd scream, holding up a plastic banana. Another favorite prop was a bicycle pump. "LET'S GET PUMPED UP!" When the mood struck, he'd break into a wild, rubber-legged jig, acting like someone whose breakfast burritos had kicked in while standing in line to use the Tiger Stadium john.

I first encountered The Brow in the late '80s. I was enjoying a mellow beer buzz one midsummer night when I was nearly blasted out of my seat by a blind-side salvo:

"STRAWBERRY SHORTCAKE! GOOSEBERRY PIE! V-I-C-T-O-R-Y!"

Ears ringing, I looked for the source of the explosion and found it in the odd little fella going berserk in the aisle. He looked to be a gnarled version of the Keebler elf, with Pierre Salinger's eyebrows, and for some reason he started waving squeeze bottles of ketchup and mustard in the air.

"THEY'LL NEVER CATCH UP!" he bellowed before aiming his second broadside straight at me. "CUZ THEY CAN'T CUT THE MUSTARD!"

Before I could come up with an appropriate response – something feeble like "Yeah! Go Tigers!" or something more genuine like "Get the hell out of the aisle so I can watch the game!" – The Brow had moved on to another section, evidently satisfied that he had done all in his power to lift the collective spirit of this particular outpost of fandom.

Although he seemed to have been around forever, the ubiquitous Brow actually was part of the local sporting scene for only a few years. He first started whooping it up in 1982, a couple of years after he retired as a Detroit schoolteacher and was casting about for another way to make himself useful.

He recognized his calling, he explained, after literally being tossed out of Cobo Arena for being a bit too demonstrative at a Pistons playoff game. His knees scraped, his pants torn, his glasses somewhere in the darkness, The Brow decided then that God had somehow shown him his true purpose in life. He would be Detroit's fan for all seasons.

Signs and condiments in hand, The Brow thus became the latest in a succession of storied Detroit superfans, a lineage that includes such characters as Gus the Dancing Vendor, who used to boogaloo down the aisles of Cobo; Patsy (The Human Earache) O'Toole, who shattered eardrums at old Navin Field; the Cusimano brothers, who launched the first octopus at Olympia; and Leon (The

---

and painting of the field every week. When the football season was over, we were there in February replacing sod, and that was tough in those conditions. Sometimes in the bleachers, the football fans would burn the redwood benches to stay warm. We always kept a stack of redwood planks under the stands for replacement."

Feneck's first responsibility for the Tigers was preparing the mound and home plate area. In 1974, he was promoted to head groundskeeper.

"As head groundskeeper, I kept close attention to how the players used the field," Feneck said. "I noticed that Aurelio Rodriguez and Don Wert liked to play on the infield grass, while Whitaker and Trammell would play on the edge of the outfield grass sometimes. I would sometimes make the diamond bigger with the skin of the infield to accommodate them.

"The Tigers' managers would talk with me often about the field, and I would make adjustments as necessary. Boston got carried

Dick Tripp / Detroit Free Press

DON WERT, AN ALL-STAR IN 1968, HELD DOWN THE HOT CORNER FROM '63 TO '70.

Courtesy Joe Crachiola

Joe Diroff lets loose a blast at Tiger Stadium. "Brow," Kirk Gibson told him, "you're a true fan."

Barber) Bradley, who heckled opponents nonstop at the Silverdome.

Unlike his predecessors, The Brow was ecumenical in his support. He showed up at every home game of every professional team in town, plus as many away contests as his pocketbook and old Dodge would permit. He also attended a variety of collegiate games. At first he had to pay to get in, but teams soon recognized his sincerity and started letting him in for free. Players and coaches took him to heart. On one occasion, the Red Wings brought him home from Edmonton on their private plane, took up a collection, then joined him in a rousing Strawberry Shortcake cheer. All this after a tough playoff loss.

As part of his mission, The Brow regularly visited the airport, setting up his lawn chair in an empty terminal in the wee hours of the morning to welcome the boys back from a road trip.

"Brow," Kirk Gibson once told him, "you're a true fan."

The Brow, who was married for 50 years and raised nine children, obviously knew something about commitment. He supported teams through good times and bad. When he sensed that some troubled soul might benefit from a private hurrah or two, he was there, no questions asked.

"I am not a man who makes judgments," he said after visiting the Red Wings' convicted druggie, Bob Probert, in jail. "I won't cast any first stones. Everybody needs someone to care. And cheer."

In 1995, The Brow became a no-show, the result of a stroke that confined him to a nursing home. When he could, he led fellow patients in cheers – keeping trim, one supposes, for the day when he could return to his regular duties at Tiger Stadium and other venues where his unfettered boosterism was sorely needed. Instead, he had a relapse and suddenly found himself sharing a skybox with Patsy O'Toole and Leon the Barber. The Brow was 74. Reading his obit, I was reminded of columnist Jim Murray's comment when Casey Stengel passed through the pearly turnstiles.

"Well," Murray said, "God is certainly getting an earful tonight."

We know the feeling. Bye, Brow. You did Detroit proud – and loud. ◆

Richard Bak is co-author of "The Corner."

---

away, claiming our crew helped the Tigers beat the Red Sox. Wade Boggs thought home plate was cocked so that it faced more to rightfield than directly to the mound. He claimed he had to adjust his stance because our pitchers would throw to the outside and still hit the plate. He finally agreed with me that it was an optical illusion."

One of the toughest chores was getting the field ready for the 1968 World Series, he said. "We had clinched the pennant at home, and the field received a lot of damage from celebrating fans. We even found box seats outside the stadium after the game.

"We made sure that didn't happen in 1984. We had mounted police for the playoffs and World Series, which helped us tremendously. A few people jumped the wall, but when they saw those charging horses, they ran back into the stands."

Besides hoof imprints in the grass, there was little damage to the field.

"The job was very demanding and time-consuming," Feneck said, "but I still enjoyed

MEMORIES
BILL NICHOLAS

When Mr. Monaghan brought in that helicopter full of pizza – that was my highlight

I'd already retired from the grocery business, the bar business and from a tool shop when I went to work at Tiger Stadium in 1969.

A big part of the time I worked in the dining rooms or VIP rooms, where the media and the players would come after the game every night. And in the WDIV room upstairs, where they had refreshments for the people the station would have up there.

For me, the stadium has all sorts of memories. I went down there when I was a kid, when Greenberg and Newhouser were playing. I've got memories as a fan and as a season-ticket holder with the Lions when they played ball there, and as somebody who worked there, too. I worked a Rod Stewart concert, and my ears were ringing for a week.

My best memory is of the World Series in '84, when Mr. Monaghan brought in that helicopter full of pizza – that was my highlight … about four times it went up and got pizza and came back, and the last couple of times Jack Morris rode along with 'em. The grounds crew and I were just sitting there, milling around, eating pizza, you know. And, naturally, sucking on a beer or two.

I thought that was great, and working the hospitality room during the World Series for NBC, with Tommy Lasorda and all the big celebrities eating the chili and the hot dogs we were serving. For me, Tiger Stadium was great. I had no qualms about nothing. ◆

Bill Nicholas – Little Bill – worked at The Corner for 27 years.

EARLY SCOREBOARD OPERATORS USED CHALK OR CHANGED NUMBERS BY HAND, BUT BY 1978 CHARLIE LEBOT USED TOGGLE SWITCHES.
BELOW: ENTERPRISING THERESA MEEHAN PARKS CARS IN 1963.

Ed Haun / Detroit Free Press

Detroit Free Press

Alan R. Kamuda / Detroit Free Press

Alan R. Kamuda / Detroit Free Press

Earl Culp sells scorebooks during a 1980 game.
Right: Curley Banks hawks hot chocolate in 1974.

Tony Spina / Detroit Free Press

Alan R. Kamuda / Detroit Free Press

The scene in '75: Get your peanuts outside the park.
Inside, Marvin Wells is the man for souvenirs in the bleachers.

it. Even when the team is on the road, you have to protect the field from the weather. I always had to stay around the house, if I wasn't at the park, in case there was a problem. Right after the last game of the season, the next day, I was already preparing for Opening Day."

It wasn't all work and no play. The playing roster has included some merry pranksters through the years: Jack Morris, Hank Aguirre, Norm Cash, Frank Lary.

"I had fun with the ground crew," said Mickey Lolich, another Tiger who provided comic relief. "I'd go sit on their tractor and get it started. They'd be sitting on the side somewhere on their little seats, and I'd put the tractor in gear and jump off. It'd take off across the outfield with three or four guys running after it. They said I made things more interesting, but they always kept a close eye on me."

"I used to have water fights with those guys," Feneck said. "You had to be careful where you walked and who was behind you.

"I remember one time running the garden tractor and grading the warning track in front of the dugout. Aguirre or Lary hooked up the hose and nearly blew me out of my seat. I got back at them good one time when they were coming out of the tunnel. They finally waved the white flag, and we called a truce."

Vendors and concessionaires also have been an integral part of the scene at The Corner. Celia Seimbor Rossi grew up in the Polish neighborhood around Martin and Michigan, a few miles west of The Corner. She and her two friends, Annie Walczak and Lottie Swiss, remain inseparable more than a half-century after they graduated together from Chadsey High School.

One of their bonding experiences was working the concession stands at Briggs Stadium.

"Hot dogs sold for 20 cents," said Rossi, who lives in Adrian. "On days when games weren't scheduled, we'd work in the commissary packing peanuts."

Occasionally, players like Greenberg and Hal Newhouser would stop in and chat with the crew, giving the girls a thrill.

Burton Historical Collection

JACK REED TOUCHES 'EM ALL, ENDING A SEVEN-HOUR MARATHON IN THE 22ND INNING IN 1962.

"It was an exciting time because Detroit won the pennant that year," she said. "It was 1945."

Whether being stuck under the stands working a counter or humping a metal box of goodies up and down concrete stairs, being on your feet for several hours usually involves more drudgery than excitement. Old-timers talk about June 24, 1962, in the same way World War II veterans talk about D-Day. It was hell, but boy, you should've been there.

A Sunday afternoon turned to twilight, and vendors' legs to jelly, as the Tigers and Yankees engaged in a seven-hour marathon before Jack Reed's home run in the 22nd inning – the only one of his career – gave the Yankees a 9-7 victory and mercifully put to bed what was then the longest game in big-league history.

That day the crowd consumed 32,200 hot dogs and 75,500 bottles of pop and beer.

MEMORIES REID CREAGER

He just laughed and pointed to my car

When I think of Tiger Stadium, I think of watching the celebration from the back of the Tigers' clubhouse after they won the 1984 World Series. I still have the sport coat with the champagne smell.

But mostly I think of my home for a couple hundred days and nights in the mid-1980s – the press box – and how I became a legend there simply for buying a new car.

That late-summer day, I completed the paperwork on my 1985 Toyota Tercel just in time to take it downtown for batting practice and pregame interviews. When I reached the parking lot for players and media – the eventual site of Tiger Plaza – the guard congratulated me. And once the game began, I told anyone who'd listen how happy I was to have the first new car of my life.

Around the fourth inning, public relations director Dan Ewald summoned me on the public-address system. It sounded like he was laughing.

When I approached him, he was laughing so hard he could barely say: "The guard at the parking lot just called. A foul ball went over the third-base roof and smashed your back windshield."

Now, press-box pranks have been known to occur – as I learned in my first week on the beat, when someone borrowed my computer for a few minutes and sent an unprintable message to my boss. So I knew that if I took the elevator downstairs and nothing was amiss, I'd face a howling multitude upon my return. But after a couple of minutes of stewing, curiosity took my legs and a sick feeling to the elevator.

When I reached the entrance to the lot, a guard said, "Are you Reid Creager?" I nodded, and he just laughed and pointed to my car. The rear window was smashed with a big hole in the middle – and I looked through a side window and saw an official American League baseball on the backseat. I picked up the ball and saw it had a thin slice under Dr. Bobby Brown's name.

In every visit to the press box since, people who don't even know me hear that story for the first time. But never from me. ◆

Reid Creager is a Free Press copy editor.

Courtesy Dwight Cendrowski

TIGER PLAZA WAS BUILT IN 1993, TOO LATE TO SAVE THE REAR WINDOW OF A REPORTER'S CAR.

Vendors might have sold more, but the concession stands were closed before game's end because of a state law prohibiting women from working more than 10 hours on Sunday.

Certain types of ballpark people have been rendered obsolete by technology. Before the public-address system, lineup changes and other announcements were made by a man with a megaphone. And the early scoreboard operators who either chalked or changed numbers by hand were replaced by an employee sitting inside a cozy control room with rows of buttons and toggle switches.

Another occupation that went the way of the dodo bird at The Corner was the organist. Bill Fox was first to climb into the loft on the extreme rightfield side of the press box when organ music was introduced to Tiger Stadium in the 1960s. Before the Ilitch regime killed the keys for good 30 years later, a handful of others filled the position. None played as long as Dan Greer.

A native Detroiter whose father was a Methodist minister, Greer first played the organ in church. He was a high school music teacher in Taylor when he started moonlighting at Olympia Stadium in 1971. That gig got him the job at Tiger Stadium when Fox retired the following spring. Greer completed a trifecta by playing for the Pistons at Cobo Arena.

"That's how many people remember me," Greer said from his home in Florida. "I'm the answer to that trivia question: 'Who's the only person ever to play for the Red Wings, Tigers and Pistons in the same season?' Except they often get it wrong and identify me as the only guy to have played for the Tigers and Lions. That's wrong. The Lions used bands. They didn't need an organist."

And for many years, neither did the Tigers. Practically every ballpark had one in place by the time the hidebound front office finally got around to it.

"I basically agreed with the general manager, Jim Campbell, who was conservative," Greer said. "He told me to just fill in the gaps: pitching changes, between innings, when there was an argument on the field. I couldn't play anything demeaning, like 'Three Blind Mice,' when somebody was arguing an umpire's call."

Greer chuckled. "Of course, nobody said I couldn't play the first couple lines from the national anthem: 'Oh, say can you see … .' I think that went over Campbell's head."

The playlist included some original compositions by Ernie Harwell, who asked the organist to try them out on the crowd.

Greer was playing "The Night Chicago Died" one evening when the Tigers had the White Sox on the ropes late in the game.

"Detroit led, 8-3, in the top of the eighth. You know, I was trying to have a little fun. Then, wouldn't you know it, the bottom falls out. Detroit commits about four or five errors, and the Sox scored eight runs." When the Sox came to bat the following inning,

"I'm the answer to that trivia question: 'Who's the only person ever to play for the Red Wings, Tigers and Pistons in the same season?' "

DAN GREER

Detroit Free Press

DAN GREER ON THE ORGAN AT THE CORNER, WHERE HE PLAYED FOR 11 SEASONS.

Craig Porter / Detroit Free Press

they were greeted with Greer's rendition of "Chicago, My Kind of Town."

For his labor, Greer made $75 a game, $150 for a doubleheader or an extremely long extra-inning affair. It worked out to about $6,000 a summer by the time he left the loft at the end of the 1982 season.

The pay is welcomed, but many ballpark people will tell you they don't really do it for the money. There are perks, like being close to history as it's being made.

When Fundaro was delivering baseballs to the umps, he had to go through the Tigers' dugout. "And that's where my biggest memory of Tiger Stadium occurred, one of the most electrifying times in my life," he recalled.

It was just before the start of the fifth game of the '84 World Series. Fundaro and several players were standing in the tunnel between the dugout and the locker room as the national anthem was playing.

"There was Tommy Brookens, myself, Alan Trammell, somebody else I can't remember. Suddenly we hear a guy going, 'It's going downtown! The blankety-blank's going downtown! These are our people. We're ending it here! We're ending it here!'

"It was Kirk Gibson, talking loud, talking to the wall, psyching himself up like for a football game.

"Now the national anthem is ending, and he walks right past us just like we don't even exist. And we all look at each other and kind of go, 'Wow!'

"That was the game he hit the home run off Goose Gossage.

"I remember when the San Diego manager went out to the mound to try to talk Gossage into walking Gibson. During time-outs, I had to walk back away from the screen to watch the crowd for any problems. They were playing 'Ghostbusters.' To see that crowd!

"When that ball cracked, it was obvious it was gone. The electricity was amazing. That was the most exciting moment of these 30 years.

"Tiger Stadium has been great. I never touched the bases or drove one into the stands, but I had my moments in the sun there, on that grass." ◆

Pitchers toe the rubber – Edward Ojeda scrubs it, making sure the mound is pitcher-perfect prior to the 1989 opener. Bill Fundaro, who worked at The Corner for 31 years, always made sure umpires had enough baseballs.

Julian H. Gonzalez / Detroit Free Press

CHAPTER 6

Midsummer classics

Courtesy Dick Clark. Opposite page: Burton Historical Collection

The All-Stars paid three visits to The Corner – in 1941, 1951 and 1971 – and on each occasion put on a demonstration of long-ball muscle. Collectively, a remarkable 15 homers were hit, including the two most famous blasts in All-Star history.

Ted Williams, the author of the most dramatic All-Star homer, considered Briggs Stadium his pet park. During his career he hit 55 home runs at The Corner, the most of any foreign field. Tall, rubbery and blessed with uncanny eyesight, the Boston outfielder was the first player to hit a fair ball out of the double-decked stadium, bombing one over the rightfield roof as a 20-year-old rookie in 1939.

The late Barney McCosky was in the Detroit outfield that day.

"I remember when I first saw Ted," he recalled in "Cobb Would Have Caught It," an oral history

ON THE FACING PAGE, RED SOX SLUGGER TED WILLIAMS AND YANKEE CLIPPER JOE DIMAGGIO SHARE LOCKER ROOM LAUGHS AFTER THE 1941 GAME.

RED SO

of the Tigers. "I think Roxie Lawson was pitching. I'm in centerfield, watching this skinny kid hitting, and – boom! – he swung and I watched the ball go over the rightfield roof in Briggs Stadium. It was foul. I said, 'Nobody can hit a ball that far.' Two innings later, he hit another one right out of the stadium (off Bob Harris). This one was fair. I just shook my head: no way. That's a good drive in a Model T Ford."

The All-Star Game had been created in 1933 to give fans an opportunity to see the best players from both leagues. On July 8, 1941, Williams was just one of a galaxy of stars assembled at Briggs Stadium for the ninth annual midsummer classic. A partisan American League crowd of 54,674 turned out on a pleasant Tuesday afternoon to watch the likes of Bob Feller, Bill Dickey, Joe Cronin, Lou Boudreau and the DiMaggio brothers (Joe and Dom) take on the National League's best. Catcher Birdie Tebbetts, first baseman Rudy York and pitcher Al Benton represented the Tigers. Del Baker, who had led Detroit to a pennant the previous season, managed the Americans.

"ARKY" VAUGHAN

Richard Bak Collection

Arky Vaughan homered twice in the '41 game, but his heroics were overshadowed by those of The Kid from Boston.

Feller started and held the Nationals to one hit, striking out four during his three innings. Whit Wyatt of Brooklyn was nearly as effective for the Nationals. The game remained scoreless until the fourth, when Williams lined an RBI double to right.

The teams exchanged sixth-inning runs, making the score 2-1 in favor of the Americans entering the seventh. Enos Slaughter led off the frame with a single to left off Washington's Sid Hudson. Williams fumbled the ball, allowing the Cardinals outfielder to take second.

This brought up Arky Vaughan, who had singled in his previous at-bat. This time the quiet Pittsburgh shortstop pulled Hudson's pitch into the upper rightfield stands, giving the Nationals a 3-2 lead. The lead grew to 5-2 when, facing Chicago's Eddie Smith in the eighth inning, Vaughan yanked another two-run homer to right.

The Americans retaliated with a run in their half of the eighth, Boston's Dom DiMaggio driving in older brother Joe with a single. The score was still 5-3 in the bottom of the ninth when the Americans filled the bags with one out against the Cubs' Claude Passeau.

At bat was Joe DiMaggio, who started the day having hit safely in 48 consecutive games. His eighth-inning double had more than a few in the stands wondering whether it extended his streak. It didn't – only regular-season games counted – though he would go on to collect a hit in eight more games after the All-Star break before his legendary streak ended at 56.

Of more immediate concern was what Joltin' Joe would do in the late-afternoon shadows of Briggs Stadium. Passeau got two quick strikes on him, then delivered a pitch that DiMaggio slapped to Boston Braves shortstop Eddie Miller. It was a made-to-order double-play ball that should have ended the game with the National League a 5-3 winner.

Instead, Brooklyn second baseman Billy Herman made a hurried throw on the relay that pulled the first baseman off the bag.

Herman's mistake left the Americans one run behind with runners on first and third, two out and Williams at bat. Passeau, a big right-hander known for his competitiveness, had fanned Williams the previous inning.

"He had a fast-tailing ball that he'd jam a left-hand batter with, right into your fists, and if you weren't quick, he'd get it past you," Williams recalled. As he came up in the ninth he lectured himself, "Damn it, you've got to be quicker, you've got to be more in front of this guy. You've got to be quicker."

With the game on the line, Passeau worked the count to two balls and one strike. Many fans who had been streaming out of the park to get an early jump on traffic had

Burton Historical Collection

"Well, it was the kind of thing a kid dreams about and imagines himself doing when he's playing those little playground games we used to play in San Diego."

Ted Williams

returned and were clotting the aisles. "The excitement in Briggs Stadium was terrific," Williams said. Passeau tried to slip a letter-high fastball past Williams, who whipped around in an all-out home run swing. The Free Press' Charlie Ward described what happened next:

"Williams swung, the crowd roared, Baker danced like a dervish as the ball struck the third deck of the rightfield stands and bounced back into the playing field. American Leaguers rushed from their dugout to congratulate the willowy Williams as he trotted around the bases in the footsteps of Gordon and DiMaggio as the American Leaguers scored a 7-5 triumph."

In his autobiography, "My Turn at Bat," Williams called the storybook swat his greatest thrill in baseball.

"Well, it was the kind of thing a kid dreams about and imagines himself doing when he's playing those little playground games we used to play in San Diego. Halfway down to first, seeing that ball going out, I stopped running and started leaping and jumping and clapping my hands, and I was just so happy I laughed out loud. I've never been so happy, and I've never seen so many happy guys."

As Baker pounded Williams on the back, a photographer asked him to give the big guy a hug for the camera. "Hell," Baker exclaimed, "I'd be willing to hug a porcupine for a hit like that!" Then he kissed Williams.

No National Leaguer lost more than Vaughan, whose two home runs, three successive hits and four RBIs – All-Star Game records – perished under one magnificent swish of Williams' bat.

The All-Star Game returned to Detroit in 1951. The 10-year hiatus would have been greater, except for special circumstances.

Detroit, oldest city in the Midwest, lit the candles for its 250th birthday that July. Civic leaders thought that a meeting between the American and National leagues – which happened to be celebrating their 50th and 75th anniversaries, respectively – would be a wonderful complement to the festivities.

Moreover, there was concern that ailing Tigers owner Walter O. Briggs didn't have long to live. Friends, family members and fellow club owners wished to give this proud and powerful man the pleasure of hosting the midsummer classic once more in his lifetime. Thus the 18th edition of the game, originally slated for Philadelphia's Shibe Park, was shifted to Detroit.

Briggs died the following January. But it was the passing of another of Detroit's legendary baseball figures that cast a pall over the '51 game.

Harry Heilmann was a direct link to a baseball past that, even in 1951, seemed like antiquity to many fans. The slow-footed San Franciscan had made his debut in the Tigers' outfield in 1914. Twenty years later, he started his broadcasting career with station WXYZ. Droll and articulate, with a cigarette

Courtesy The Designated Hatter

Briggs Stadium was decked out for two celebrations in 1951: the All-Star Game and Detroit's 250th birthday. Above: Jackie Robinson was one of seven Brooklyn Dodgers at The Corner for that year's midsummer classic.

Richard Bak Collection

TIGERS GEORGE KELL AND VIC WERTZ WERE AMONG THE AMERICAN LEAGUE FLAG BEARERS. BELOW: HARRY HEILMANN, WHO DIED ON THE EVE OF THE ALL-STAR GAME IN 1951, INTERVIEWS DIZZY TROUT (RIGHT) AND BIRDIE TEBBETTS SOME YEARS EARLIER.

dangling from his smoke-stained fingertips, Heilmann loved to spin yarns about the fabled names he had played with and against: Cobb, Ruth, Wahoo Sam, Shoeless Joe. A couple of generations of Detroiters had grown up watching Heilmann slug the ball or listening to his voice. But as baseball people began arriving in Detroit during the All-Star break, they learned that "Ol' Slug," who'd been ailing for months, was fading fast.

Third baseman George Kell was one of three Tigers suiting up for the Americans. Pitcher Fred Hutchinson and rightfielder Vic Wertz were the others.

"I remember the night before the All-Star Game, there was a banquet honoring the all-time Tiger team," Kell recalled. "I was fortunate enough to have been chosen. Ty Cobb was there, along with others like Gehringer and Greenberg. The only one missing that night was Harry Heilmann, who was in the hospital battling cancer. The next morning we learned he had passed away the night of the banquet. He was 56.

"I knew Heilmann very well. He influenced my broadcasting career more than anybody. At spring training in 1950, he had a show on WJR that was broadcast from Lakeland, Fla. He asked me if I would join him on those broadcasts to answer questions from the fans. In the spring of 1951 when he became ill, I did the show myself. It was my first broadcasting experience."

Burton Historical Collection

July 10, 1951, was a sunny Tuesday, with temperatures climbing into the middle 80s. Flags flew at half-mast in honor of Heilmann, and players, umpires and spectators observed a moment of silence. Then Cobb threw out the first ball, and 52,075 people in sheer dresses, summer suits and straw hats settled in to see if the underdog National League could win back-to-back All-Star games for the first time.

It could and did, rolling to an 8-3 victory.

Richard Bak Collection

George Kell, who homered for the home team in the 1951 game, catches up on his reading.

The Nationals roughed up five American League pitchers for 12 hits, including four home runs. The tone was set when the Phillies' Richie Ashburn doubled off the Browns' Ned Garver on the first pitch of the game. He ultimately scored on an error, giving the Nationals a 1-0 lead.

The junior circuit tied the score in the second inning when Ferris Fain's triple off the Phillies' Robin Roberts scored Yogi Berra. But Berra's batterymate, Eddie Lopat, the junk-ball specialist for the Yankees, came on in the fourth inning and immediately surrendered a home run to the Cardinals' Stan Musial. A few minutes later, the Boston Braves' Bob Elliott poled a two-run homer for a 4-1 lead.

Despite the Nationals' overwhelming display of power and finesse, and the fact that he struck out to end the game, Kell remembered it as "a great day. My parents, wife, children and others from Arkansas were there. I hit a home run and played all nine innings. My teammate, Vic Wertz, one of my all-time favorites, also hit a homer."

Both Tigers homers were solo shots and shaved the National League's lead to one, 4-3, entering the sixth. But Hutchinson walked Jackie Robinson, one of seven Brooklyn Dodgers on the roster, to open the inning, and Gil Hodges followed with a home run. The next inning, Hutchinson surrendered another run as Robinson surprised everybody by laying down a perfect two-out bunt to score Ashburn from third. All Kell could do was watch the ball trickle toward the bag and hope it would roll foul. It didn't, and the Nationals' lead grew to 7-3.

In the eighth, Pittsburgh's Ralph Kiner closed out the scoring with a bases-empty home run off Boston's Mel Parnell.

Coming at a time when there was an intense rivalry between the leagues and a real difference in their style of play, the loss stung the junior circuit's pride. Since the 1930s, the American League had dominated the World Series and All-Star Game, but now some observers noticed a shifting in the balance of power.

"A few years ago, you'd never expect the National League to smash four homers in one of these games," Kiner said afterward. "We weren't known for power, but times do change."

Twenty years later, when the All-Stars paid their third and final visit to The Corner, the times had indeed changed, inside and outside the ballpark. Primacy had passed to the National League, which had been more aggressive in signing black athletes during the intervening years.

The '70s were a controversial and radical decade, particularly in sports. A minor spat in the week leading up to the 1971 All-Star Game perfectly captured the tone of the era.

Entering the break, each league's leading pitcher was black. In the American League, Oakland's Vida Blue was having a sensational rookie season. The flashy, bowlegged left-hander was 17-3 and tops in strikeouts, inviting comparisons to Denny McLain's 31-win season three years earlier.

In the National, Pittsburgh's Dock Ellis

Tony Spina / Detroit Free Press

had a 14-3 record, which made him the logical choice to start the All-Star Game on July 13. His last victory came at the expense of the Cincinnati Reds, managed by Sparky Anderson. Afterward, Ellis blasted Anderson and the baseball establishment.

"I know I don't have a chance to start because Anderson doesn't like me," he said. "Besides, they'd never start one 'brother' against another 'brother.' "

Anderson, set to manage the Reds' Lee May and several other black stars against Earl Weaver's American League squad, couldn't figure out Ellis' beef.

"I don't know why he said I didn't like him. I don't even know him. I've only spoken with him once – at dinner last winter.

"I'll tell you this much: I'd like to have him on my club. And if he didn't like me, I wouldn't care."

When it came time to fill out the official scorecard, Anderson penciled in Willie Mays – playing his 22nd All-Star Game – as his centerfielder and leadoff batter. At the bottom of the card he wrote Ellis' name as starting pitcher.

The Americans' 28-player squad included four Tigers: Al Kaline, Mickey Lolich, Norm Cash and Bill Freehan. Cash was tied for the league lead with 20 home runs, and Lolich was en route to a 25-win, 376-inning season that probably would have won him the Cy

THE 1971 LINEUP INCLUDED SPARKY ANDERSON, WHO MANAGED THE NATIONAL LEAGUE. "I HAVE TO ADMIT I WAS VERY NAIVE ABOUT ALL-STAR GAMES THEN," HE SAID. "I NEVER UNDERSTOOD THAT YOU WERE SUPPOSED TO WIN."

Young Award if it hadn't been for Blue's tremendous year.

"To participate in the game, representing the Tigers in my hometown with that array of talent, was special," said Freehan, playing in his eighth straight game. "Take a look at the players on each of those teams: Willie Mays, Hank Aaron, Johnny Bench, Roberto Clemente and a lot of others who are either Hall of Famers or future Hall of Famers."

The game was held on a warm Tuesday night in front of a full house of 53,559. Tiger Stadium was conservatively dressed, as always. There were giant red, white and blue stars painted on the outfield grass and some bunting fluttering in the stiff 30-miles-per-hour wind, but that was all. Management's philosophy was that the players, not the surroundings, were supposed to be the centerpiece. But again, the stadium's hitter-friendly environment became the biggest part of the story.

The Nationals built a quick 3-0 lead off Blue, as Bench and Aaron drilled opposite-field home runs into the upper deck in right. "Anything hit in the air to right tonight – look out," broadcaster Curt Gowdy warned a national television audience after Aaron's first extra-base hit in 20 All-Star appearances.

In an article leading up to the game, the Free Press had asked, "Can Any of the Stars Clear Roof?" In the bottom of the third

All: Associated Press

Cincinnati's Johnny Bench and Pittsburgh's Roberto Clemente were two of six future Hall of Famers to homer in the '71 game.

Atlanta's Hank Aaron and Minnesota's Harmon Killebrew also reached the seats and the Hall.

inning, Reggie Jackson provided the answer.

Oakland's 25-year-old slugger, who throughout his career displayed a flair for the dramatic, wasn't supposed to be at Tiger Stadium. But Weaver had named him a last-minute substitute for injured Tony Oliva. Before leaving for Detroit, Jackson jokingly had been warned by teammate Sal Bando, "Don't strike out and embarrass us."

With Luis Aparicio on first base after a leadoff single, the left-handed-hitting Jackson pinch-hit for Blue.

The Sporting News

Reggie Jackson watches his All-Star homer sail out of sight and into legend. "I couldn't have hit it any farther if I stood at second base and hit it with a fungo bat," he said.

Ellis, firing nothing but fastballs, built a 1-2 count on Jackson. The tall right-hander came in with another, but by now Jackson had timed his delivery. Jackson wrapped his bat around it, then watched in fascination as it rocketed toward the stands in right.

The ball rose … and rose … and crashed into the base of the light tower atop the rightfield roof. There was no telling how far the ball would have traveled if the light tower hadn't violently interrupted its flight.

"I can't get over how quickly the ball got out of here," marveled Gowdy's sidekick, Tony Kubek, over the air.

Tigers manager Billy Martin, coaching first base, later disagreed with those who called Reggie's blast the hardest-hit ball ever seen. "It didn't knock the light tower down, did it?" he cracked.

The entire stadium was still buzzing when, a couple of minutes later, Frank Robinson sent another Ellis pitch screaming toward the seats in lower right. The second two-run homer of the inning gave the Americans a 4-3 lead that they never relinquished.

There was more long-distance hitting to come. Kaline started the bottom of the sixth inning with a pinch-hit single off Chicago's Fergie Jenkins, then trotted home when Harmon Killebrew hit a full-count sinkerball into the upper deck in left.

Kaline's run turned out to be the winner when Pittsburgh's Clemente capped the scoring with an eighth-inning solo blast off Lolich, who pitched the last two innings for a save.

The 6-4 victory was the junior circuit's first since 1962, but just as noteworthy was the home run barrage. Six had been hit, matching the record set at Briggs Stadium 20 years earlier (and tied at the 1954 game in Cleveland). Most impressive, each had been smacked by a future Hall of Famer.

"The game was memorable in many ways," observed the next day's Free Press, "mostly because it was the last of these All-Star classics that will ever be played in Tiger Stadium.

"We should have our new stadium in another 20 years or so." ◆

MEMORIES EVA NAVARRO

Dad just shook his head at me in disbelief

I was introduced to baseball by my father. Wherever he was, the ballgame was either on the TV or the radio. Whenever he got out of his car, he would listen to the game on his transistor radio so that he wouldn't miss a pitch. If it were not for Tiger baseball, I'm not sure I would have had such a special relationship with my father.

I'm the youngest of seven children. With a family of that size, there naturally was a competition among the siblings for Dad's attention. He would primarily only take me to Tiger Stadium. We would always arrive early to watch batting practice and sit in the lower-deck rightfield bleachers. Everyone out there knew Jesse Navarro. My best memories of my father are going to all those games and watching my hero, Norm Cash, perform.

Cash was always my favorite because he always made the game seem like so much fun. I remember punching out his name on the 1971 All-Star Game ballot at least a thousand times, using names and addresses from the phone book. As it turned out, Dad and I were lucky enough to get our $8 All-Star Game tickets in the mail. We sat in the rightfield upper deck, section 403, and watched Norm and numerous future Hall of Famers play one of the most exciting All-Star Games ever. To see players like Willie Mays, Hank Aaron, Roberto Clemente and Johnny Bench at Tiger Stadium was unbelievable. To share this game with Dad was my all-time favorite moment at the ballpark.

Courtesy Eva Navarro

EVA NAVARRO AND HER FATHER, JESSE, ATTENDED THE 1971 ALL-STAR GAME AT THE CORNER, WHERE SHE SNAPPED A PREGAME PHOTOGRAPH OF ST. LOUIS FIRST BASEMAN JOE TORRE.

Another favorite moment was when the Tigers beat the Red Sox at the end of the 1972 season to win the division. I remember jumping over the railing and picking up infield dirt and stuffing it into my pocket. Dad just shook his head at me in disbelief. But with a smile he said, "You are about as crazy as they come."

My father died in 1987, just before the Tigers won the division again. I still go to games, but not as many. It hasn't been the same without him. A year after he died, I became an active member of the Tiger Stadium Fan Club. I did everything from participating in the famous hug of the stadium and passing out literature to collecting signatures to place the stadium issue on the ballot.

Even though we ultimately lost, at least through our efforts we were able to see the Tigers play there a few more years. When the Tigers finally leave our great ballpark, I will have another large void in my life. ◆

Eva Navarro, a legal secretary living in Dearborn, grew up in southwest Detroit.

MEMORIES SPARKY ANDERSON

Can you imagine . . . Gehrig and Ruth and, my God, Greenberg?

Oh, the first thing that comes to mind when I think of that stadium is the American Legion World Series in 1951. I was 17 then and playing shortstop for the American Legion team in Los Angeles. It was called Briggs Stadium then, and when you came up to it for the first time, you were so awed because it was so big. It looked like stadiums used to look like.

We played four games there, and I think I did fairly decent. I got hit in the elbow, in the crazy bone, and I played the last two games with it tucked in real close to me. But you know, I was such a sensational fielder that it didn't really bother me. We won the whole thing. We beat White Plains, N.Y., in the final game.

There are just so many memories for me there, you know. When I was managing Cincinnati, I managed the National League team there in the 1971 All-Star Game. That was the game where Reggie Jackson hit the light tower on the rightfield roof. I have to admit I was very naive about All-Star Games then. I never understood that you were supposed to win. I thought you were supposed to play everybody and have a good time. But I found out that I didn't do good because we lost. I got mail on top of mail, and people weren't happy with me.

The most special memory about that stadium for me will always be, naturally, winning the World Series in '84. But the special, special memory is the first game I managed there as manager of the Tigers.

I was so tired. I'd been in all day with owner John Fetzer, and I'd never even met my players until they came in the dugout. But when I went up to the plate with the lineup card, the crowd gave me a standing ovation. I'll never forget that. I said to myself, "You know what, these people really are fans because they don't do this in Cincinnati."

You know, no fooling, every single time I came off the freeway, right there at Trumbull, when you turn and see the stadium, oh, it's a magnificent sight. It is a beautiful sight if you are a baseball fan. That stadium, that's baseball the way I was raised.

Detroit Free Press

SPARKY ANDERSON'S MEMORIES OF THE CORNER INCLUDE AN ALL-STAR GAME AND NOT ONE BUT TWO WORLD SERIES.

I used to sit in the dugout sometimes when things weren't going good – you've got to put your mind somewhere else sometimes – and I'd think, "Can you imagine, in this place there used to come here Gehrig and Ruth and, my God, Greenberg? I wonder just now, with this ball, where he'd hit it."

What Tiger Stadium has is history. The new places are beautiful – don't get me wrong – I think they're needed. But they have no history, and baseball has always been based on history. But we can't sit around and worry about that. Things change. ◆

Sparky Anderson spent 17 seasons at The Corner, the longest tenure of any manager in Tigers history.

MEMORIES **FRANK TANANA**

Man, oh man, talk about dreams being fulfilled!

When I was a cocky young pitcher – relatively new in the league, probably about 21 years of age – at a game in Tiger Stadium, I threw a couple too close to Willie Horton. I kind of knocked him down, and he started walking out to the mound. To say the least, I was slightly concerned.

When he got close to me, our catcher and the umpire kind of put their hands on him, and that kind of set Willie off a little bit, and he began to challenge the entire team. He didn't have any takers, naturally. Thankfully, Mickey Stanley was able to kind of settle him down and somewhat get things in order. They sent me to the dugout, and the umpires kicked Ralph Houk, who was the Tigers manager, and Willie out, and I was allowed to continue.

Being the cocky young kid that I was, I gave kind of a smirky sort of grin into their dugout when we were about ready to start – kind of a "Ha-ha, I'm still in and you guys are kicked out" – and Ralph and Willie didn't like that, so they came out again; and again, thankfully, Willie was intercepted by Mickey, but he got close enough to me to begin to poke me in the chest with his finger, and I was kind of happy that was all he was doing. I tried to tell him I was just trying to pitch him inside and, of course, he didn't want to hear any of that.

That's one Tiger Stadium memory that is very vivid. But I have wonderful memories of going there as a kid, trying to get to Bat Day. My dad and I would come out, and a neighbor, Mr. Mack, would bring me to night games, and we'd sit just above the Tiger dugout in the first row of the upper deck, and what a tremendous seat that was to watch my heroes play ball.

I pitched in Tiger Stadium in my senior season in the Catholic League Championship. I went to Catholic Central, and we lost to Holy Redeemer. It was the summer of '71, and I pitched four innings of perfect ball, but then my shoulder was just killing me, so I said I couldn't take any more of this pain and went to first base. I thought for sure I would never get drafted then, but California took me No. 1, and I signed with them that summer.

Courtesy Joe Crachiola

TEAMMATES MOB FRANK TANANA AFTER HE PITCHED THE PENNANT CLINCHER AGAINST TORONTO ON THE LAST DAY OF THE 1987 SEASON.

I spent most of my career pitching other places, but when I came home in '85, it was awesome. My first game wearing that English D, I was every bit as excited as I was ever in baseball. The adrenaline was pumping, and I was very, very excited and ended up beating New York, 2-0, at Tiger Stadium in the first game I ever pitched for them.

Returning home was just huge. Man, oh man, talk about dreams being fulfilled! And then to have it last for seven more years.

I was fortunate enough to pitch a couple of Opening Days for the Tigers, and what I remember about one of them was someone asking Sparky why he was starting me, and he said: "Well, I got to throw somebody." There was Sparky in his own inimitable way, just boosting me up big-time.

One game that does stand out in my memory, though, was the last game of the '87 regular season, the memory of beating Jimmy Key, 1-0, on the last day of the regular season to clinch the division. That will never leave me. I fielded a ground ball and had an underhand flip to Darrell Evans at first for the final out, and what a celebration we had. ◆

Frank Tanana grew up in Detroit.

PLAYING THE FIELD

For better or for worse, music long has been a part of the scene at The Corner. Brass bands were a regular feature at Bennett Park, though their playing ability and song selection often were questionable. Many had the irritating tendency to strike up "Marching Through Georgia" whenever Ty Cobb, whose ancestors had fought for the Confederacy, came to bat. "Someone ought to hand some of these enterprising brass band leaders a few tips in American history," one reporter grumbled in 1910.

"The Star-Spangled Banner" was performed only occasionally at ballparks until World War II, when the national anthem was widely adopted by baseball officials as the perfect patriotic prelude to that most American pastime. Its ritualistic significance was underscored by the uproar over Jose Feliciano's guitar-strumming, red-white-and-bluesy rendition of the song before the fifth game of the 1968 World Series at Tiger Stadium. The blind singer's unconventional performance made the front page of the New York Times and caused him to be labeled as everything from a misguided artist to a Viet Cong sympathizer. Feliciano meant no disrespect. But as crotch-grabbing Roseanne Barr would learn in another park on another day, you just don't mess with the national anthem.

Richard Bak Collection

Detroit Free Press

Performances of note at The Corner included open-air opera in 1935, Perry Como in 1954 and Jose Feliciano – seated with guitar on the facing page – in 1968.

As pitching changes and scheduled doubleheaders became more prevalent during the postwar years, organ music came along as a way of filling dead time. Even Denny McLain occasionally felt the urge to climb into the organ loft and treat the Tiger Stadium crowd to his version of "Satin Doll."

By the 1980s, organists at Tiger Stadium and other ballparks were being replaced by rock standards played over state-of-the-art sound systems. The Tigers' hopelessly unhip front office managed to alienate fans by continually playing John Denver's "Thank God I'm a Country Boy" throughout the summer of 1984. "I could care less," Jim Campbell told his critics. "I'm a baseball man, not a stage-show manager."

Through the years, the field was occasionally rented for concerts. The most ambitious of these was the "Opera Under the Stars" series that Frank Navin staged in 1935 in collaboration with the Board of Commerce and local theater owner J.J. Shubert.

That summer, Cincinnati's Crosley Field hosted the first major league game under the lights. Although Navin insisted that artificial illumination would be the death of baseball, the Tigers' owner had no compunction about experimenting with staging operettas at night. Floodlights were strategically placed around the edge of Navin Field's upper deck, their powerful beams directed at the portable stage hurriedly built on the infield at the conclusion of each afternoon game.

The Free Press reported on the final dress rehearsal of "The Student Prince," which opened the series of week-long plays on Saturday night, June 8, 1935:

"Overhead the stars were blazing, but they seemed of very low candlepower compared with the brilliance of the floodlights pouring onto the stage.

"Home plate was gone. It had vanished under the largest outdoor stage in captivity. The screen behind the plate had vanished to make way for batteries of multicolored lights.

"And the dugouts! From them stemmed no flood of

Detroit Free Press

guys wearing suits labeled Tigers or Indians. Instead, there were strange, shadowy figures moving out to that mysterious place called "backstage." Eight lackeys in bright red uniform and gold braid.

"What would Hughie Jennings think!"

About 9,000 people paid between 25 cents and $1.65 a seat to watch the debut of Opera Under the Stars. They sat in the four upper and lower sections directly behind home plate. The orchestra was squeezed between the stage and the grandstand.

In all, a dozen week-long operettas and musical comedies – a total of 84 nightly performances – were scheduled. They went on, rain or shine, noted the Free Press, "since the audience is protected even if it rains and the actors will follow the axiom of the theater that 'the show must go on.' Even the scenery is waterproof."

Each performance was aired live over radio station WJR and sponsored by General Motors. To keep noise from outside the park from intruding, streetcar employees were stationed at intervals along the tracks to caution motorists to slow their cars to 5 m.p.h. Despite such widespread community involvement, mediocre crowds and Navin's death that fall sealed the fate of open-air opera in Detroit.

During the 1950s, Briggs Stadium hosted such popular acts as Pat Boone, Nat King Cole and Perry Como. Cole and Como joined Patti Page and Sarah Vaughan in a "Star Night" show that attracted 25,000 fans to The Corner on July 23, 1954. Tickets cost $4.50. The singing stars and several local disc jockeys began the evening by circling the field in convertibles.

"Gee," said Como, stepping onto the lawn usually traversed by Harvey Kuenn and Ray Boone, "I haven't had so much fun since I quit barbering."

It would be nearly another 40 years before the next big-time concerts were held at the ballpark. On Sept. 25, 1993, music lovers paid $35 a ticket to see Rod Stewart rock the old park. In subsequent years, the Eagles and Kiss performed there. For the Eagles' Glenn Frey, who grew up in Royal Oak, playing this particular venue was a dream realized – in a way.

"I always wanted to play centerfield at Tiger Stadium," he said. "I just thought I'd have a glove instead of a guitar." ◆

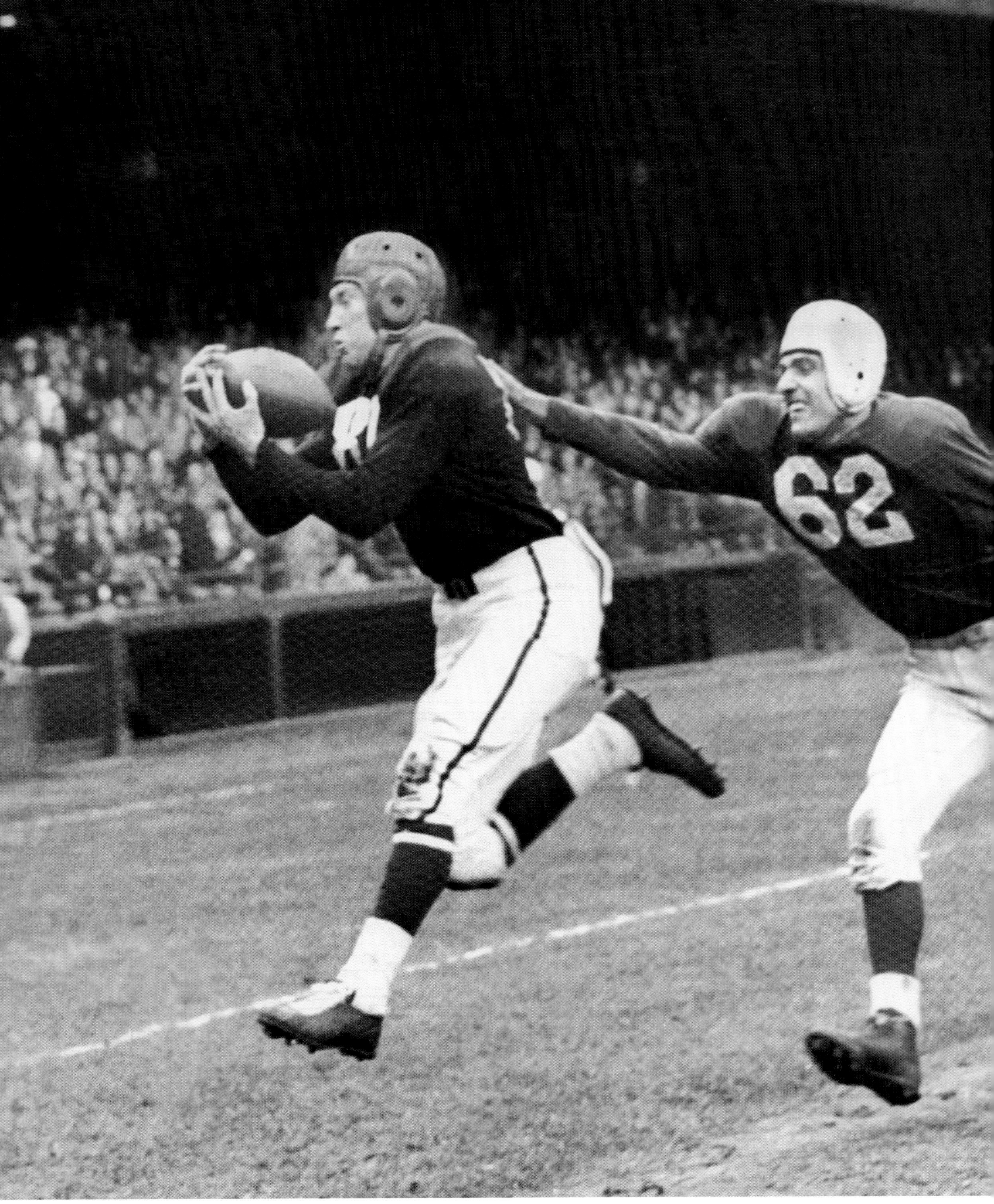
62

The Corner's other tenants, the Lions, were NFL ne'er-do-wells in the years after World War II. John Greene, who went to Michigan, played seven seasons and made this touchdown catch at Briggs Stadium in 1948.

Detroit Free Press

CHAPTER 7

A different breed of cat

Wayne Walker was a fresh-faced, potato-fed, 21-year-old kid from Idaho when he got his first look at Briggs Stadium all dressed up for football in 1958.

"It was a Saturday night exhibition game against the Giants," recalled the linebacker-turned-broadcaster.

"Growing up, I was a big baseball fan, so I knew about the park. I remember getting off the bus and going through the tunnel and onto the field. I never even bothered to look at the locker room. To a kid from Boise, it was like seeing the seventh wonder of the world. It was just what a ballpark was supposed to look like.

"I thought to myself, 'If this isn't from central casting, then what is?' "

Walker went on to play more football at The Corner,

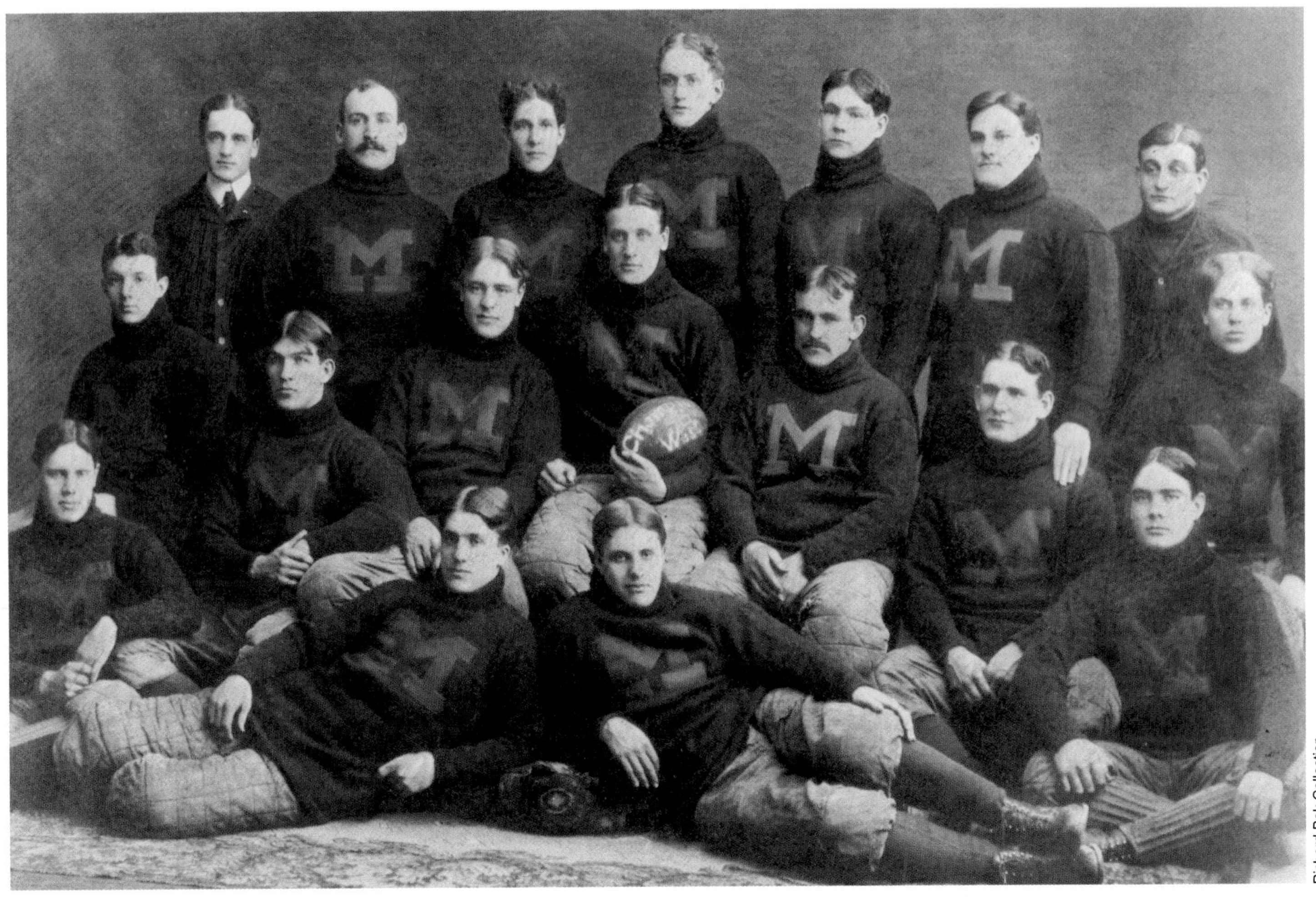

Richard Bak Collection

THESE WOLVERINES VENTURED TO THE CORNER AND DEFEATED ILLINOIS, 12-5, ON NOV. 12, 1898. "HAIL TO THE VICTORS" WAS HEARD ON SEVERAL OCCASIONS AT BENNETT PARK AT CENTURY'S TURN.

15 seasons, than any other Lion. That and his off-season job as a television sports reporter gave him an intimate acquaintance with the quirks of the old green stadium.

"I saw a lot of baseball games there," he said, "but I really liked the stadium for football, too. Both teams were on the same side of the field, and that really led to some 'back and forth' on the sidelines, something you didn't get at a lot of other places.

"I found out pretty quick how small the locker rooms were, especially the visitors'. The few times I was in the visitors' locker room, I thought, 'This must be worth three points for us because these other guys must be so depressed.' "

Forty Buick-sized footballers squeezed into a room built for 25 baseball players – a major reason the Lions left downtown for Pontiac's plastic pastures at the end of the 1974 season. Before that happened, however, a long succession of prep, collegiate, semipro and professional teams stretching back to Bennett Park days managed to provide their share of autumnal thrills and early winter chills.

From the beginning, Tigers owners looked to football as a way of keeping the revenue stream flowing. At the turn of the century, the field hosted annual visits from the University of Michigan, though squeezing the gridiron into the narrow confines of Bennett Park was a challenge. The improvised seating and poor sight lines didn't dampen the ardor of the thousands of Wolverines supporters who descended on The Corner with noisemakers, megaphones and giant yellow and blue chrysanthemums.

The 1901 game between Fielding Yost's Michigan 11 and Pop Warner's Carlisle squad was front page news in the Free Press. More than 8,000 boisterous fans dammed up behind barbed-wire fences to root the Wolverines to a 22-0 victory.

"The largest crowd that ever turned out to a football game in Michigan was at Bennett Park yesterday to do honor to the sturdy young heroes with the big yellow M's on their sweaters," the Free Press reported. "The 'man with the M' was 'it' yesterday. He could have the homage of every girl in the crowd, and when the brunette saw him select the young woman with the blue eyes and golden hair she was not a bit spiteful. She knew he did it just because the yellow and blue were Michigan's colors… ."

The Wolverines went on to finish an undefeated, unscored-on season with a 49-0 thrashing of Stanford in the first Rose Bowl game. The popularity of Yost's famous "Point-a-Minute" national championship teams ended the Wolverines' visits to The Corner; the park simply couldn't handle the throngs.

Frank Navin was able to accommodate larger-sized crowds with the opening of Navin Field in 1912. The Detroit Heralds, the city's premier semipro squad, rented the field for its 1916 schedule. Games with long-time rivals like the Dayton Cadets and Columbus Panhandles regularly drew a few thousand. On Nov. 11, 1917, a benefit game between the Heralds and the Camp Custer All-Stars attracted 16,000.

Richard Bak Collection

ACTOR-ACTIVIST PAUL ROBESON PLAYED AN NFL GAME AT NAVIN FIELD IN 1921.

Even as professional football teams began renting the park in the 1920s, The Corner continued as the site of occasional collegiate action. The apex of the amateur game's popularity arrived Oct. 5, 1951, when Notre Dame defeated the University of Detroit, 40-6, before a crowd of 52,331. At the time, not even Bobby Layne's Lions had ever attracted a greater number to Briggs Stadium.

Most people mistakenly believe professional football in Detroit began with the Lions. Actually, they were the fifth attempt to launch a National Football League franchise in the city. Four previous tries occurred during the Roaring '20s. The Detroit Heralds played the 1920 season, the NFL's inaugural campaign, at Mack Park before folding. The Heralds were followed by the equally unsuccessful Tigers (1921), Panthers (1925-26) and Wolverines (1927). The Wolverines played their home schedule at the University of Detroit's Dinan Field. The Tigers and Panthers tried to make a go of it at Navin Field. No matter the venue, all quickly discovered that public taste ran more toward collegiate and high school action.

The first NFL game at The Corner was between the Tigers and Dayton Triangles on Sunday, Oct. 9, 1921. No attendance figures were given, though the Free Press noted that the game "was played under fine weather conditions and a good-sized crowd was on hand to cheer the home team, something that has been lacking in past games here."

The Tigers, dressed in snazzy new orange-and-black uniforms, won, 10-7. The winning score was delivered by Tillie Voss, a familiar face around local gridirons. The former University of Detroit standout and ex-Herald end returned a blocked kick 65 yards for a touchdown. The Tigers had adopted the name of their baseball cousins, looking to capitalize on their popularity, but their victory proved to be the only one of the campaign. The turnstiles quit spinning and the club went under, but not before hosting one other game of note.

On Oct. 16, 1921, the Akron Pros demolished the home team, 20-0, behind the skillful play of two black stars. One was wingback Fritz Pollard. The other was end Paul Robeson, a true Renaissance man playing his only NFL season. In years to come, the powerful and imposing orator, actor,

THE NFL AT THE CORNER

DETROIT TIGERS

FIRST GAME:
Oct. 9, 1921
Detroit 10, Dayton 7

LAST GAME:
Oct. 23, 1921
Rock Island 14, Detroit 0

DETROIT PANTHERS

FIRST GAME:
Sept. 27, 1925
Detroit 7, Columbus 0

LAST GAME:
Nov. 28, 1926
Green Bay 28, Detroit 0

DETROIT LIONS

FIRST GAME:
Oct. 18, 1938
Washington 7, Detroit 5

LAST GAME:
Nov. 28, 1974
Denver 31, Detroit 27

United Press International

When Panthers point man Jimmy Conzelman announced Red Grange (above) and the Chicago Bears were coming to town, Detroiters turned out in droves to buy tickets to see the famous "Galloping Ghost." But Grange suffered a leg injury and pulled out of the game. "A few hours before the game was about to start," Conzelman said, "I looked out the window and saw a long line at the box office. I remember thinking to myself, 'What a great sports town. Grange isn't going to play, but they're still lining up to buy tickets.' Then I got the news from the ticket man. They were lining up to get refunds."

singer and activist would be a regular visitor to Detroit, performing in downtown theaters and participating in various civil rights causes. A hero to African Americans and white liberals in the '40s and '50s, few knew that this internationally famous figure had once lugged a football around Navin Field for the better part of a Sunday afternoon.

The second NFL presence at The Corner was the Detroit Panthers, who were owned, coached and quarterbacked by Jimmy Conzelman of St. Louis. The energetic Conzelman, one of pro football's pioneers and a natural promoter, paid $50 to the league as a franchise fee and agreed to lease Navin Field for $1,000 a game. That was a healthy rent, and Conzelman immediately looked for ways to induce Detroiters to come down to The Corner.

He managed to interest Notre Dame's famous backfield, the "Four Horsemen," in playing the 1925 season in Detroit. As part of their contract, he also got them to perform skits and a clog dance on stage while their coach played the piano. Unfortunately for Conzelman, the vaudeville act fell apart when one of the Horsemen, his nostrils evidently flaring at the smell of greasepaint, decided to take a job with the recreation department in Davenport, Iowa.

Though the Horsemen never played at The Corner, famous names like Jim Thorpe, George Halas and Curly Lambeau did visit Navin Field during the Panthers' two autumns there. The Panthers' lineup was heavy with local sandlotters and ex-collegiate stars, including the irrepressible tackle and placekicker Gus Sonnenberg.

Sonnenberg, a stumpy, barrel-chested farm boy from Ewen, Mich., had starred at the University of Detroit. He loved to show off by tipping over cars and yanking signposts out of cement. Like Robeson, a greater destiny awaited him after he left Navin Field's gridiron. He would soon become the country's best-known wrestler, a fixture at Olympia and other venues, pulling down an estimated $1 million in ring earnings before his premature death of leukemia. The colorful Sonnenberg was dubbed "The Flying Dutchman" for a favorite football tactic that he transferred to the ring. He would leap at an opponent, wrap his arms around the fellow's legs, then slam him to the mat.

Richard Bak Collection

Jim Thorpe was a Canton Bulldog when he played at The Corner in 1925.

In 1934, local radio magnate George A. Richards bought the Portsmouth Spartans, moved the team from the small mill town in southern Ohio to the Motor City, and renamed them the Lions.

Some of the game's brightest stars were on the roster, including backs Dutch Clark, Glenn Presnell, Ernie Caddel and Ace Gutowsky. Playing their home games at Dinan Field, the Lions won the NFL title in their second season, beating the New York Giants, 26-7, in Detroit on a cold, wet December Sunday in 1935.

Having outgrown Dinan Field, the Lions

MEMORIES JOE SCHMIDT

I was tickled we won because I could pay off that two-door Chevy

John Collier / Detroit Free Press

TWO LIONHEARTED PLAYERS OF THE '50S AND '60S, JOE SCHMIDT AND ALEX KARRAS, IN 1975.

Back when there were only 12 teams in the league, Briggs Stadium was the most comfortable stadium in which to practice and play. It was always a very friendly environment. There was nothing like being there on a beautiful autumn day with the sun out, the smell of the freshly cut grass and the people sitting so close it felt like you could reach out and touch them.

When I started in 1953, I was only 21. I didn't even think I would make the team. To then make the team and be on a national broadcast on Thanksgiving Day and the world championship game, both from Briggs Stadium, delighted me and the folks back home in Pittsburgh.

That '53 title game ... I had just purchased a new car and I thought, "If we win it, it'll take me out of the hole." I remember standing on the sidelines when Bobby Layne hit Jim Doran with the winning touchdown to beat Cleveland for the championship. Our winning payoff was $2,400, and the losers got $1,800. The $600 difference was a lot of money back then. I was tickled we won because I could pay off that two-door Chevy.

Needless to say, Bobby Layne was a unique individual who marched to his own drummer. He always got a lot more credit than he deserved for some of the off-field escapades. Not to say some of them didn't happen. He was simply a fun-loving guy who loved the camaraderie and closeness with his teammates. He was always ready to play football and had the capability to rally the team from what looked like disaster. He made everybody around him play at a little higher level. Mechanically he was not a great thrower, but he always got the ball there.

Another wonderful season was 1957. Tobin Rote did a magnificent job filling in for Bobby after he hurt his ankle. In the title game, we paid off a debt to the Browns for the '54 championship game in which they knocked the daylights out of us. Cleveland made five turnovers, and we got on them real fast. They never recovered from the first half. When the game ended, I went to the official to retrieve the game ball. Fans came onto the field and tried to get the ball. I ended up getting lifted up and carried off the field. There are still a lot of people floating around the city who remember and cherish those days.

The 1962 Thanksgiving Day game was obviously my favorite. It was the only game Green Bay lost that year. We played so well – partly out of frustration over our defeat in Green Bay earlier. That was a game which we never should have lost.

Our defensive team that year was one of the best of all-time, but we never get enough recognition because we ended up second. In that Thanksgiving game, we really moved the defense around a lot and did a lot of blitzing. We just turned the guys loose. Alex Karras just killed Jerry Kramer that day, and the rest of the Fearsome Foursome played so well. Bart Starr ended up getting sacked 11 times. Green Bay just got to a point where they didn't know how to handle us.

You know, in '62 I think we would have won the whole thing if we'd still had Bobby. He was playing with Pittsburgh that year. We lost three games by a total of eight points, and he would have made a difference. ◆

Straight-shooting Joe Schmidt helped define the emerging position of middle linebacker during his 13 seasons with the Lions. He spent another six years at The Corner as head coach before leaving the game for good in 1972.

Courtesy Betty Steen

At 330 pounds, middle guard Les Bingaman was an imposing figure on the Briggs Stadium sideline. Half his size, but still a force, was all-purpose back Doak Walker.

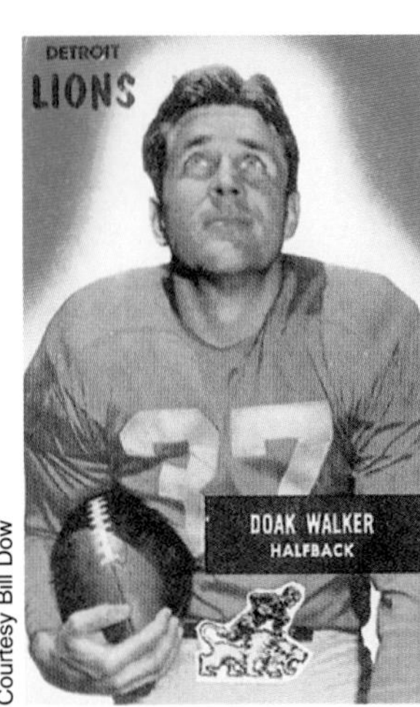

Courtesy Bill Dow

Courtesy Betty Steen

The Lions and their mascots moved from their lair at University of Detroit Stadium to Briggs Stadium in 1938.

moved to Briggs Stadium during their fifth season. Their first game at The Corner was a 7-5 loss to Washington on Oct. 18, 1938. Nearly 43,000 showed up, paying between 55 cents and $2.20 for a seat. For the year, the Lions averaged a little better than 30,000 per game. Except for 1940, when Tigers owner Walter O. Briggs had a change of heart and booted his leather-helmeted tenants out for a year, the Lions called The Corner home for the next 36 seasons.

Much as Ty Cobb is the cornerstone of baseball history at The Corner, Layne is the centerpiece of Lions lore. Under Layne, the Lions of the Eisenhower decade became one of the dominant teams of the NFL and its most glamorous, helping sell the game to a country waking up to the joys of watching televised football on Sunday.

There was all-purpose back Doak Walker, Layne's old high school buddy from Texas. The Heisman Trophy winner from Southern Methodist University led the league in scoring as a rookie in 1950 and was All-Pro in five of his six NFL seasons. "He wasn't the fastest guy in the world," recalled teammate Leon Hart, the giant end who had won the Heisman the year before at Notre Dame, "but he had quickness and a change of pace and change of direction. He had football savvy."

Other cast members included tackle Lou Creekmur, who perfected the practice of the leg whip; defensive back Jimmy (The Hatchet) David, who loved to rub opponents' noses into the Briggs Stadium turf; Jack Christiansen, one of the greatest kick returners and pass defenders in league history; and Les Bingaman, the 330-pound middle guard who anchored the defense until Joe Schmidt came along. They were more than teammates, insisted Yale Lary, the crew-cut defensive back and punter. They were silver-and-blue soulmates.

"When I went to the Lions in 1952, Doak and Bobby said I was their rookie," said Lary, who became a banker in his native Texas following his football career.

"I was their rookie until the day they died. Even after we all retired, whenever we would

Bert Emanuel / Detroit Free Press

Courtesy Bill Dow

Who's the boss? Quarterback Bobby Layne and coach Buddy Parker won two championships together. "Look, guys," Layne would tell his teammates, "there's one chief, and I'm the chief and y'all the Indians."

Courtesy Bill Dow

End Leon Hart, Layne's teammate for eight seasons, won the Heisman at Notre Dame and was an All-Pro on offense and defense for the Lions in the 1950s.

Richard Bak Collection

Associated Press

talk, Doak would call me '28' and I would call him '37.' Those were our uniform numbers. My work phone number even has Bobby's number, Doak's number and my number in it. We were one big family."

The Lions were dominated by the personality of their paunchy, soulful leader, dutifully following his lead from huddle to watering hole.

"Bobby's favorite nickname was 'Sweet Bobby,' " Lary said. "In our team meetings at the Stadium Bar across from the stadium, Bobby would say, 'Look, guys, there's one chief, and I'm the chief and y'all the Indians.' He was all the way the chief.

"Bobby left a wide path whatever he did. I remember going with him to the Flame Show Bar to see B.B. King. They wanted to shut down, but Bobby would wad up a hundred-dollar bill and stick it in the saxophone player's sax. They kept playing as long as Bobby dumped those bills."

Alternately staggering and swaggering through life, Layne might never have led the Lions to championship heights without the guiding genius of Raymond (Buddy) Parker. Parker – a back on the Lions' 1935 world champions and an assistant when Layne joined the club in 1950 – was promoted to head coach at the end of the 1951 season.

"Buddy Parker never gets the credit he deserved," said Schmidt, the prototypical middle linebacker and one of several Hall of Famers to play under Parker. "They always talk about Cleveland's coach, Paul Brown, as an innovator and how great he was. The bottom line is that Buddy consistently won."

It was Parker who came up with the idea of the two-minute drill at the end of halves, who instructed his offensive backs to "run to daylight" and his defensive backs to play the bump-and-run. It was Parker who brought in aging veterans like fullback Pat Harder and center Vince Banonis from other clubs to add experience to his nucleus of young talent. His moves paid off, time and again.

"He was quiet and superstitious," Schmidt said. "He motivated in his own quiet manner. If you didn't produce, you would be replaced. That in itself was a motivation because we never knew what he was thinking."

Between 1951 and 1957, a span of seven autumns, the Lions won four divisional titles and finished second twice, each time losing out on the last day of the season. They played six postseason games and lost just once, claiming the NFL championship in 1952, 1953 and 1957. Only a loss to the

Buddy Parker gets carried away at Briggs Stadium after the Lions won their second straight championship in 1953. They added a third title in 1957, the first season that fullback John Henry Johnson (above) played for the Lions.

"They always talk about Cleveland's coach, Paul Brown, as an innovator and how great he was. The bottom line is that Buddy consistently won."

Joe Schmidt

Browns in Cleveland in the '54 title game kept the Lions from becoming the first team to win three straight championships.

The first NFL playoff game at The Corner was between Detroit and Los Angeles on Dec. 21, 1952. The Lions had finished the regular season in a flat-footed tie at 9-3 with the Rams, who were the defending league champs and boasted such household names as quarterbacks Norm Van Brocklin and Bob Waterfield, end Elroy (Crazy Legs) Hirsch, and defensive back Dick (Night Train) Lane. The game was played on a gloomy, foggy Sunday before 47,645 fans. With Pat Harder scoring a then-record 19 points, including two touchdown runs, the Lions whipped Los Angeles, 31-21. The following Sunday in Cleveland, the Lions beat the Browns, 17-7, to win the title.

On Dec. 27, 1953, they made it two championships in a row, squeaking past the Browns, 17-16, in the first NFL title game played at The Corner. This was a classic Layne comeback, featuring a flurry of wobbly passes and his trademark self-confidence. Trailing, 16-10, with the clock winding down, Layne told his teammates, "Just give me the time, boys, and I'll get you downfield and back into that All-Star Game at Chicago." He then drove his team 80 yards for the winning score.

"I will always remember Bobby throwing that ball with just a couple of minutes left to Jim Doran over Warren Lahr's head to win the game," Lary said. "Warren never got over it, bless his heart."

A PRIDE OF LIONS STOPS CLEVELAND'S LEW CARPENTER IN THE 1957 TITLE GAME. THE LIONS WON, 59-14, THEIR LAST CHAMPIONSHIP AT THE CORNER.

Burton Historical Collection

Dick Tripp / Detroit Free Press

On Dec. 29, 1957, the Lions claimed their third championship in six years with a 59-14 rout of the Browns at Briggs Stadium. It capped the most chaotic season in team history, one that saw the abrupt preseason resignation of Parker, a season-ending broken leg sustained by Layne, and a series of impossibly dramatic comeback victories, including a special playoff in San Francisco that put the Lions in the title game. Assistant coach George Wilson, who succeeded Parker, acquired quarterback Tobin Rote from Green Bay before the season, and Rote threw for four touchdowns and ran for another against the Browns. Afterward, delirious Detroit fans carried him and Schmidt, the team captain, off the field on their shoulders.

Nobody would have dared predict in those heady moments that the Lions would never play another postseason game at Michigan and Trumbull – that, in fact, at the end of the 20th Century they would still be waiting to win their next NFL championship. But a dizzying downward spiral, characterized by quarterback controversies, clubhouse dissension and myriad coaching changes, dropped the Lions into the league's middle echelons for the remainder of their stay at The Corner.

Which is not to say there weren't moments and personalities to keep people passing through the turnstiles. Nearsighted tackle Alex Karras, snowball-ducking head coach Harry Gilmer, recalcitrant errand boy Joe Don Looney – "If you want a messenger, call Western Union" was the fullback's legendary response to Gilmer's request to carry a play to the huddle – all made major deposits in the memory banks of Lions fans.

"I always considered myself an entertainer," said Gail Cogdill, a split end from Washington State. "I just wish I could have entertained a little bit more. The fans at Tiger Stadium were pretty entertaining, too. Of all the places I played, the Detroit crowd was the most fantastic, whether we were winning or losing. I remember looking up and seeing fires in the stands and fights coming all the way down the middle of the centerfield bleachers."

Without question, according to old Lions, the most memorable football game at The Corner was the wipeout of Green Bay on Thanksgiving afternoon in 1962. Cogdill had the finest game of his nine-year Lions career, scoring twice on passes from Milt Plum, as the Lions dominated the previously unbeaten Packers, 26-14, before a national TV audience. It was revenge for the bitter 9-7 loss in Green Bay a few weeks earlier, when an errant toss by Plum had set up Paul Hornung's winning field goal.

"I remember Alex Karras throwing his

GAIL COGDILL WAS A FAN FAVORITE AND THREE-TIME PRO BOWL RECEIVER DURING HIS NINE SEASONS AT THE CORNER IN THE 1960S.

Courtesy Bill Dow

ROGER BROWN, ALEX KARRAS, SAM WILLIAMS AND DARRIS MCCORD FORMED THE "FEARSOME FOURSOME" OF THE 1960S.

helmet at Plum after that first game," Cogdill said from his home in Washington. "It really wasn't Milt's fault. George Wilson called the play, and Terry Barr just slipped trying to catch the ball that was intercepted."

When the teams assembled at The Corner for their rematch, the Lions were still steaming.

"The field was soft and wet," Cogdill said. "Because of the baseball field, they threw grass over the infield and they still expected you to do something on it. We tried to run patterns away from that area."

Midway through the first quarter, Cogdill split the secondary and ran underneath a perfect throw from Plum.

"When we scored right off the bat, that was the inspiration. The guys on the sideline said, 'We got them; we can tear these guys apart!' Don Shula was our defensive coach, and he really inspired the defensive unit. The defense then motivated the offense. The defense pressured Bart Starr all day, they were so fired up."

Before most of the country had taken its first bite of turkey, the Lions were devouring the Packers, 26-0. Only a couple of late Green Bay touchdowns made the final score more presentable. Roger Brown, the 300-pound tackle, was a one-man gang, tackling Starr for a safety and causing a fumble that was run in by fellow Fearsome Foursome member Sam Williams. By game's end, Starr had been sacked 11 times for 110 yards in losses; the league's leading rusher, Jim Taylor, had been held to 47 yards; and the myth of Packers invincibility had been shoved into coach Vince Lombardi's face. Lombardi was so upset, he ended the Packers' longstanding tradition of being the Lions' Thanksgiving Day opponent after a 13-13 tie in 1963.

The annual Turkey Day game was not the only treasured football tradition at The Corner. Every November between 1938 and 1967 the champions of the Catholic and Public School leagues met in the Goodfellows Game, a benefit event that during its 30-year run raised nearly $1 million for one of the city's favorite charities.

The inaugural Goodfellows Game was

Associated Press

TAKEN IN AN INSTANT

Fifty-four thousand of us saw him topple over on the cold Tiger Stadium grass and take his final breath as Dick Butkus waved frantically for somebody – anybody – to help. On Oct. 24, 1971, Chuck Hughes died the most visible death in the history of the NFL, taken in an instant when a blood clot lodged in an already clogged artery killed him with 62 seconds left in the Lions' 28-23 loss to the Chicago Bears. He was a lean wide receiver from Texas, 6-feet, 180 pounds, with hands that were quicker than his feet. He had just run a pass pattern, but Greg Landry instead threw an incompletion to Charlie Sanders. Hughes turned toward the Lions' forming huddle, took a couple of steps, threw both hands to his chest and fell face-first at the 25-yard line. ◆

By Charlie Vincent

Detroit Free Press

Nov. 26, 1938, on a snowy field at Briggs Stadium. Heavily favored Hamtramck High was upset by Catholic Central, 19-13. The first points were registered by John McHale, the father of Tigers president John McHale Jr. The Catholic Central center lugged a Hamtramck pass 45 yards for a touchdown, one of two interceptions that CC returned for scores that afternoon. McHale went on to play parts of five seasons as a Tigers first baseman in the 1940s before entering baseball's executive ranks.

At its peak in the late '50s and early '60s, the Goodfellows Game drew crowds approaching 40,000. The spectators often included a Dearborn kid named Gary Danielson.

"As a kid, my dad had taken me to Tiger Stadium several times to see the Lions and the annual Goodfellows Game," he said. "In 1967, I remember seeing Mel Farr score a long touchdown for the Lions, and that same year I played in the last Goodfellows Game."

Divine Child, behind Danielson, upset top-ranked Denby, 14-7.

"I was a junior, and just a few games earlier I had been converted to quarterback. I scored the last touchdown on a rollout into the centerfield end zone."

Danielson went on to star at Purdue and later played nine seasons for the Lions, beginning in 1976. By then, however, the team he had cheered on from the bleachers – where frostbitten fans were known to break up the boards for fires – was playing inside the climate-controlled Pontiac Silverdome.

"You know," Danielson said, echoing a sentiment felt by many hard-core football fans, "I think the Lions kind of lost their identity when they left Tiger Stadium."

The Lions, tired of their second-class status, had a football-only stadium built for them by taxpayers. The facility was ready in time for the start of the 1975 season.

The Lions' last game at The Corner was Nov. 28, 1974, a Thanksgiving Day contest with Denver. It was a dismal finale. Steve Owens, the Lions' first 1,000-yard rusher, tore up his knee at the end of the longest run of his career and never played again. His replacement, Leon Crosswhite, scored the last NFL touchdown at The Corner on a short run in the waning minutes. Errol Mann, who on that day eclipsed Doak Walker as the Lions' all-time scorer (a record later surpassed by Eddie Murray), booted the extra point, making the final score 31-27 in favor of Denver.

Save for rare exceptions like 1985's Coleman Young Classic between Southern University and Tennessee State University, no more gridirons have been chalked onto the lawn at Tiger Stadium since the Lions left.

"The last time I was at Tiger Stadium," Lary said, "it was in the early '80s, just before Bobby died. Bobby and I were up there for an alumni golf outing. We stopped at the Stadium Bar and then walked across to the stadium's side entrance where we had always walked in. They were working on the field, so we just walked out onto the grass and reminisced."

The two teammates spent 15 or 20 minutes resurrecting old roars inside the nearly vacant stadium. Then they turned their backs on the empty stands and left The Corner for good. ◆

Jimmy Tafoya / Detroit Free Press

NOV. 28, 1974: DENVER'S JON KEYWORTH HURDLES INTO THE END ZONE AS THE LIONS CLOSE OUT 36 YEARS AT THE CORNER.

HEAR THEM ROAR

Three largest Lions crowds at The Corner

Sept. 28, 1964

59,203

GREEN BAY 14, LIONS 10

Nov. 14, 1954

58,431

LIONS 48, SAN FRANCISCO 7

Oct. 12, 1969

58,384

GREEN BAY 28, LIONS 17

MEMORIES **BILL McGRAW**

All around me in the dark stands were high school kids necking

Members of my g-g-generation can recall precisely what they were doing the day President John Kennedy was shot. I sat in the Tiger Stadium bleachers for the first time that night.

It was Nov. 22, 1963, at the annual Goodfellows charity game between Detroit's best Catholic and public high school football teams. I was 12, an avid prep sports fan and the guest of a neighbor, who was the game's referee.

It was an especially exciting evening for an east-sider because playing for the title were two Kelly Road pigskin powers, Notre Dame and Denby.

Sitting alone in the cozy lower deck, on one of those narrow, wooden benches that were later replaced by wider metal seats, I quickly realized it was an unusual night. The president was dead, it was cold and misty, and all around me in the dark stands were high school kids necking.

A priest went on the field at halftime and led a prayer for JFK. A girl in a maroon St. Ambrose jacket cried. People talked about a guy named Lee Harvey Oswald. After Denby won, 7-0, the announcer invoked the name of the late president in pleading with fans to remain in their seats.

Police on huge, frisky horses stood guard in front of our section, but as I watched, dozens of students scaled the fence and jumped on the field, heading to the end zone to tear down the goalposts.

The entire evening was a memorable introduction to life in the cheap seats. ◆

Bill McGraw is a Free Press reporter.

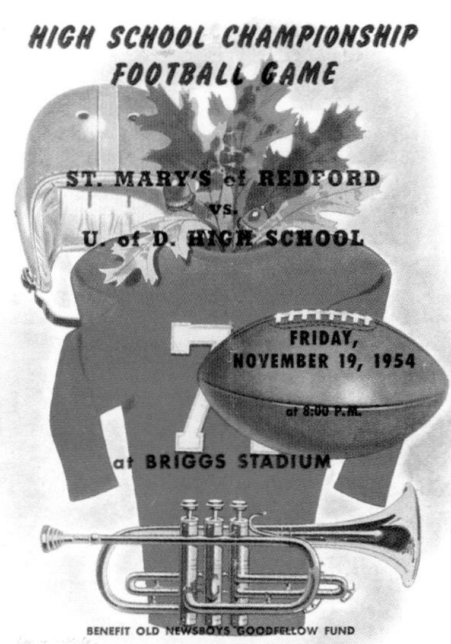

Courtesy Dick Clark

KEEPING SCORE ◆ GOODFELLOWS GAMES AT THE CORNER

YEAR	RESULT	ATTENDANCE
1938	Catholic Central 19, Hamtramck 13	20,857
1939	University of Detroit 20, Catholic Central 0	23,120
1940	Cooley 6, St. Theresa 6	14,861
1941	Cooley 47, St. Theresa 6	30,715
1942	Catholic Central 46, Hamtramck 0	26,495
1943	Catholic Central 8, Cooley 0	17,500
1944	Mackenzie 3, Holy Redeemer 0	30,054
1945	Catholic Central 19, Denby 19	22,140
1946	Cooley 21, St. Anthony 13	35,201
1947	Denby 14, Redford St. Mary 0	28,528
1948	Denby 28, Redford St. Mary 0	39,004
1949	St. Anthony 19, University of Detroit 13	34,038
1950	Redford 7, St. Gregory 6	30,119
1951	Redford St. Mary 23, Western 6	29,283
1952	Redford St. Mary 13, University of Detroit 6	25,776

YEAR	RESULT	ATTENDANCE
1953	Pershing 21, Lourdes 7	29,454
1954	University of Detroit 23, Redford St. Mary 20	30,593
1955	Pershing 13, Redford St. Mary 7	29,830
1956	De La Salle 26, Denby 20	28,343
1957	Redford St. Mary 25, Southeastern 6	34,538
1958	Redford 27, Redford St. Mary 7	38,896
1959	St. Ambrose 13, Cooley 7	30,062
1960	Denby 21, Catholic Central 18	39,196
1961	St. Ambrose 20, Pershing 13	37,157
1962	St. Ambrose 19, Cooley 0	37,763
1963	Denby 7, Notre Dame 0	23,500
1964	St. Ambrose 20, Southeastern 0	15,000
1965	Notre Dame 14, Denby 14	25,435
1966	St. Ambrose 33, Denby 19	12,337
1967	Divine Child 14, Denby 7	15,186

CHAPTER 8

The long ball

Tiger Stadium was buzzing this Sunday afternoon. It was only the third inning and already, seven home runs had been hit. The ball was jumping around the old park like Sparky Anderson after his 20th cup of coffee.

Chad Curtis opened the barrage, his first-inning drive off Chicago's James Baldwin landing in the leftfield seats. He was followed a few minutes later by Cecil Fielder, whose blast into the centerfield bleachers brought in another three Tigers runs.

Tony Spina / Detroit Free Press

The summer of '61 belonged to Roger Maris, whose record-breaking 61 homers included five hit at The Corner. Above: He connects on Sunday afternoon, Sept. 17.

The next inning, Curtis and Fielder repeated their act off Baldwin. But then the White Sox started flexing their muscles, banging three home runs in a row, driving starter David Wells from the mound.

By the end of the day, Detroit and Chicago hitters had, in the modern vernacular, "gone yard" 12 times. The Tigers accounted for a club-record seven homers, including two by Kirk Gibson and one by Lou Whitaker, though the White Sox overcame a six-run deficit and won the battle of the scoreboard, 14-12.

"It stunk," Anderson said. "It was awful." That was the losing manager's grumpy assessment. From a fan's perspective, the bombardment had been fun to watch – and to count. The dozen dingers on May 29, 1995, established a major league record for home runs by both clubs in a game. It broke the old mark first set on June 23, 1950, between the Tigers and Yankees at Briggs

Stadium. That night, an inside-the-park home run by Hoot Evers with two out in the bottom of the ninth inning delivered a wild, 10-9 Tigers victory and capped a barrage of 11 home runs.

Old-timers in the crowd that evening might have experienced a sense of deja vu watching Evers' mad dash. It could just as easily have been Wahoo Sam Crawford or Donie Bush steaming around the sacks, for the leisurely home run trot was practically unheard of during the dead-ball era.

Bennett Park, like all turn-of-the-century ballyards, was not designed for long-ball hitters. In 1904, for example, Detroit and visiting batters combined for seven home runs in 79 games at The Corner. The cavernous outfields, coupled with a mushy ball and a conservative approach to batting, made the sight of a fence-clearing drive a rare experience. Most round-trippers were of the inside-the-park variety. When Ty Cobb won batting's triple crown in 1909, all nine of his home runs (including six at Bennett Park) required him to leg it out at full gallop.

The gradual elimination of trick pitches, the introduction of several fresh balls during games, and the friendlier dimensions of new parks like Navin Field resulted in a rapid escalation of balls sailing into the seats in the years following World War I. The old, one-base-at-a-time philosophy suddenly was replaced by a swing-from-the-heels mentality that saw an upsurge in scoring, strikeouts and attendance.

The Corner has since served as a launching pad for generations of bashers. Homeboys Hank Greenberg, Al Kaline and Fielder feasted on the short fences, and visiting deities like Babe Ruth and Ted Williams declared the site their favorite foreign field. The Corner's transfiguration from a pasture where fly balls went to die to a cozy home run haven reached its peak in 1996. That season, 230 home runs were hit at Tiger Stadium, an average of nearly three per game.

More home runs have been hit at The Corner than at any other venue – somewhere around 11,000, if one counts Western League, playoff, World Series and All-Star games. And that number threatens to grow by two, three or even a dozen with every passing game.

Richard Bak Collection

Teammates swarm Hoot Evers after his home run gave the Tigers a wild, 10-9 win over the Yankees in 1950. The teams combined for 11 homers that night.

Along with quantity has come quality. There were, of course, the All-Star home runs of Williams and Reggie Jackson, as well as dramatic postseason shots by Gibson and Pat Sheridan.

But how many people remember that Ruth and Mickey Mantle hit the longest home runs of their careers at The Corner? Or that during an August game in 1986, Mark McGwire, then a rookie third baseman just called up by Oakland, smacked his first big-league tater at Tiger Stadium?

Walt Terrell was the pitcher.

The ball smashed into the seats with such velocity that Terrell wryly suggested McGwire was trying to get a head start on tearing down the old park.

Before that happens, a look back is in order. What follows is a grab bag of some of the more memorable regular-season home run performances at The Corner.

Burton Historical Collection

The Captain, George Stallings, hit the first-ever home run at The Corner.

George Stallings, April 28, 1896

George Stallings, the leftfielder and captain of the Tigers, didn't hit many home runs, but he did hit the first round-tripper at Michigan and Trumbull.

In the first inning of the first game at The Corner, Stallings lifted an easy fly ball to the outfield, which was ringed with hundreds of spectators. The Columbus outfielder, a fellow

Burton Historical Collection

PITCHER ED SUMMERS HIT THE ONLY TWO HOMERS OF HIS CAREER ON A DAY WHEN TEAMMATE TY COBB WAS SIDELINED.

named Butler, was converging on the ball when he collided with a late-arriving fan. While Butler lay stretched out on the grass, unconscious, Stallings circled the bases for an easy inside-the-park home run.

Later that afternoon, Stallings' teammate, Jack Fifield, became the first pitcher to homer at The Corner. Fifield would have had another, too, if a Columbus player hadn't tripped him while he was rounding third base.

Ed Summers, Sept. 17, 1910

With Cobb, the major leagues' reigning home run champion, out of the lineup with an eye injury, pitcher Ed (Kickapoo) Summers took it upon himself to provide the punch one Saturday afternoon at Bennett Park.

Summers, a switch-hitter, spanked a pair of two-run homers while pitching the Tigers past Philadelphia, 10-2. The first went to rightfield, the second to left. Each drive landed just inside the foul line and bounded over the fence, which counted for a home run in those days.

This was quite an achievement for anyone in the dead-ball era, particularly a pitcher. In fact, newspapers reported that it was the first time in modern big-league history that a pitcher had accomplished the feat.

"The day will live long in the history of Detroit baseball," one scribe wrote. "Ty Cobb, with one eye bandaged, sat on the bench to see a new batting king arise, at least for one day."

"Ty Cobb, with one eye bandaged, sat on the bench to see a new batting king arise, at least for one day."
NEWSPAPER STORY

Cobb need not worry. Summers' home runs turned out to be the first and last of his five-year big-league career.

Babe Ruth, June 8, 1926

Babe Ruth loved hitting at Navin Field, and this moon shot demonstrated why. In the fifth inning, Ruth walloped a Lil Stoner pitch far over the 12-foot wall in right-centerfield.

How far? Newspaper accounts describe the ball landing on the other side of Trumbull, bounding over several parked cars and rolling down Cherry Street before finally

Detroit Free Press

BABE RUTH HIT THE 700TH HOMER OF HIS CAREER AT NAVIN FIELD IN 1934. THAT FALL, HE JOINED HANDS WITH WORLD SERIES FOES, FROM LEFT: CARDINALS DIZZY DEAN AND FRANKIE FRISCH, TIGERS MICKEY COCHRANE AND SCHOOLBOY ROWE.

being chased down on Brooklyn Avenue – two blocks from the park – by a kid on a bike. New York beat writers reported that the ball had traveled more than 600 feet from home plate to the point where it landed. Local sports writer Harry Salsinger calculated the ball came to a halt 885 feet from the plate.

Ruth's drive has come down in history as the longest of his career. It probably was, though the distance typically cited – 626 feet – should be viewed with skepticism. The computerized measuring system currently in place in major league parks suggests that the 500- and 600-foot drives commonly attributed to sluggers like Ruth and Mantle were probably off by 100 feet or more.

In those days, before engineering entered the game, there was no precise method of measuring home run distances. The figures were a blend of rough math and simple guesswork, with a big pinch of hyperbole thrown in. There was no regard for the law of physics, which tells us that once a batted ball reaches its highest point, it has already lost most of its velocity and thus falls from the sky in a rapidly declining trajectory.

Even allowing for exaggeration, however, the Babe's blast clearly was the mightiest of the 60 homers he hit at Navin Field and probably the longest home run ever seen at The Corner.

Babe Ruth, July 13, 1934

The aging Sultan of Swat was in his final year as a Yankee when he hit a milestone homer at Navin Field. Facing Tommy Bridges in the third inning, Ruth fouled off several full-count offerings before driving the ball over the fence in right for a two-run homer, the 700th of his career.

"Get that ball!" Ruth yelled as he circled

MEMORIES WILLIE HORTON

To hit a ball up there scared the devil out of me – I mean, wow!

George Waldman / Detroit Free Press

I grew up on Canfield and Sixth Street. When they'd drive the garbage truck in through the centerfield gate, I'd sneak into the park to watch the game and see all those guys. I always thought a big-league player was from another planet.

I guess the memory that comes to me first when you say "Tiger Stadium" is of my first game there. I was 15 years old and playing for Northwestern High School. We beat Cass Tech for the city championship. I hit my first home run in Tiger Stadium that day, way up there where Reggie Jackson later hit his in the All-Star Game. To hit a ball up there scared the devil out of me – I mean, wow! I'd never played in a big park, and it was like I was dreaming, anyway. The umpire had to tell me to run.

Whew, boy, memories of Tiger Stadium. I've got a lot of them.

I've been involved with the Tigers all my life. I signed with them when I was 17 and then went back and finished my senior year of high school. I thought I was going to sign with the Yankees as a catcher. They had sent me a catcher's glove, but on the way downtown my dad said, "Let's stop at Tiger Stadium and meet Judge (Damon) Keith." At the time, Judge Keith was a lawyer. When we got there, my dad said, "Well, we've decided you're going to sign with the Tigers."

Just as I was getting ready to sign the contract, my dad grabbed my wrist and said, "If you can't make a total commitment now that your life belongs to the fans, don't sign that contract." And that was the way I always tried to live.

I was fortunate because I've been a part of that organization since I was a baby. Tiger Stadium's important to me because it's more than just playing baseball. I grew up there; they raised me.

Jerry Heiman / Detroit Free Press

TOP: WILLIE HORTON SCOUTED OUT THE CORNER FROM THIS GATE AS A KID. ABOVE: HE POSES WITH SCOUT LOU D'ANNUNZIO IN 1961.

I played my first game there as a Tiger in 1963, and I hit my first homer off Robin Roberts as a pinch hitter to tie the game in the ninth inning. I hit it in the upper deck by the flagpole. But my dad didn't see it because he got put in jail that night.

See, my dad would never take seats down by the dugout, down where the players got their tickets for their families. He raised me up in the bleachers, and that's where he would sit. That game he and another guy got into it. The guy said, "Well, if that's your son, you'd be down there where the families sit." They've got that little lockup down at the park, and they put him in there. When the game was over, my mom and brother and me were waiting after everybody else had left the ballpark, saying, "Where's Poppa? Where's Poppa?"

Finally, after the park was empty, he showed up. But back then, the way you were raised, you didn't ask the old man, "Where you been?" We just got in the car. It was a long time before I ever knew what happened. ◆

Willie Horton played for other teams in the final years of his career, but Detroit remains his home.

the bases in his familiar mincing-step style. A groundskeeper and a couple of police officers left the park and returned a few minutes later with 17-year-old Lennie Beals.

Beals was one of several youngsters outside the park who saw the ball sail over Trumbull and down Plum Street.

"We all started down Plum after the ball," Beals said, "and there was a little freckle-faced kid who could really run. But I got there first. I'm sure glad I went out for track at school."

For his trouble, Beals got $20 and a pair of new baseballs.

No. 700 home run was important to Ruth, who normally didn't place much stock in records. At the time, it represented more than twice as many home runs as any other player had hit.

Hank Greenberg, Sept. 10, 1934

The game's first Jewish superstar had never been particularly religious, but as the Tigers pursued their first pennant in 25 years, Greenberg wrestled with the problem of following the dictates of his faith and became front-page news.

At issue was whether he should play on Rosh Hashanah, the first day of the Jewish new year, or spend the day in spiritual reflection. Greenberg consulted a local rabbi, who discovered references to children playing in the Talmud. A precedent! And so on the day in question, the Tigers' leading run producer took his familiar position at first base.

In true storybook fashion, Greenberg hit two solo home runs, including the winner in the bottom of the ninth, beating Boston, 2-1. The Free Press ran a front-page headline in Yiddish: "Happy New Year, Hank."

Eight days later, Greenberg sat out Yom Kippur, the Jewish day of atonement. When he walked into his synagogue for prayer, the congregation gave him an ovation as heartfelt as any he ever received at The Corner. Free Press poet Edgar Guest wrote:

We shall miss him on the field
and we shall miss him at the bat
But he's true to his religion
and I honor him for that!

Detroit Free Press

HAMMERIN' HANK GREENBERG WAS A .319 HITTER DURING HIS 12 SEASONS AT THE CORNER. HE LED THE LEAGUE IN HOME RUNS AND RBIS FOUR TIMES EACH AND WAS NAMED MVP IN 1935 AND 1940.

Vic Wertz, May 15, 1952

Art Houtteman's oversized shoes and Vic Wertz's clutch bat. That was the winning formula when Virgil Trucks became only the second Tiger to toss a no-hitter at The Corner. It was an unusual season of highs and lows that saw the Tigers' veteran right-hander finish 5-19, the worst record of his 17-year big-league career, but still manage to throw a second no-hitter against the Yankees in New York.

Three weeks earlier at Briggs Stadium, Houtteman had lost a no-hitter to Cleveland when Harry (Suitcase) Simpson singled with two out in the ninth. On this spring afternoon, Trucks, suffering from swollen feet, borrowed Houtteman's spikes for his outing against Washington.

There were only 2,215 at The Corner. The rest of Detroit had turned out for a downtown parade honoring Gen. Douglas MacArthur. Trucks kept the Senators hitless through nine innings. But Detroit batters had little luck against Bob Porterfield. The game

MEMORIES TOM PANZENHAGEN

Courtesy Panzenhagen family

HAPPY BIRTHDAY: ALICE PANZENHAGEN AT THE CORNER ON HER 75TH, IN 1988.

It was just the two of us on a Sunday in 1962

My mom liked to sit in the reserved seats behind third base, lower deck, near the back. I can picture her now. We must've gone to a hundred games together.

Our first was against the Yankees in 1961. Our last was against the Angels in 1995. In between we saw the Tigers clinch the '68 pennant on Don Wert's single in the ninth and, a couple of weeks later, watched them go down three games to one in the World Series.

"It's over," I said.

"Don't be discouraged," she said. "They might just come back."

We saw Reggie Jackson launch one off a light tower in the '71 All-Star Game. And Gibby's two homers in the fifth and deciding game of the '84 Series sailed right over our heads.

Mom loved the Tigers and listened to every game on radio. She loved taking me and the neighborhood guys to The Corner. Of course, we kids couldn't sit still for long, not with foul balls and souvenirs to chase down. So Mom would take her seat, and we'd run wild, always returning about the eighth inning.

It was just the two of us on a Sunday in 1962, though. I remember the Tigers and the dreaded Yanks were tied after nine that day. The game stretched on and I got bored, I hate to admit. I wanted to play some ball, not watch any more of it, so Mom reluctantly agreed to take me home. Hours later, with dusk approaching, I walked home from the sandlot and there she was, sitting on the porch, transistor to her ear.

The Tigers game we went to that day was just ending, after 22 innings and seven hours. It was a classic, and she would've enjoyed watching every minute of it had I not begged her to go home. But what I remember about the moment is how she laughed good-naturedly at my amazement when she told me about the marathon game.

And then we played catch. I can picture her now. ◆

Tom Panzenhagen is an assistant sports editor of the Detroit Free Press and editor of "The Corner."

KEEPING SCORE ◆ LONG GONE

Thirty-five home runs have cleared the roof since Tiger Stadium was double-decked in 1938. All but four were hit over the rightfield grandstand. Those hit over the leftfield roof are indicated by an asterisk.

DATE	BATTER, TEAM	PITCHER, TEAM
May 4, 1939	Ted Williams, Red Sox	Bob Harris, Tigers
June 18, 1956	Mickey Mantle, Yankees	Paul Foytack, Tigers
Sept. 17, 1958	Mickey Mantle, Yankees	Jim Bunning, Tigers
Sept. 10, 1960	Mickey Mantle, Yankees	Paul Foytack, Tigers
June 11, 1961	**Norm Cash, Tigers**	Joe McClain, Senators
May 11, 1962	**Norm Cash, Tigers**	Don Schwall, Red Sox
July 27, 1962	**Norm Cash, Tigers**	Eli Grba, Angels
July 29, 1962	**Norm Cash, Tigers**	Bob Botz, Angels
Aug. 3, 1962	* Harmon Killebrew, Twins	Jim Bunning, Tigers
Aug. 23, 1964	Don Mincher, Twins	Fred Gladding, Tigers
May 18, 1968	* Frank Howard, Senators	Mickey Lolich, Tigers
July 6, 1969	Boog Powell, Orioles	Denny McLain, Tigers
Aug. 28, 1969	**Jim Northrup, Tigers**	George Lauzerique, A's
Aug. 18, 1977	**Jason Thompson, Tigers**	Catfish Hunter, Yankees
Sept. 17, 1977	**Jason Thompson, Tigers**	Dick Tidrow, Yankees
June 14, 1983	**Kirk Gibson, Tigers**	Mike Brown, Red Sox
Oct. 2, 1983	Cecil Cooper, Brewers	Dave Rozema, Tigers
May 12, 1984	Reggie Jackson, Angels	Juan Berenguer, Tigers
June 24, 1984	**Ruppert Jones, Tigers**	Tom Tellmann, Brewers
May 13, 1985	**Lou Whitaker, Tigers**	Burt Hooton, Rangers
Sept. 10, 1986	**Kirk Gibson, Tigers**	Chris Bosio, Brewers
April 17, 1988	George Brett, Royals	Jeff Robinson, Tigers
Aug. 25, 1990	*** Cecil Fielder, Tigers**	Dave Stewart, A's
June 21, 1991	**Mickey Tettleton, Tigers**	Kirk McCaskill, Angels
June 26, 1991	**Mickey Tettleton, Tigers**	Jaime Navarro, Brewers
May 1, 1994	**Kirk Gibson, Tigers**	Jack McDowell, White Sox
May 21, 1994	**Chad Kreuter, Tigers**	Jaime Navarro, Brewers
May 17, 1996	**Melvin Nieves, Tigers**	Alex Fernandex, White Sox
July 6, 1996	Carlos Delgado, Blue Jays	Omar Olivares, Tigers
Sept. 15, 1996	**Tony Clark, Tigers**	Rocky Coppinger, Orioles
April 21, 1997	* Mark McGwire, A's	Brian Moehler, Tigers
June 17, 1997	Bobby Bonilla, Marlins	Todd Jones, Tigers
July 2, 1997	**Tony Clark, Tigers**	Juan Acevedo, Mets
May 28, 1999	**Karim Garcia, Tigers**	Jaime Navarro, White Sox
June 9, 1999	Brant Brown, Pirates	Willie Blair, Tigers

Mickey Mantle hit three homers over the rightfield roof, including this one off Jim Bunning on Wednesday afternoon, Sept. 17, 1958.

remained scoreless. With two out in the ninth, and Trucks resigned to having to extend his no-hitter through extra innings, Wertz came to bat.

Two innings earlier, the Tigers' left-handed slugger had doubled off Porterfield, only to be picked off. This time Wertz swung at Porterfield's first offering and sent it flying toward the seats in upper right. It crashed into the nearly empty stands, sealing a 1-0 victory and Trucks' no-hitter.

Trucks was so excited that he leaped up from the bench, cracking his skull into the cement roof of the dugout. Those who didn't know better thought the pitcher's stunned look was the result of Wertz's dramatic poke.

"I finally made it out to home plate," Trucks recalled, "where I gave Wertz the biggest hug I knew how to give. But my head was still buzzing."

Babe Birrer, July 19, 1955

For one big-league afternoon at Briggs Stadium, Werner (Babe) Birrer hit and pitched in a fashion true to his nickname.

In a game against Baltimore midway through his only season with Detroit, the 6-foot, 200-pound right-hander came on in relief of starter Frank Lary. The Tigers were clinging to a 5-4 lead, but a close game turned into a rout thanks to a pair of three-run homers by Birrer.

The first came in the sixth inning, when Birrer drove one of George Zuverink's deliveries off the upper deck in left. The following inning, he lined an Art Schallock pitch into the lower pavilion in left-center. The Tigers wound up winning, 12-4, as Birrer also pitched four innings of scoreless relief.

It was a shame that Birrer batted only twice. Another turn would have given him a chance to challenge a couple of hitting records for pitchers. In 1945, Jim Tobin homered three times in a game for the Boston Braves. And Birrer's six RBIs fell one shy of the mark set by the Yankees' Vic Raschi in a 1953 contest with the Tigers at Yankee Stadium.

"I just went up there and swung like I always do," shrugged Birrer, who a year earlier hit 29 homers playing the outfield for the

Wally Steiger / Detroit Free Press

7th Army Corps in Germany. "I don't have the eye or the coordination to be a punch hitter, so I always go for the long ball. I just happened to connect with a couple."

Mickey Mantle, Sept. 10, 1960

Sports writers in the '50s invented the term "tape-measure home run" to describe Mantle's prodigious blasts. An odometer might have been a more appropriate measuring stick for the one he hit off Paul Foytack, his third roof-topper at The Corner since 1956.

Batting left-handed against the Detroit right-hander, Mantle propelled the ball toward the light tower atop the roof in right-centerfield. It sailed through the tower, banged off a pipe, then disappeared. According to Paul Susman, who wrote an article in Baseball Digest describing his investigation of the historic blast, startled press box observers agreed it was the longest ball they had ever seen hit. Their informal impressions were borne out by the calculations of mathematical expert Bob Schiewie, who assisted Susman.

Their research revealed that the ball crossed Trumbull (110 feet wide) and landed on the fly in the Brooks Lumber Yard. Workers pinpointed the exact spot the ball hit the ground.

"We measured the depth of the stands, Trumbull Avenue, and the distance to where the ball was seen on the fly," Susman wrote. "The final measurement came out to 643 feet, making this a new record for precisely measured home run distance, surpassing Mantle's previous 565-foot shot in Washington's Griffith Stadium in 1953."

Asked about the home run today, all Foytack can say with certainty is that "Mickey sure hit the hell out of it." Which is something mathematicians and casual fans can all agree on.

Roger Maris, April 26, 1961

Once again, Foytack was a footnote to a historic Yankees home run. New York was in town and Roger Maris, destined to break Ruth's single-season home run mark, had gone the first 10 games of the season without reaching the seats.

Detroit Free Press

CAB DRIVER JOE MARTIN HAS SOMETHING BELONGING TO NORM CASH – THE BALL STORMIN' NORMAN KNOCKED OVER THE RIGHTFIELD ROOF ON JUNE 11, 1961. CASH, WHO LAUNCHED FOUR ROOF SHOTS AMONG HIS 373 HOMERS AS A TIGER, WAS HONORED WITH A DAY IN 1973.

This day, Foytack relieved starter Don Mossi and faced Maris in the fifth inning. If memory serves him right, it was an inside fastball that the quiet 26-year-old rightfielder got hold of.

Kiss it good-bye. Maris' solo home run in front of a meager gathering of 4,676 fans kick-started a personal odyssey of glory and grief in pursuit of baseball's most hallowed record. Of the 61 round-trippers he hit that summer, numbers 23, 24, 57 and 58 also came at Tiger Stadium.

As Maris' first victim, Foytack was a popular interview when Mark McGwire overhauled Maris' mark in 1998.

"I get reminded of that all the time," the West Bloomfield resident said. "I used to kid Roger and say, 'You owe me $400 a month. Without me, there would be no record.' And he'd say, 'You're absolutely right. But I'm not sending you any money.' "

Norm Cash, June 11, 1961

For the first 23 years that the stadium was double-decked, only two players – Ted Williams and Mantle – had cleared the roof. In the opener of a Sunday doubleheader against Washington, Detroit's bandy-legged

NORM CASH DAY
Tiger Stadium • August 12, 1973

Courtesy Eva Navarro

first baseman became the third player, and the first Tiger, to accomplish the feat.

Norm Cash's smash came off Joe McClain, a rookie right-hander, in the fourth inning of a game the Tigers lost, 7-4. It sailed out of sight between the foul line and the light tower and was retrieved by a cab driver, Joe Martin, who happily posed for pictures afterward.

The Tigers managed to gain a split, thanks chiefly to Cash's production. For the day, he had three home runs and three singles. He even uncharacteristically stole a base.

"I guess it was the biggest day I ever had," the 26-year-old Texan drawled in the clubhouse. Stormin' Norman could afford to be nonchalant. He would go on to hit three more roof-clearing shots the following season, giving him four for his career. No player has had more.

Tommy Matchick, July 19, 1968

Of the 30 games the Tigers won in their last at-bats in 1968, several role players unexpectedly rose to the occasion. The most memorable of these occurred in the opener of a weekend series with Baltimore, the Tigers' nearest rival in the standings.

More than 53,000 fans were shoehorned into Tiger Stadium on a muggy Friday night. Down, 4-2, in the ninth, the Tigers clawed back within a run. With two out and Bill Freehan on first, the game boiled down to a confrontation between ace reliever Moe Drabowsky and seldom-used Tommy Matchick.

The slightly built reserve infielder battled Drabowsky to a full count. Then the right-handed reliever grooved one. Matchick, a career .215 hitter with little power, whipped

Ira Rosenberg / Detroit Free Press

TOMMY MATCHICK REMEMBERS THE BIGGEST HIT OF HIS CAREER, A HOMER OFF RELIEF ACE MOE DRABOWSKY IN 1968.

around from the left side of the plate. Miraculously, the ball sliced through the humid air and smashed into the overhang in rightfield, giving the Tigers a stunning 5-4 victory and sending the crowd into hysterics.

"I just wanted to make contact," the Tigers' newest hero explained. "It was the biggest hit of my career."

And 1968 was the biggest year of Matchick's otherwise undistinguished six major league seasons. Of the four home runs he hit in the bigs, three came in the Year of the Tiger. Each was stroked at Tiger Stadium.

Lindy McDaniel, Sept. 28, 1972

Lindy McDaniel's name doesn't usually come to mind in discussions of the most notable home runs hit at The Corner. It should. In one of the last games before the advent of the designated-hitter rule in 1973 made hitting pitchers obsolete in American League parks, McDaniel cracked the final four-bagger by a pitcher at The Corner.

National Baseball Library

YANKEES PITCHER LINDY MCDANIEL DIDN'T NEED A DESIGNATED HITTER WHEN HE CAME TO BAT AGAINST MICKEY LOLICH IN 1972.

It came in the ninth inning of a 1-1 game between the Tigers and Yankees. Mickey Lolich was on the mound, trying to keep Detroit one-half game behind the Red Sox in the final week of a torrid pennant race. In this situation, the 36-year-old reliever was perhaps the least likely person to reach the seats off the Tigers' ace.

But McDaniel, with just two home runs in a career stretching back to 1955, unexpectedly connected to leftfield, giving New York a 2-1 lead. The Tigers tied it, but the Yankees won it in the 12th on their third solo shot of the night off Lolich.

Afterward, manager Billy Martin criticized his own pitcher's performance at bat and on the bases. Lolich had bunted through a pitch on an attempted squeeze and failed to advance on a wild pitch. If nothing else, Lolich's ineptitude served as a reminder why, come next April, the pitcher's spot in the Tigers' batting order was going to be filled by a real hitter, Gates Brown.

Fred Lynn, June 18, 1975

Several visiting players have hit three home runs in a game at The Corner, including Ted Williams and George Brett. But none of them has been as productive with the trifecta as Boston rookie Fred Lynn was on a muggy Wednesday night against one of the Tigers' most hapless teams.

In the first inning, the 23-year-old centerfielder drilled a three-run homer off Joe Coleman. The next inning, he cranked a two-run homer against the Tigers' starter. This time the ball bounced off the roof in right.

The score had grown to 8-1 against Lerrin LaGrow in the third when Lynn tripled over Danny Meyer's head in left to send two more Bosox scurrying home. Lynn slowed down to a single in his next two at-bats. But with two on in the ninth, he hammered a Tom Walker pitch into the upper deck in right. This made the final score 15-1, with Lynn accounting for 10 runs with a single, triple, and three home runs. One more RBI and he would have matched Tony Lazzeri's league mark.

Lynn went on to lead Boston into the World Series, earning Most Valuable Player and Rookie of the Year awards along the way. He was acquired 13 years later by Detroit, but by then he was only a shadow of the hitter who had once single-handedly dismantled the Tigers.

Dave Bergman, June 4, 1984

Maybe it was because the Friday night game was nationally televised. That it involved America's pet team and second-place Toronto certainly added to its impact. In any event, pinch-hitter Dave Bergman's winning blast off Roy Lee Jackson, capping a mesmerizing pitcher-batter duel, remains the second-best-remembered home run of the Tigers' last championship season. Only Kirk Gibson's World Series blast off Goose Gossage has the same staying power.

The talent-laden Blue Jays, looking to creep within 3½ games of the Tigers, blew a

Tony Spina / Detroit Free Press

OUTTA SIGHT: IN 1990 CECIL FIELDER HIT 51 HOME RUNS AND BECAME THE FIRST TIGER TO CLEAR THE ROOF IN LEFT.

3-0 lead in the seventh inning when Howard Johnson bounced a Dave Stieb delivery off the foul pole in right. It was still tied, 3-3, when Bergman came to bat with two on and two out in the bottom of the 10th.

For the next seven minutes, Bergman faced down the Blue Jays' ace reliever, patiently fouling off pitch after pitch while the count grew full.

"It was getting toward midnight," Bergman said. "Somebody had to get a hit."

Jackson's 13th pitch was a slider, maybe six inches off the ground. Bergman got underneath it and sent it flying toward the upper deck in right, where it landed among a knot of delirious fans. It was the first Tigers home run for Bergman, acquired in a trade with Philadelphia, and it put the demoralized Jays 5½ games behind Detroit.

"You know they were going after him hard," joked Tom Brookens, batting .159 at the time. "They saw me on deck."

Cecil Fielder, Aug. 25, 1990

According to longtime groundskeeper Frank Feneck, it almost takes a howitzer to send a ball over the leftfield grandstand. The roof is 94 feet high and 340 feet from home plate, making roof shots in that direction one of the most difficult feats in baseball.

"Climb up to the roof and look down, and you won't believe how high and hard they have to hit the ball to do that," he said.

Through 1998, only four players had cleared the leftfield roof. Three were visitors – Harmon Killebrew, Frank Howard and McGwire – and one was a Tiger.

Fielder joined the exclusive circle of sluggers in a game against Oakland during his first season in Detroit. In the fourth inning, with Alan Trammell on first and two out, Big Daddy powered a 3-1 fastball from right-hander Dave Stewart toward the roof. It bounced twice before plopping over the edge and onto the street below.

"That's the longest home run I've had hit off me," marveled Stewart, who had surrendered an upper-deck shot to Fielder in the first inning. "I'd have a chance to send my family to Paris on that one."

Sammy Sosa, June 25, 1998

On the last day of August in 1937, Rudy York capped a month-long rampage by drilling a pair of home runs against Washington at Navin Field. That gave the Tigers' backstop 18 round-trippers for the month, a record that stood 61 years until Sammy Sosa and the rest of the Chicago Cubs paid their first visit to The Corner since the 1945 World Series.

The previous night, Sosa tied York's mark with a first-inning blast. On this Thursday evening, the Cubs' rightfielder led off the seventh by taking a Brian Moehler pitch to the opposite field. It landed several rows back in the upper deck, causing the thousands of Chicago fans in the half-filled park to chant "Sam-my! Sam-my!"

Sosa acknowledged the fans and the toppling of York's record with a curtain call – a rarity for a visiting player at Tiger Stadium. In the bottom of the inning, however, the Tigers' Tony Clark earned his own curtain call after his game-deciding, three-run homer whistled over the 440-foot sign in dead center.

"I'll do the same thing tomorrow that I did today – go up there and keep swinging," said Sosa, who would go on to hit 66 home runs for the season, after the Tigers' 6-4 victory.

Homer-happy fans at The Corner would have it no other way. ◆

Reuters

JUNE 25, 1998: SAMMY SOSA HAS A BOUNCE IN HIS STEP AFTER HITTING HIS 19TH HOME RUN OF THE MONTH, BREAKING RUDY YORK'S RECORD.

THE MANY AND THE FEW: BOSTON'S TED WILLIAMS, WHO HIT 55 HOMERS AT THE CORNER, SWINGS FOR THE SEATS. REGGIE SANDERS CONNECTS FOR A HOME RUN – ONE OF ONLY THREE IN A BRIEF CAREER – IN HIS FIRST MAJOR LEAGUE AT-BAT IN 1974.

Tony Spina / Detroit Free Press

KEEPING SCORE ◆ HOMER HEAVEN

Most home runs by teams in a game at The Corner

(Major league record indicated by asterisk)

- **Opening Day, 6** — April 7, 1986, Boston (4), Detroit (2).
- **Regular season, 12 *** — May 29, 1995, Detroit (7), Chicago (5).
- **Night, 11 *** — June 23, 1950, New York (6), Detroit (5).
- **All-Star, 6 *** — July 10, 1951, National League (4), American League (2); July 13, 1971, American League (3), National League (3).
- **World Series, 4** — Oct. 14, 1984, Detroit (3), San Diego (1).

Most home runs by a player in a game at The Corner

- **Game, 3** — Many times (last: Bobby Higginson, June 30, 1997, vs. NY Mets).
- **Doubleheader, 4** — Charlie Maxwell, May 3, 1959, vs. New York.
- **Season, 39 *** — Hank Greenberg, 1938.
- **Lifetime, 226** — Al Kaline, 1953-74.
- **World Series, 2** — Alan Trammell, Oct. 13, 1984, vs. San Diego; Kirk Gibson, Oct. 14, 1984, vs. San Diego.
- **All-Star, 2 *** — Arky Vaughan, National League, July 8, 1941.

Most lifetime home runs by visiting players at The Corner

- **60** — Babe Ruth, Boston and New York, 1915-34.
- **55** — Ted Williams, Boston, 1939-60.
- **52** — Jimmie Foxx, Philadelphia and Boston, 1927-42.
- **42** — Mickey Mantle, New York, 1951-68.
- **37** — Yogi Berra, New York, 1946-63.

Tony Spina / Detroit Free Press

Most home runs in a season by visiting players at The Corner

- **9** — Jimmie Foxx, Philadelphia, 1932.
- **7** — Jimmie Foxx, Boston, 1937; Yogi Berra, New York, 1951; Gus Zernial, Philadelphia, 1953; Mickey Mantle, New York, 1956; Roger Maris, Cleveland and Kansas City, 1958; Gary Geiger, Boston, 1963; Mark McGwire, Oakland, 1987.

Richard Bak Collection

New York's Yogi Berra and Philadelphia's Jimmy Foxx enjoyed the friendly confines.

KEEPING SCORE ◆ DEBUT DINGERS

Of the 76 major-leaguers since 1876 to hit a home run in their first big-league at-bat, three accomplished this rare feat at The Corner.

DATE	PLAYER	PITCHER
May 3, 1963	Buster Narum, Baltimore	Don Mossi, Detroit
Sept. 1, 1974	Reggie Sanders, Detroit	Catfish Hunter, Oakland
June 29, 1984	Andre David, Minnesota	Jack Morris, Detroit

Jimmy Tafoya / Detroit Free Press

YEARBOOK

By Bill McGraw

1968

Strangers hugged and kissed along Woodward Avenue after the Tigers won the pennant and World Series

As in many places in the United States and western Europe, 1968 was a tumultuous year in Detroit, which was buffeted by youth rebellion, Vietnam war protests and embittered reactions to the assassinations of the Rev. Martin Luther King Jr. and Robert Kennedy.

But Detroit also was recovering from another momentous event, the previous summer's civil disorder. The 1967 riot – or rebellion, depending on your point of view – overshadowed virtually everything that happened in Detroit in 1968.

With 43 deaths, at least 1,000 injuries, 7,231 arrests and 2,509 buildings looted or burned, the civil disorder was one of the worst in American history.

In 1968, newly formed organizations such as New Detroit Inc. and Focus:HOPE began working on rebuilding the city. Detroit then was the country's fifth-largest city, with a population of about 1.6 million, but it was shrinking rapidly.

The 1967 disorder did not start the exodus from the city. Historians say flight began after World War II, when the auto industry decentralized and cut jobs, and Packard and Hudson – not to mention numerous suppliers – shut down. University of Michigan historian Sidney Fine notes that Detroit lost nearly one quarter of its white population during the 1950s, and its nonwhite population doubled to about one-third of city residents.

The abandonment of Detroit by whites accelerated in the 1960s as suburbs such as Warren, Troy and Livonia flourished. Some residents and business owners who remained in Detroit installed bars on their windows and Plexiglas shields around their cash registers, a physical reflection of the burgeoning crime rate and rampant paranoia. Downtown, nonetheless, remained southeast Michigan's busiest commercial center, and massive celebrations, in which strangers hugged and kissed, took place along Woodward Avenue after the Tigers won the pennant and World Series.

Detroit Free Press

Race was an issue everywhere, and "Black Power!" was a slogan popular with many African-Americans. In the auto plants, many blacks fought what they called "Uncle Toms" and "honky-dog racists" in both the companies and the UAW by forming the Dodge Revolutionary Union Movement and similar groups.

As blacks approached 50 percent of the city population, they began to assert their rights in many white-run Detroit institutions such as the school system and Recorder's Court. Despite the racial tension, some black and white fans danced together after the Tigers' pennant victory,

Ira Rosenberg / Detroit Free Press

Detroiters clashed in 1967, but city streets were a clamorous place in September 1968, when the Tigers won the pennant.

and black and white fans shouted, "Willie Horton, unite our city!"

Blacks and whites also celebrated Motown Records, Detroit's homegrown music machine on W. Grand Boulevard, which dominated the charts along with the Beatles, Rolling Stones and another Detroit product, Aretha Franklin. Motown founder Berry Gordy, a former assembly line worker and the most famous example of a growing number of black business leaders, renovated a fabulous home on Boston Boulevard with a swimming pool and backyard golf greens.

While Motown's music rarely got political, Edwin Starr captured the widespread opposition to American involvement in Vietnam by recording "War." Starr proclaimed: "War! Huh! Good Gawd, y'all. What is it good for?"

Rebellious young people clashed with police at Detroit's Balduck Park, in Royal Oak and at Northland Center.

Detroit contributed to the international counterculture with innovative, high-energy rock music, especially by Iggy and the Stooges and the MC 5, whose popular anthem, "Kick out the jams," helped spread the White Panther Party's bawdy agenda of rock 'n' roll, dope and sex in the streets. ◆

CHAPTER 9

October heroes

Courtesy The Designated Hatter

THE TIGERS CLAWED THEIR WAY TO A MEMORABLE WORLD SERIES CLASH WITH THE CARDINALS IN 1934. FIFTY YEARS LATER, KIRK GIBSON EPITOMIZED THE ROAR OF '84.

For a franchise as old as the Tigers, championships have been few and far between. Never mind the Western League days or the first three years of the American League, when there was no World Series and winning the pennant was the sole objective. In 96 seasons since the fall classic began in 1903, the Tigers made it to baseball's ultimate showdown nine times, winning the whole enchilada on four occasions: 1935, 1945, 1968 and 1984. There also have been a handful of half-pennants since the leagues adopted a playoff format in 1969. The Tigers grabbed the Eastern Division flag – thus qualifying for the American League Championship Series – in 1972, 1984 and 1987. However, the only time they won the ALCS and advanced to the World Series was in '84.

At first blush, it doesn't seem like a heck of a lot to show for a century of labor at The Corner. Still, among American League teams only the Yankees have made more World Series appearances. And Detroit's four championships, while matched or exceeded by nine other big-league clubs, are still more than historic franchises such as Cleveland, the Philadelphia Phillies and both Chicago teams have won during the same period.

Ty Cobb learned how elusive a World Series championship can be. Detroit's pennant winners of 1907-08-09 played in the fourth, fifth and sixth modern World Series. Manager Hughie Jennings, who had been a star shortstop with the Baltimore Orioles of the National League during the 1890s, was eager to show his old employer that the junior circuit was the real deal.

There's nobody around who can talk about those days, which is just as well. After the Tigers' sad-sack performances all three Octobers, Ban Johnson was left grumbling.

"We do all right in the World Series," the league president said, "except when that damn

Mary Schroeder / Detroit Free Press

National Leaguer, Jennings, gets into it. Then we get the hell beaten out of us."

The first World Series game at The Corner took place Oct. 11, 1907. The Chicago Cubs, featuring the fabled infield of shortstop Joe Tinker, second baseman Johnny Evers and first baseman Frank Chance, whipped the Tigers, 6-1. Most of the 11,306 spectators at Bennett Park recognized the Cubs' third baseman, Harry Steinfeldt, from his days as a Western League Tiger.

The following afternoon, Detroiters stayed away in droves as the Cubs completed a sweep with a 2-0 blanking. The Tigers were handcuffed by pitchers Orvie Overall, Ed Reulbach, Jack Pfiester and Three Finger Brown. In five games (the first game in Chicago had ended in a 3-3 standoff), Cobb – the American League's leading batter and base stealer – hit .200 with no RBIs and no stolen bases. "The wonderful Ty Cobb," New York writer Joe Vila observed, "dwindled from a world-beater to a lame amateur." Sam Crawford, runner-up to Cobb on the league's batting list, was marginally better, hitting .238.

Richard Bak Collection

Richard Bak Collection

Top: Fans circle Bennett Park for the 1907 World Series, first ever at The Corner. Above: Tigers pitcher Bill Donovan looks on as the rival managers meet.

When the teams met in a rematch the following October, the Tigers improved to the extent that they actually won a game. Unfortunately, Chicago won the other four, including all three played at Bennett Park. The finale was a 2-0 loss that attracted 6,210 spectators on a wintry afternoon. The turnout remains the record low for a World Series game and had some out-of-town pundits predicting that Detroit would not remain a major league city for too many more years. Cobb had his finest postseason, batting .368, but the team only hit .203 against one of the greatest pitching staffs of all time.

The Tigers were more competitive against a new opponent in the 1909 World Series, but the result was the same. The tussle between Pittsburgh and Detroit was billed as a showdown between each league's greatest star: Cobb vs. Honus Wagner. The Pirates' bowlegged shortstop outperformed his rival as Pittsburgh took the seventh game in Detroit, 8-0. Babe Adams, an unheralded 12-game winner during the regular season (12-3), won his third of the series on a blustery Saturday afternoon at Bennett Park. The Tigers remain the only American League team to drop three World Series in a row.

Again heading into the off-season a loser,

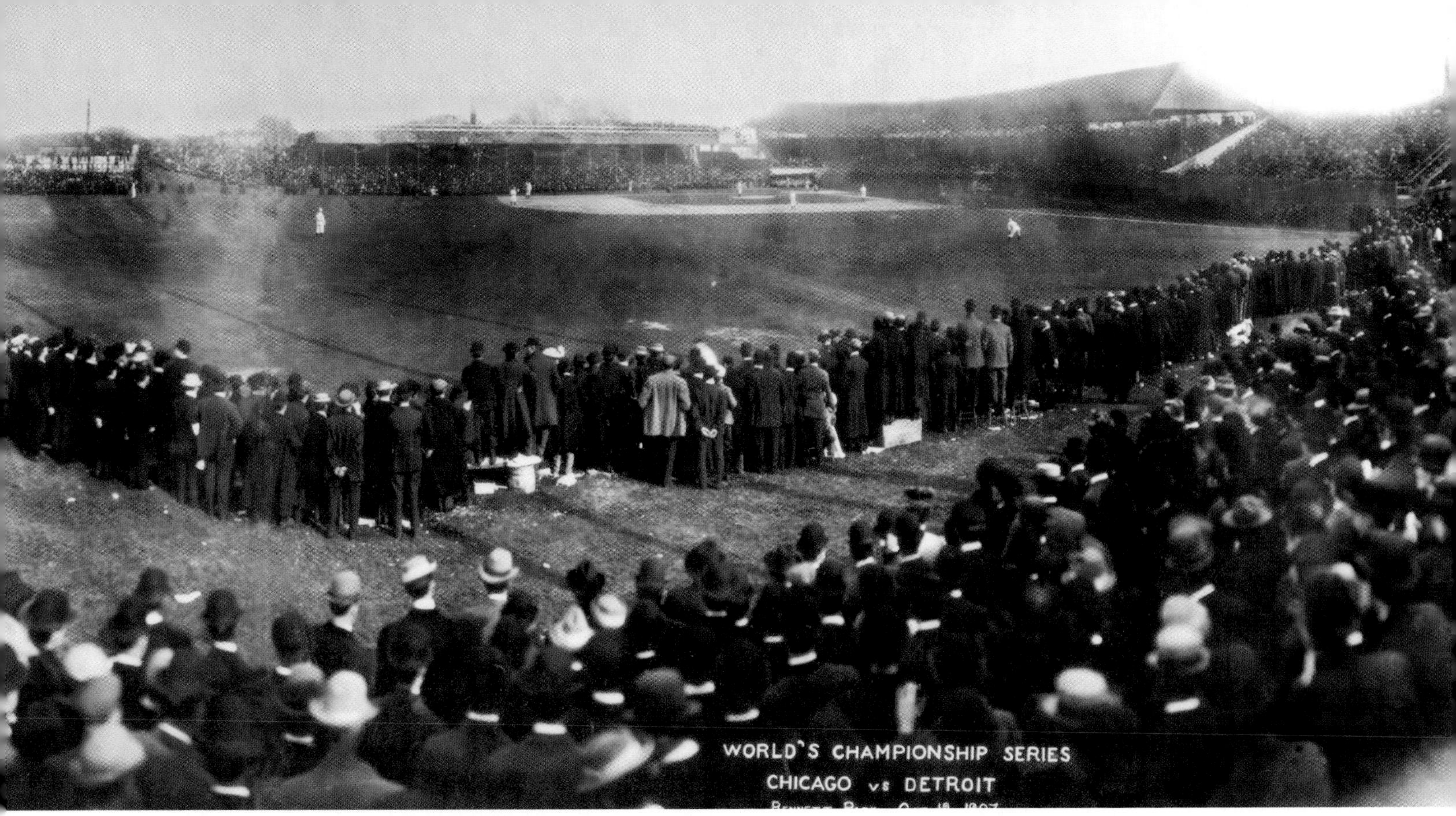

Burton Historical Collection

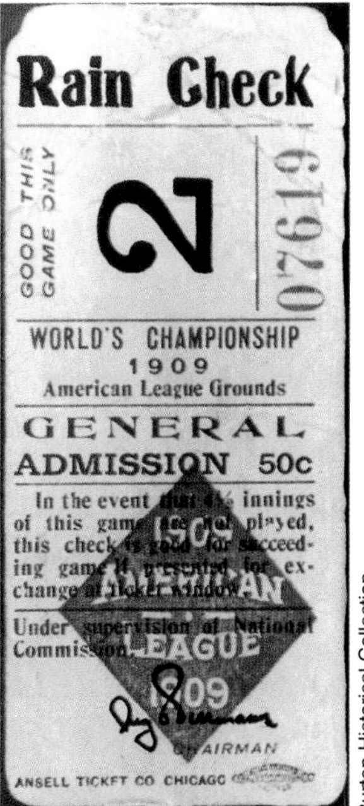

Rain Check

GOOD THIS GAME ONLY

2

07619

WORLD'S CHAMPIONSHIP
1909
American League Grounds

GENERAL
ADMISSION 50c

In the event that 4½ innings of this game are not played, this check is good for succeeding game if presented for exchange at ticket window.

Under supervision of National Commission.

CHAIRMAN

ANSELL TICKET CO. CHICAGO

Burton Historical Collection

During the 1909 World Series, fans who balked at paying 50 cents for a general admission seat instead found a perch in the wildcat stands on the other side of the leftfield fence. But owner Frank Navin hung strips of canvas to block their view.

Burton Historical Collection

In 1934, downtown Hudson's hung a seven-story banner commemorating the Tigers' first pennant in 25 years.

MEMORIES BILLY ROGELL

I first played at Navin Field in 1925 with the Red Sox. The field had rocks and everything else in it. I'd have a pocketful of rocks by the end of the game. It wasn't like the carpet that the players have today. To tell you the truth, though, of all the parks I played in, it was my favorite. That's why I was happy when I came to Detroit in 1930.

In 1933, I remember talking with Mr. Navin, and he mentioned there was a chance we might get Babe Ruth as the manager. Ruth went on a long trip to Japan and told Navin he would talk to him when he got back. When Cochrane's name came up, he didn't have the $100,000 to buy him from Philadelphia. He didn't want to wait for Ruth, so he wound up borrowing the money from Mr. Briggs.

Mickey was one hell of a guy who simply liked to win. So did I. He never bawled you out in public and never showed anybody up. We had Greenberg, a great ballplayer. I felt sorry for that poor bugger. Being Jewish, he took so much abuse. They called him "Christ Killer" and all that. I don't know how he kept his cool.

An umpire, Brick Owens, cost us the '34 Series against the Cardinals. In the sixth game at Navin Field we had two men on and nobody out when he called Cochrane out on a play at third. Owens was 20 to 30 feet away from the play. We should have scored three runs; instead we wind up losing the game, 4-3.

In the seventh game we got creamed, 11-0. The whole problem started with a pop fly. Dizzy Dean hit a pop fly to Goslin in left, and he should have caught the damn ball. I don't know if he ever saw it. Marv Owen and Goose used to go at it all the time. Marv would tell him, "Goose, you should give Billy half your salary. He covers half of leftfield for you." That opened the gates. They scored seven runs that inning.

Later, Ducky Medwick was the showboat sliding into third. Marv Owen had the ball and he was in foul territory. To keep from stepping on him, Marv fell on top of Medwick. Medwick then started kicking him. Hell, Marv wouldn't hurt a fly. But Medwick was part of the Gas House Gang, and I guess he had to live up to that reputation.

You know, in the '35 Series against the Cubs, we lost Greenberg in the second game with a broken wrist. Flea Clifton then played third base while Marv Owen was moved to first. Flea never gets credit, but he played third as good as anybody I ever saw.

My all-time favorite moment at the park was in the sixth game of the Series. In the top of the ninth with the score tied, Stan Hack tripled off Tommy Bridges. I never saw a guy so determined not to let another guy get a hit. Tommy got the next three batters out. We ended up winning the Series in the bottom of the ninth when Goslin hit that broken-bat single to score Mickey. I was the happiest guy in the world. ◆

Billy Rogell was a Tiger throughout the '30s.

An umpire, Brick Owens, cost us the '34 Series against the Cardinals

OUT OF UNIFORM: A DAPPER BILLY ROGELL AT NAVIN FIELD IN 1933.

Detroit Free Press

Burton Historical Collection

BROTHER ACT: HUB AND GEE WALKER (ON THE LEFT) WERE TIGERS TEAMMATES IN 1935, THE YEAR DETROIT WON ITS FIRST WORLD CHAMPIONSHIP. ON THE RIGHT ARE PITTSBURGH'S PAUL AND LLOYD WANER, IN TOWN FOR AN EXHIBITION GAME. RIGHT: OH, BROTHER – IN THE '34 SERIES, DIZZY DEAN BLEW THE TUBA AND BEAT THE TIGERS TWICE AT NAVIN FIELD.

Richard Bak Collection

Cobb stayed optimistic. He was, after all, only 22 years old. His best years were ahead; certainly there would be more World Series to come.

Unfortunately for Cobb, there weren't. When he retired 19 years later, the failure to get one more kick at the can was his biggest regret, one that ate at him into old age.

"I was too young when that part of my career happened," he said in his autobiography. "I regret I never got a crack at the World Series during my peak years."

It took another 25 years before the Tigers played in another World Series. The 1934 Series with the "Gas House Gang" Cardinals went the limit and was one of the most contentious ever played. St. Louis fielded a colorful, braggadocios lineup that included shortstop Leo (The Lip) Durocher and 30-game winner Dizzy Dean.

Accounts of the Series typically boil it down to the riotous seventh game played at Navin Field, but The Corner hosted three other contests. All were played before large, boisterous crowds that topped 40,000. About half were jammed into the massive bleacher section Navin erected in leftfield. Carpenters had to remove the wall and were forced to build around one of the few remaining houses on Cherry Street, but nobody was

Courtesy The Designated Hatter

THE 1934 TIGERS ELECTRIFIED DETROIT DURING THE DEPRESSION, BATTING .300 AS A TEAM AND WINNING 101 GAMES.

complaining. The gerrymandered stands meant greater shares for the players, a substantial boost to Navin's take, and the opportunity for even more fans in the most baseball-mad town in Depression-era America to take in the action.

The teams split Games 1 and 2 at Navin Field before traveling to Sportsman's Park. There the Tigers won two of three to return to Detroit one victory away from their first World Series championship.

The city was primed for a celebration as the clubs assembled at Navin Field for Game 6. Detroit's pitching sensation, 24-game-winner Schoolboy Rowe (24-8), went up against Dean's brother, Paul, a.k.a. Daffy. It was an umpire's daffy decision at third base that cost the Tigers the game, with an obviously bad call short-circuiting a sixth-inning rally during which the Tigers knotted the game at 3. In the seventh, with Mickey Cochrane still steaming behind the plate, Dean smacked a run-scoring single off Rowe that held up for a 4-3 Cardinals victory.

Eldon Auker, who had gone 15-7 in his second big-league season, was Cochrane's choice to pitch the seventh game the following afternoon. Auker, a jug-eared 24-year-old with an unusual submarine motion, had beaten the Cardinals in Game 4. His opponent this time was Dizzy Dean, who'd dropped a 3-1 decision to Tommy Bridges in Game 5. Dean was pitching on one day's rest. But given new life and with the entire baseball world as his audience, the showboating speedballer was intent on humiliating the Tigers. As the crowd filed in, Dean clowned around with the band and baseball clown Al Schacht. He snatched a tiger rug from Schacht and paraded around the field, telling everybody, "I got that Tiger skin already." He strolled over to where Auker was warming up and said, "Hey, podnah, you don't expect to get anybody out with that shit, do ya?"

In 1999, Auker was one of only four Tigers from the 1934-35 pennant winners still alive. "I remember some things very distinctly," he said, rolling back the years from his Florida home.

"In the third inning the bases were loaded and I had two men out. Frank Frisch fouled off five or six pitches and then hit a soft liner to Greenberg. He thought it was hit harder and jumped up and tipped it with his mitt.

Both: Richard Bak Collection

Cardinals leftfielder Ducky Medwick stands his ground as 17,000 bleacherites pelt him with fruit and vegetables. Medwick's hard slide into third baseman Marv Owen (left) precipitated a melee at Navin Field. Facing page: visiting St. Louis fans hoisted home plate after the Cardinals won Game 7.

Detroit Free Press

"The ball rolled into the drainage ditch near the stands. (Rightfielder) Pete Fox came in to get it, but he kicked the ball towards the dugout. Cochrane ended up fielding the ball, but three runs scored on the play. I was then replaced. I believe Mickey brought in Rowe, and he couldn't get anyone out, and then Tommy Bridges came in. They scored seven runs that inning."

The all-purpose Dizzy contributed two hits that inning and frustrated Detroit batters the rest of the way. His grandstanding antics and obvious delight from the Tigers' futility incited the 40,902 sulking spectators. The fireworks exploded in the sixth inning, when Joe (Ducky) Medwick slid hard into third baseman Marv Owen while running out a triple.

"I remember Medwick sliding into Marvin with his spikes letter-high," Auker said. "He tore Marvin's shirt, and he got upset. They got into a little scuffle, but no one got hurt."

When Medwick took his position in leftfield in the bottom of the inning, the score had grown to 9-0, and the 17,000 fans crammed into the temporary bleachers were screaming for his scalp. A barrage of bottles, fruit, vegetables, sandwiches and balled-up scorecards was hurled at him. Medwick played catch with a piece of fruit, but his nonchalance inspired a fresh round of missiles.

"The fans that had been waiting out all night for a ticket got pretty upset," Auker said. "It was very unsportsmanlike by the fans, but we were behind, and frustration just broke out."

It took nearly 20 minutes of interruptions, personal intervention by baseball commissioner Judge Kenesaw Mountain Landis, and a police escort off the field for Medwick before play could continue. Dean mopped up the few remaining Tigers batters as the Cardinals rolled to an 11-0 victory. To a man, every Tiger felt to his dying day the pangs of humiliation and bitterness about the Series' outcome.

"Was St. Louis the better club?" Owen repeated an interviewer's question not long before his death in 1991. "The best way for me to answer that is to say we won it all the next year."

Cochrane's troops went into the 1935

Courtesy The Designated Hatter

PLAYERS AND UMPIRES STAND AT ATTENTION BEFORE THE START OF THE 1935 WORLD SERIES AT NAVIN FIELD. IN THEIR FIFTH FALL CLASSIC, THE TIGERS FINALLY WOULD EMERGE VICTORIOUS, DEFEATING CHICAGO IN SIX GAMES.

Richard Bak Collection

World Series eager to avenge themselves against the Cardinals, but the Cubs upset those plans by overhauling the Gas House Gang in the final days of the season. Because Wrigley Field couldn't be made ready in time, the Cubs surrendered home-field advantage to Detroit.

The first two games were held at Navin Field. Lon Warneke spun a four-hitter as the Cubs won the opener, 3-0, but Bridges and Hank Greenberg paced the Tigers' 8-3 victory the following afternoon. Greenberg hit a two-run homer, chasing Chicago starter Charlie Root in the first inning. Bridges went the distance, scattering six hits.

Despite losing Greenberg for the Series because of a broken wrist, Detroit eked out a pair of one-run wins at Wrigley Field, seizing a 3-1 Series lead. However, the Cubs rallied, winning Game 5, 3-1, before the clubs boarded trains for the return trip to Detroit.

Oct. 7, 1935, looms large on the calendar of Tigers fans. It was a cool, sunny Monday, the kind of day of which pleasant autumnal memories are made. None could be more pleasant than the one Bridges provided this

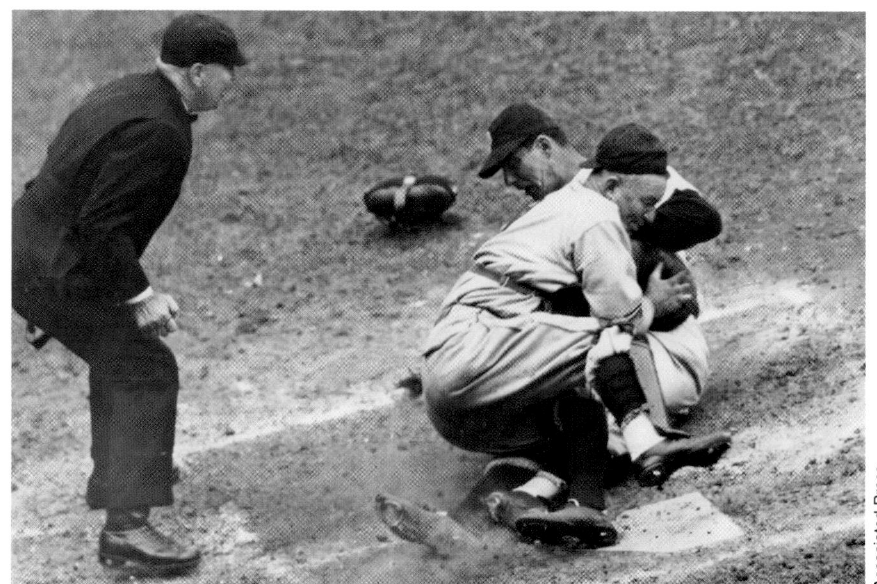

Associated Press

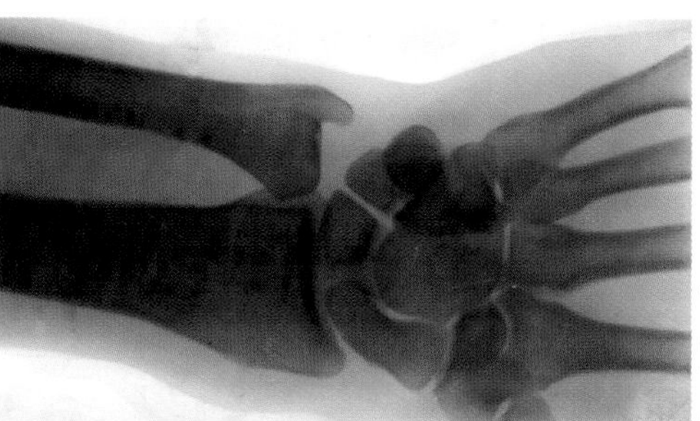

Detroit Free Press

An X-ray reveals the broken wrist Hank Greenberg suffered in a home-plate collision with Cubs catcher Gabby Hartnett (above). Greenberg was sidelined, but the Tigers went on to win the Series and downtown streets like Lafayette were clogged with confetti.

Detroit Free Press

afternoon. In the ninth inning of a taut struggle tied at 3, the little right-hander surrendered a leadoff triple to Stan Hack. Inside the suddenly hushed park, he then proceeded to pitch himself out of a suffocating jam and into the hearts of an entire city.

"So there's the leading run on third base with nobody out," Cubs first baseman Phil Cavarretta told Donald Honig many years later. "But we never got him home. Billy Jurges was the next batter and he struck out. Then Larry French, the pitcher, came up. He bounced back to Bridges. Augie Galan made the third out, on a fly ball that came too late."

Relief and fresh enthusiasm greeted the Tigers as they came to bat in the bottom of the ninth.

"With all the great players they had over the years, like Cobb, Harry Heilmann and all the rest, they had never won a World Series," Cavarretta said. "Just a year before, the Cardinals had beaten them in seven games. So that pump was primed. Those fans were on the edges of their seats, waiting for it."

Cavarretta had a hand – literally – in the Tigers' history-making rally. With one out and Cochrane on first base with a hit, "Gehringer came up and, boy, did he hit a shot right at me! It was one of those instances when you see a man swing a bat and a split second later there's a line drive exploding right on top of you. … More in self-protection than anything else, I threw up my gloved hand. The ball tore right on through, and I was just about able to stop it with my bare hand. If I had knocked it down with my glove, I could have gone to second and forced Cochrane. But the ball had really stung my bare hand and I was in so much pain that I didn't want to risk a throw to second. I was afraid it might wind up in leftfield. So I took the sure way out and stepped on first. But that got Cochrane to second."

Up stepped Goose Goslin, one of the best clutch hitters in the game's history. French tried to jam him with an inside pitch, but Goslin got enough of it to send it floating over the head of the second baseman before dropping softly onto the grass in short rightcenterfield.

Cochrane, off with the crack of the bat, raced around third and scored standing up, igniting a civic celebration that everyone agreed was more spirited and sustained than any seen before. The streets remained clotted with merrymakers blowing horns, pounding drums, hoisting drinks and throwing confetti until early the following morning. Some people even fired machine guns out office windows.

"The entire town was gaga," was Charlie Gehringer's recollection one-half century later. "I tried to take a friend downtown, but golly, everything was blocked up. You couldn't cross the streets, the city was such a mess. Seemed like everybody was downtown, whoopin' and hollerin.' "

By the time the Tigers next made it into the postseason, in 1940 against Cincinnati, Navin Field had been made over into Briggs Stadium. Players calculating their World Series shares certainly appreciated the difference between the Tigers' expanded home, which averaged 54,053 paying customers for three games, and Crosley Field, which averaged 29,942 admissions in the four games it hosted.

The melodrama of the series revolved around Detroit's 21-game winner, the much-traveled Louis Norman (Bobo) Newsom. Bobo was a gruff, bear-like, beer-drinking right-hander who would make an incredible 17 different stops during a career that stretched from 1929 to 1953. In Detroit, he stayed at the same downtown hotel as Greenberg.

Despite Newsom's reputation, "Bobo

Both: Courtesy The Designated Hatter

In a span of six seasons, the Tigers played two World Series at The Corner, losing in 1940 but winning in 1945.

wasn't really a troublemaker," Greenberg said. "He just liked to brag, and he usually could back up his bragging because he was quite a pitcher."

The series was knotted at two games apiece when Newsom took the mound for the fifth game, Oct. 6 in Detroit. Newsom had pitched the Tigers to a 7-2 victory in the opener in Cincinnati, then awoke the next morning to find out that his father, who had been in the stands, had died of a heart attack. While the Series continued, Newsom went home to bury his father.

That was the prologue to Game 5, which Newsom and Greenberg turned into an 8-0 rout. Greenberg cracked a three-run homer in the first inning while Bobo, fighting back tears and vowing to "win one for Dad," allowed just three hits. The largest crowd yet to watch a baseball game in the city – 55,189 people – felt a tug on their collective heartstrings. The Tigers had been favored going into the Series, but now destiny seemed on their side. It wasn't to be, however. The Series returned to Crosley Field, where the Reds won twice – including a 2-1 victory over Bobo in the finale – capturing the championship.

Newsom was long gone by the time Briggs Stadium hosted its second World Series, but Greenberg was still the backbone of the team. Returning to The Corner after spending four prime years in the Army, Greenberg had batted .311, powering the Tigers into the 1945 Series against the Cubs. The figure led the league, though Greenberg lacked the number of at-bats to qualify for the batting title.

Because of wartime travel restrictions, the schedule called for three games in Detroit before shifting to Wrigley Field for the balance of the Series. The Cubs pounded Tigers ace Hal Newhouser, 9-0, in the opener. The next afternoon, Virgil Trucks, recently released from the Navy, twirled the 4-1 equalizer. The winning runs came off the bat of Greenberg, who hit a three-run homer in the fifth inning.

In Game 3, Cubs curveballer Claude Passeau blanked the Tigers, 3-0, before 55,500 shivering customers – the largest postseason crowd ever at The Corner.

Both: Richard Bak Collection

MUCH-TRAVELED BOBO NEWSOM LANDED WITH THE TIGERS IN 1940, WINNING 21 GAMES DURING THE REGULAR SEASON AND TWO MORE IN THE WORLD SERIES AGAINST CINCINNATI.

"He was a great pitcher, but I think he pulled a snow job on the umpires and us," Tigers second baseman Eddie Mayo said of Passeau. "He had rheumatic hands and he had to kind of twist the ball in his glove to get a grip on it. We were all so naive. He's saying it's cold, he's got arthritic fingers, but he must've had sandpaper in there because he shut us out on one hit."

With cold bats and facing the Herculean task of having to win three of the next four games on enemy turf, the Tigers were longshots. But they pulled it off, Newhouser grabbing a 9-3 decision in the seventh game, giving Detroit fans their second world's championship.

Having seen their team participate in four World Series within 12 years, Tigers fans felt confident that the postwar era would produce a few more postseason appearances. Although the Tigers came tantalizingly close

MEMORIES MICKEY LOLICH

I sort of nonchalantly unscrewed every single lightbulb in the scoreboard

I remember warming up before the fifth game of the World Series in '68. I was a very regimented person as far as what time I stepped out of the dugout and went down to the bullpen and what time I started my warm-ups, how long it took me to warm up, when I would finish, when I would walk back to the dugout.

Well, I was in the process of going through my warm-up, I was right on track, and all of a sudden some guy by the name of Jose Feliciano went into a rendition of the national anthem that took forever to sing. He was the first guy ever to interpret the national anthem rather than just sing it. He totally threw me off my routine because he started singing in the middle of my warm-up – which was not normal – and he took so long to sing, I went through a cool-down period while I was waiting for him to finish. So after he's finished, I'm almost starting all over again and that's when the umpire comes down to get me and tells me I'm supposed to be out on the mound.

I went out and pitched the first inning and gave up three runs to the Cardinals, primarily because I was not ready to pitch. I hadn't thrown any breaking balls or anything like that. I wasn't in the mode to be pitching a ballgame yet. But we came back to win, 5-3.

Tiger Stadium was my office and my home for 13 years, and some of the memories will be with me forever.

Dick Tripp / Detroit Free Press

Richard Lee / Detroit Free Press

MICKEY LOLICH SHOWS HIS GAME FACE DURING THE 1960S AND A DOUGHNUT-MAKER'S DEMEANOR AFTER HIS PLAYING DAYS.

I remember one Sunday I was shagging balls in leftfield, and in the course of batting practice, I was leaning up against the scoreboard on the leftfield fence. I sort of nonchalantly unscrewed every single lightbulb in the scoreboard.

When the game started, they turned on all the scoreboards in the ballpark and one didn't light up. I guess the electricians kind of went nuts trying to figure out why the one scoreboard didn't work. They checked the circuit breakers and everything, and when they couldn't figure out what was wrong, they called in somebody from Edison, who was working on triple-time because it was a Sunday.

So the Edison guy came to the ballpark and checked everything out. It's now about the third or fourth inning and one of the grounds crew guys remembered I had been standing out by the scoreboard. Between innings he went out there and turned one light bulb and it came on, and when he turned the second one, it came on. But they could do only so much between innings. It took a couple of innings to get all the bulbs screwed back in.

I guess it cost the club quite a bit of money, but when general manager Jim Campbell found out what had happened, he just sort of chuckled. ◆

Southpaw Mickey Lolich turned out the lights on the St. Louis Cardinals by winning three games in the '68 World Series.

Tony Spina / Detroit Free Press

on several occasions – finishing second in 1946, 1947, 1950, 1961 and 1967 – it took another 23 years before the bunting was hung at The Corner for a World Series game.

In the fall of 1968 the opponents were the St. Louis Cardinals, looking to win their second straight world's championship and third in five years. Leftfielder Lou Brock, a superb blend of speed, power and intimidation, was the catalyst of the Cards' offense. The mound staff was fronted by the equally intimidating Bob Gibson, whose fastballs had produced 13 shutouts and a record-low 1.12 ERA.

After splitting two games in St. Louis, the Tigers returned to The Corner for the middle three contests. St. Louis won the first two, 7-3 and 10-1, putting it within a game of the title. The Tigers not only lost the games but embarrassed themselves in front of their fans and a national television audience by trying to drag out the Game 4 rout, played on a rainy Sunday, in hopes of having the game canceled before it went the minimum $4^{1/2}$ innings.

Tom Venaleck / Detroit Free Press

Courtesy The Designated Hatter

In 1968, the Tigers' first pennant in 23 years had fans camping out for days in order to buy Series tickets. David Yaroch (left) woke up to find he was 2,000th in line.

The fifth game was played on a Monday afternoon, and the Cardinals quickly jumped on Mickey Lolich. But then they got a little cocky.

"We were down, 3-2, in the fifth inning and Brock was on second when Julian Javier hit the ball," leftfielder Willie Horton recalled. "I fielded it and threw it all the way to Bill Freehan on the fly. If Brock had slid, he'd have scored, but he came in standing and Freehan put the tag on him. Of all the plays, that's the one that stands out. That was the turning point for us to go on and win the World Series."

Actually, there were a couple more turning points in the pivotal fifth game. Having stemmed the Cardinals' tide, the Tigers still needed a run to tie things. In the bottom of the seventh, manager Mayo Smith let Lolich bat for himself, and the portly southpaw – a .110 career hitter – blooped a single to right. After a walk and a single loaded the bases, Al Kaline came to the plate in the

Tony Spina / Detroit Free Press

Bill Freehan blocks the plate in the pivotal play of the '68 Series, and to this day fans wonder why Lou Brock didn't slide.

With his trademark leg kick, Denny McLain delivers during the '68 World Series. The 31-game winner lost his first two starts against the Cardinals but won Game 6 in St. Louis.

Both: Tony Spina / Detroit Free Press

THE RACIAL DIVIDE OF THE '60S NARROWED, AT LEAST TEMPORARILY, IN 1968, AND DETROITERS JUST WANTED TO CELEBRATE AFTER THE TIGERS WON GAME 7 IN ST. LOUIS.

most pressurized at-bat of his career.

Kaline's very presence involved a subplot. Injured during the season, the man who had waited 16 seasons to play in a World Series returned to find the outfield positions in the capable hands of Horton, Mickey Stanley and Jim Northrup. Smith solved the dilemma of where to play the king Tiger by shifting Stanley from centerfield to shortstop. The gamble – one of the biggest in World Series history – worked. Stanley, the finest natural athlete on the club, fielded his new position nearly flawlessly while Kaline led all Detroit batters with 11 hits and eight RBIs.

Left-hander Joe Hoerner was on the mound.

"The Cardinals had been pitching me low and away all through the series," Kaline recalled, "and I figured that Hoerner would do the same thing."

Sure enough, Hoerner's third pitch was low and away. Kaline, counting on that, whacked the ball over the second baseman's head into right-centerfield. Two runs scored, giving the Tigers a 4-3 lead. Norm Cash concluded the uprising with a run-producing single, making the final 5-3.

As they had in 1945, the Tigers went on to win the Series in their opponent's backyard. In Game 6, Denny McLain – who had lost both of his starts – finally won, the Tigers smashing the Redbirds, 13-1. And then the Game 7 duel between Lolich and Gibson – each looking for his third win – was broken open by Curt Flood's infamous misplay of Northrup's line drive in the seventh inning. It went for a two-run triple, propelling the Tigers to a 4-1 victory that had everybody back in Motown behaving like Martha and the Vandellas – dancin' in the streets.

Four Octobers later, Detroiters were left singing a sadder tune. By now, baseball had split each league into two divisions, creating a postseason tournament officially called the League Championship Series. Fans called it the playoffs. The 1972 pairing was Detroit vs. Oakland. It featured the aging remnants of the '68 champions, managed by Billy Martin, against up-and-coming stars like Reggie Jackson, Catfish Hunter, Vida Blue and Joe Rudi.

Tony Spina / Detroit Free Press

Frustrated fans scaled the screen after the Tigers lost the deciding fifth game of the 1972 playoffs.

The swashbuckling, mustachioed A's took the first two games on the coast before flying to Detroit for the balance of the five-game set. Tradition-soaked Detroit fans evidently had not warmed to the idea of playoffs. There also was some residual bitterness after a players strike that had caused 86 games to be canceled at the start of the season. For these reasons, attendance for the first two games at The Corner averaged less than 40,000.

Those who did show up saw Joe Coleman set a playoff record with 14 strikeouts in a

MEMORIES ALAN TRAMMELL

The first thing that comes to mind when I think of Tiger Stadium is of winning the World Series in 1984, and the feeling of that stadium and the electricity you felt when the place was getting 35,000 or 40,000 people on a regular basis. Sometimes you'd almost think the darn place was going to fall down, the way the people stomped their feet. The stadium would shake a little bit.

I remember standing out there during batting practice – back when we had the old green seats all over – and looking up there at the upper deck, and when somebody would hit a ball up there, you could see the seats splinter, especially in rightfield, when no one was out there.

Before they started doing the renovation and putting the aluminum siding on the outside, you would come around the corner of the freeway and as you got closer, you could see the paint was all chipped off on the outside. Basically, if you didn't see the light towers, it kind of looked like an old warehouse.

When I first got here, I was just overwhelmed by the stadium, about how close the people were to the field. I had grown up in San Diego, where the stadium was new and with a big parking lot all around it. When I first saw Tiger Stadium, I wondered where all the people parked.

There are things about the stadium that the fans probably don't know, but which I'll always remember. For instance, we didn't have air conditioning in the locker room until 1982. We didn't have all the modern conveniences that the new

When I first saw Tiger Stadium, I wondered where all the people parked

stadiums do, but we managed to get by. The showers didn't work all the time; we ran out of hot water.

After a rain it would sometimes flood down in the runway between the locker room and the dugout. So, to get to the dugout, we'd have to walk through the crowd in the corridor and go out on the field where the grounds crew did, down by the bullpen.

That runway was always kind of musty. I called it "the dungeon" down there. Actually, sometimes you'd go down there if you got upset, but you couldn't do much because the walls were all concrete. You couldn't hit the walls or anything because you'd break your hand. If a guy wanted to break a bat or something, he couldn't do it. There wasn't enough room.

I know I went down there a couple of times wanting to do something, and it was kind of funny; it was so frustrating that I'd just say, "Ah, forget it." I'd go back and put my bat back in the bat rack and just say, "Well, it's not worth it."

I remember when Lou Whitaker and I were called up at the end of the 1977 season. We flew in from Montgomery, Ala., and went right to the stadium, and by the time we got downstairs the game had started. So we just put on our uniforms and walked through that runway to the dugout.

They gave me No. 42 and Lou something like 44 or 46. I didn't want to wear 42. I wasn't a 42. But I was 19 years old and very nervous, and as a kid I certainly wasn't going to say anything. I was just glad to have a uniform. But when we got to spring training the next year, Lou was No. 1 and I was No. 3, and I thought those were neat numbers.

When Tiger Stadium is gone, a piece of me will be gone, along with everybody else who played there. But I do know to compete in this day and age, you have to have a new stadium. It's not for you or me, it's for our kids and grandkids. They don't want to come see baseball like we did; they want the amenities. I think that's the way you have to look at it now. They want more than just the ballgame. ◆

Alan Trammell was a fixture at shortstop for two decades, playing more games at that position than any other Tiger in history.

Detroit Free Press

TEAMMATES FOR 19 SEASONS, LOU WHITAKER (ABOVE) AND ALAN TRAMMELL WERE BLESSED WITH A WORLD CHAMPIONSHIP IN 1984.

Mary Schroeder / Detroit Free Press

3-0 victory in Game 3 and a thrilling comeback in the 4-3, 10-inning win the following afternoon. The Tigers, who had been on the brink of elimination practically the entire series, suddenly were one victory from moving on to the World Series against Sparky Anderson's Cincinnati Reds.

More than 50,000 packed Tiger Stadium in a celebratory mood, but the A's spoiled the party with a 2-1 victory. A controversial call in the fourth inning put George Hendrick in position to score the winning run on Gene Tenace's only base hit of the series. Toward the end, frustrated bleacherites tossed smoke bombs, firecrackers, toilet paper, bottles and garbage onto the field, forcing Hendrick to wade through ankle-deep debris in centerfield to catch the final out of the game.

The Year of the Tiger had such an impact on the community that it was inevitable that every subsequent Tigers team would be measured against it. "I'm sick of hearing about the '68 Tigers," Jack Morris admitted at one point.

To Morris' credit, in 1984 he and his teammates did something about it.

The Tigers of Morris, Gibson, Parrish, Hernandez, Whitaker and Trammell not only broke the '68 team's record of 103 regular-season wins (104-58), they smoked Kansas City (3-0) and San Diego (4-1) in October to deliver the franchise's fourth World Series championship.

The Tigers already were up two games to none in the best-of-five ALCS when they left Kansas City for home. They clinched a World Series berth with a 1-0 victory over the Royals at The Corner, then four days later opened the World Series in San Diego.

The underdog Padres lost the opener, 3-2, but came back to win the second game on Kurt Bevacqua's three-run homer in the fifth. As he circled the bases, Bevacqua blew kisses to the delirious crowd. "That pushed our desire to win even higher," said Kirk Gibson, taking note in rightfield.

Third baseman Marty Castillo was the surprise hero of Game 3, smacking a two-run homer, pacing the Tigers to a 5-2 victory before the first of three straight capacity crowds. The series MVP was Alan Trammell, a San Diego native who hit .450 with a pair of two-run homers. Both of them came in Game 4, a 4-2 victory that put Detroit on the cusp of the title.

Mary Schroeder / Detroit Free Press

MARTY CASTILLO, A PART-TIMER FOR ALL FIVE OF HIS MAJOR LEAGUE SEASONS, WAS AMONG THE HEROES OF '84.

But it was Gibson, the team's emotional engine, who slapped an exclamation mark on the end of a remarkable season. Blending an old-fashioned linebacker mentality with a New Age visualization technique he had learned in the off-season, Gibson practically willed the Series to end on a gray Sunday at Tiger Stadium. "I wanted to finish off the Padres now," he said, "and not mess around with any sixth or seventh games."

Gibson was as good as his word, hitting a two-run homer in the first inning as Detroit bolted to a 3-0 lead. San Diego tied the score in the fourth, but Gibson's football instinct drove him to try to score from third base on a shallow fly to right in the fifth. Gibson slid so furiously that he shredded the knee of his uniform pants, but the surprising dash

BUBBA'S BIG NIGHT

By Roddy Ray

The day the Tigers won the '84 World Series, Kenneth Neal (Bubba) Helms was an unknown Lincoln Park 17-year-old who had left school in the eighth grade. Helms became something of a celebrity the next day, when a photo of him, holding high a Tigers pennant while standing by a burning police car outside Tiger Stadium, appeared in newspapers across the United States. He was not identified in the photo.

"I was jumping in front of every camera I could," said Helms, who with his friends had drunk "a fifth of Jim Beam, smoked a few bad ones" and gone downtown to join what became a postgame melee.

A photographer working for the Associated Press snapped the picture, and "it was used virtually across the board," said Brian Horton, photo enterprise editor at the wire service's New York headquarters. "It seemed to be the picture that was used of events happening outside the stadium."

Helms, who told the Free Press he had nothing to do with setting the police cruiser on fire, came away with souvenirs that included wiring he ripped from the burning car. He said he didn't mind revealing his identity because "I didn't do nothing. I just got my picture taken."

Helms said he watched the first seven or eight innings of the game at home and then drove with three friends to the stadium. "It was one big party," he said. "It was great."

As he and his friends approached the stadium, they noticed a parked armored truck. "Me and my friend went up there, and we jumped on top of it," he said. "We was up there screaming and dancing and stuff." The other two were "just down there looking up at me, going 'Bubba! Bubba! Get 'em!' " said Helms, who stood 6-2 and weighed 190 pounds.

Helms said he then went to one of the steel doors of the stadium to try to see the victors. "They started closing the door, and I ran up there and grabbed it," he said, motioning upward with clenched fists. "It started going back up. Then they started coming after us. ...

"I was pretty drunk, and I ran over to this wall. I wanted to climb up on top where everybody else was.

Robert Kozloff / Associated Press

From dancin' in the streets to wild in the streets: Bubba Helms became a symbol of anarchy after the Tigers won the World Series in 1984.

So I started climbing up this pole, and they come up and hit me with a club on the side of the head ... security or somebody."

Then, Helms said, he heard a "whoosh" and saw a car on fire. "I just ran right over there," he said.

Helms said one of his friends, who had been picking up returnable cans and bottles, tried to dissuade him. "I gotta get my picture taken!" Helms said he told the friend.

Helms said about nine photographers were taking pictures of the burning car, and he "just jumped right in front of them and stood as still as I could." One of the photographers told him to get out of the way, but Helms only made an obscene gesture and yelled an obscenity. Other than that, Helms said, he did not talk with the photographers.

"I was too drunk," he said. "I was just having a good time. It was the best time in my whole life. Serious." ◆

Roddy Ray was a Free Press reporter.

returned the lead to Detroit, 4-3.

The score was 5-4, Detroit's favor, when Gibson batted in the eighth. There were runners on second and third and one out. The situation called for an intentional walk, but Goose Gossage talked manager Dick Williams out of it. The fireballing reliever had owned Gibson since striking him out in his first big-league at-bat nine years earlier.

This time, however, Gibson yelled over to Anderson, who had become the Tigers' manager in 1979: "Ten bucks says they pitch to me and I crank it!"

It unfolded exactly as Gibson had visualized. He sent Gossage's second fastball deep into the upper deck in rightfield.

"I can remember the thunder of the crowd as the ball disappeared into the sea of screaming fans," Gibson would later write in his book, "Bottom of the Ninth." "I remember the feeling of triumph, of having rid myself of all the past ugliness, as I trotted around the bases on the sweetest victory lap imaginable. The game was over. The World Series was ours. They knew it. We knew it. Everyone knew it.

"I almost killed some of the guys with high fives as I crossed home plate. I couldn't contain myself as I turned toward the dugout, feeling the emotions from the crowd and, really, from an entire baseball city. I took a giant-sized, celebratory leap that was captured by Detroit Free Press photographer Mary Schroeder. It captured in that instant all of the excitement, the intensity, the desire and the commitment to be a World Champion."

Gibson rose to the occasion in the Tigers' memorable drive to their next postseason appearance, the 1987 ALCS against Minnesota. An extra-inning home run saved the Tigers from getting swept in Toronto and started a late September turnaround in which they overtook the Blue Jays for the Eastern Division flag on the final weekend. The Tigers went into Minnesota boasting the majors' top record (98-64) and best offense. They left humbled by a team sporting one of the worst records of any postseason team ever (85-77).

Gibson said: "We had beaten Minnesota something like 11 or 12 out of 13 times during the regular season, and they came in and kicked our butts in the championship series. We spent everything we had in the Toronto series and didn't realize it."

Pat Sheridan only postponed the outcome. With Detroit down, two games to none, and losing in the eighth inning of the third game, 6-5, the bespectacled, blade-like outfielder yanked a two-run homer, producing a 7-6 win, the Tigers' only victory of the series.

A 5-3 loss the next day featured a baserunning gaffe by the usually heads-up Darrell

The '84 Tigers clinched the pennant, the playoffs and the World Series at The Corner, each time turning neighborhood streets into parking lots. In the wake of the World Series win, Lance Parrish toasted Detroit's delirious fans, who poured through the turnstiles in record numbers that year.

Detroit Free Press

Mary Schroeder / Detroit Free Press

Courtesy Joe Crachiola

KEEPING SCORE ◆ POST PARADE

The Tigers have played 35 postseason games at The Corner, including 28 World Series games. Their home record in the postseason is 16-19.

1907 World Series

GAME	DATE	ATTENDANCE	OUTCOME
Game 4	Oct. 11	11,306	Cubs 6, Tigers 1
Game 5	Oct. 12	7,370	Cubs 2, Tigers 0

1908 World Series

GAME	DATE	ATTENDANCE	OUTCOME
Game 1	Oct. 10	10,812	Cubs 10, Tigers 6
Game 4	Oct. 13	12,907	Cubs 3, Tigers 0
Game 5	Oct. 14	6,210	Cubs 2, Tigers 0

1909 World Series

GAME	DATE	ATTENDANCE	OUTCOME
Game 3	Oct. 11	18,277	Pirates 8, Tigers 6
Game 4	Oct. 12	17,036	Tigers 5, Pirates 0
Game 6	Oct. 14	10,535	Tigers 5, Pirates 4
Game 7	Oct. 16	17,562	Pirates 8, Tigers 0

Tom Venaleck / Detroit Free Press

WHAT COULD BE BETTER THAN HOLDING A HANDFUL OF WORLD SERIES TICKETS IN 1968?

1934 World Series

GAME	DATE	ATTENDANCE	OUTCOME
Game 1	Oct. 3	42,505	Cardinals 8, Tigers 3
Game 2	Oct. 4	43,451	Tigers 3, Cardinals 2 (12)
Game 6	Oct. 8	44,551	Cardinals 4, Tigers 3
Game 7	Oct. 9	40,902	Cardinals 11, Tigers 0

1935 World Series

GAME	DATE	ATTENDANCE	OUTCOME
Game 1	Oct. 2	47,391	Cubs 3, Tigers 0
Game 2	Oct. 3	46,742	Tigers 8, Cubs 3
Game 6	Oct. 7	48,420	Tigers 4, Cubs 3

1940 World Series

GAME	DATE	ATTENDANCE	OUTCOME
Game 3	Oct. 4	52,877	Tigers 7, Reds 4
Game 4	Oct. 5	54,093	Reds 5, Tigers 2
Game 5	Oct. 6	55,189	Tigers 8, Reds 0

1945 World Series

GAME	DATE	ATTENDANCE	OUTCOME
Game 1	Oct. 3	54,637	Cubs 9, Tigers 0
Game 2	Oct. 4	53,636	Tigers 4, Cubs 1
Game 3	Oct. 5	55,500	Cubs 3, Tigers 0

1968 World Series

GAME	DATE	ATTENDANCE	OUTCOME
Game 3	Oct. 5	53,634	Cardinals 7, Tigers 3
Game 4	Oct. 6	53,634	Cardinals 10, Tigers 1
Game 5	Oct. 7	53,634	Tigers 5, Cardinals 3

1972 American League Championship Series

GAME	DATE	ATTENDANCE	OUTCOME
Game 3	Oct. 10	41,156	Tigers 3, A's 0
Game 4	Oct. 11	37,615	Tigers 4, A's 3 (10)
Game 5	Oct. 12	50,276	A's 2, Tigers 1

1984 American League Championship Series

GAME	DATE	ATTENDANCE	OUTCOME
Game 3	Oct. 5	52,168	Tigers 1, Royals 0

1984 World Series

GAME	DATE	ATTENDANCE	OUTCOME
Game 3	Oct. 12	51,970	Tigers 5, Padres 2
Game 4	Oct. 13	52,130	Tigers 4, Padres 2
Game 5	Oct. 14	51,901	Tigers 8, Padres 4

1987 American League Championship Series

GAME	DATE	ATTENDANCE	OUTCOME
Game 3	Oct. 10	49,730	Tigers 7, Twins 6
Game 4	Oct. 11	51,939	Twins 5, Tigers 3
Game 5	Oct. 12	47,448	Twins 9, Tigers 5

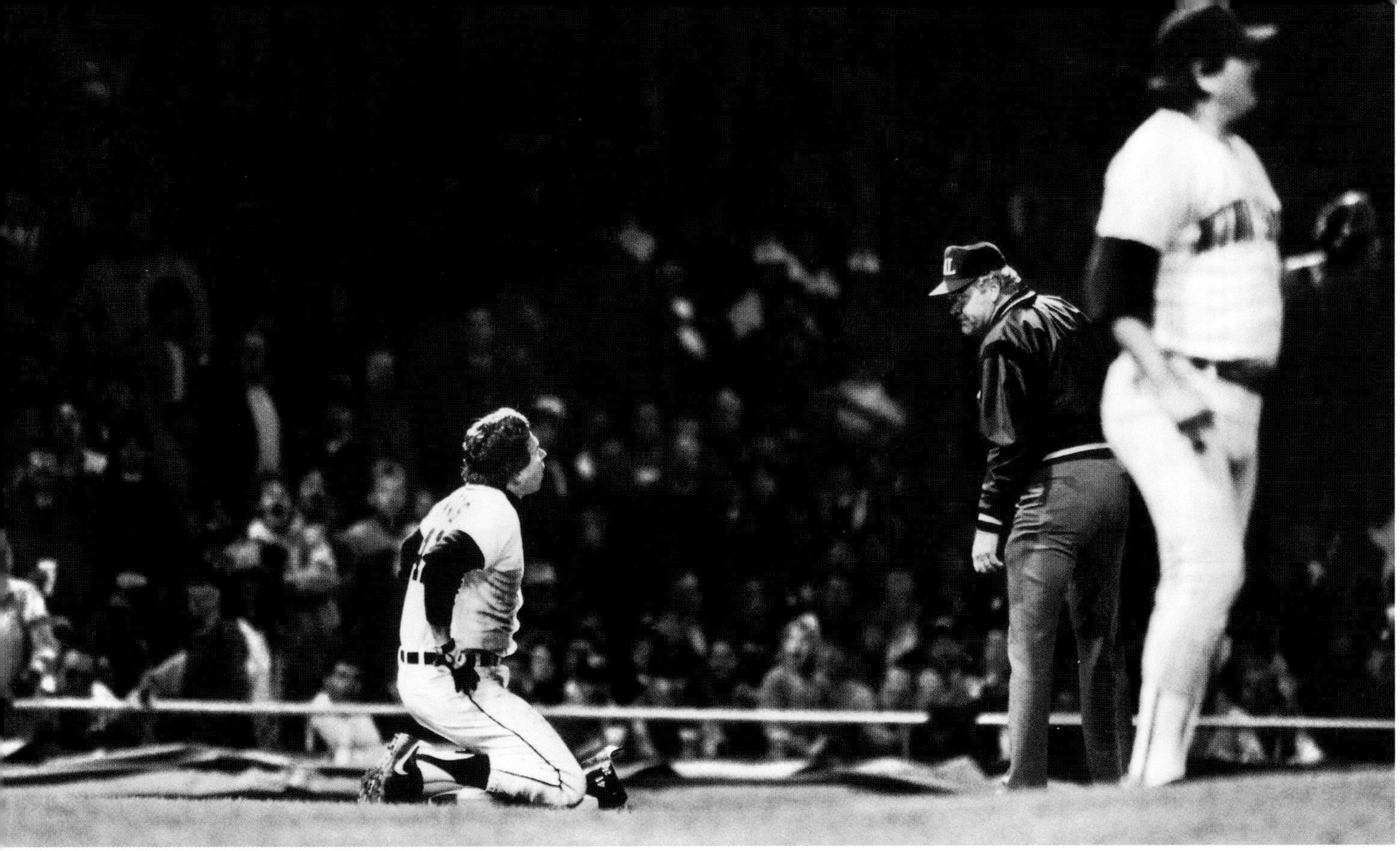

Daymon J. Harley / Detroit Free Press

Courtesy Joe Crachiola

Santa was no help to the '87 Tigers, who lost to the Twins in the playoffs.

Evans. Representing the tying run late in the game, the old pro was unaccountably picked off third base. All he could do was kneel in the dirt, weakly arguing his case with the umpire, before returning in embarrassment to the dugout.

There's no denying that, in Octobers past, Detroit fans have been boorish and sometimes downright violent in their reaction to losing. But the last postseason game played at The Corner, a 9-5 loss that closed the '87 playoffs, had a moment that demonstrated the class and affection that knowledgeable fans are capable of expressing.

As Evans walked to the plate for his first at-bat, he expected to hear from the fans about his boneheaded play on the previous day. He did, but not in the way he expected.

"That was a fantastic thing," said Ernie Harwell, who from his perch in the broadcast booth heard the thousands of scattered hand claps quickly jell into a single sustained ovation.

"The nice thing about it was that it was not contrived. It was not staged. It was spontaneous, and that's what I really love. I hate these scoreboards that say, 'More noise, more noise!' It was just a display by the fans of their devotion to Evans." ◆

Detroit Tigers

Darrell Evans, a Tiger for only five seasons, remained a fan favorite even after he was picked off third base, a turning point in the 1987 playoffs.

Teammates for 19 seasons, Alan Trammell and Lou Whitaker share a final moment at The Corner as Tram acknowledges the cheers during the home finale of 1995, Lou's last season.

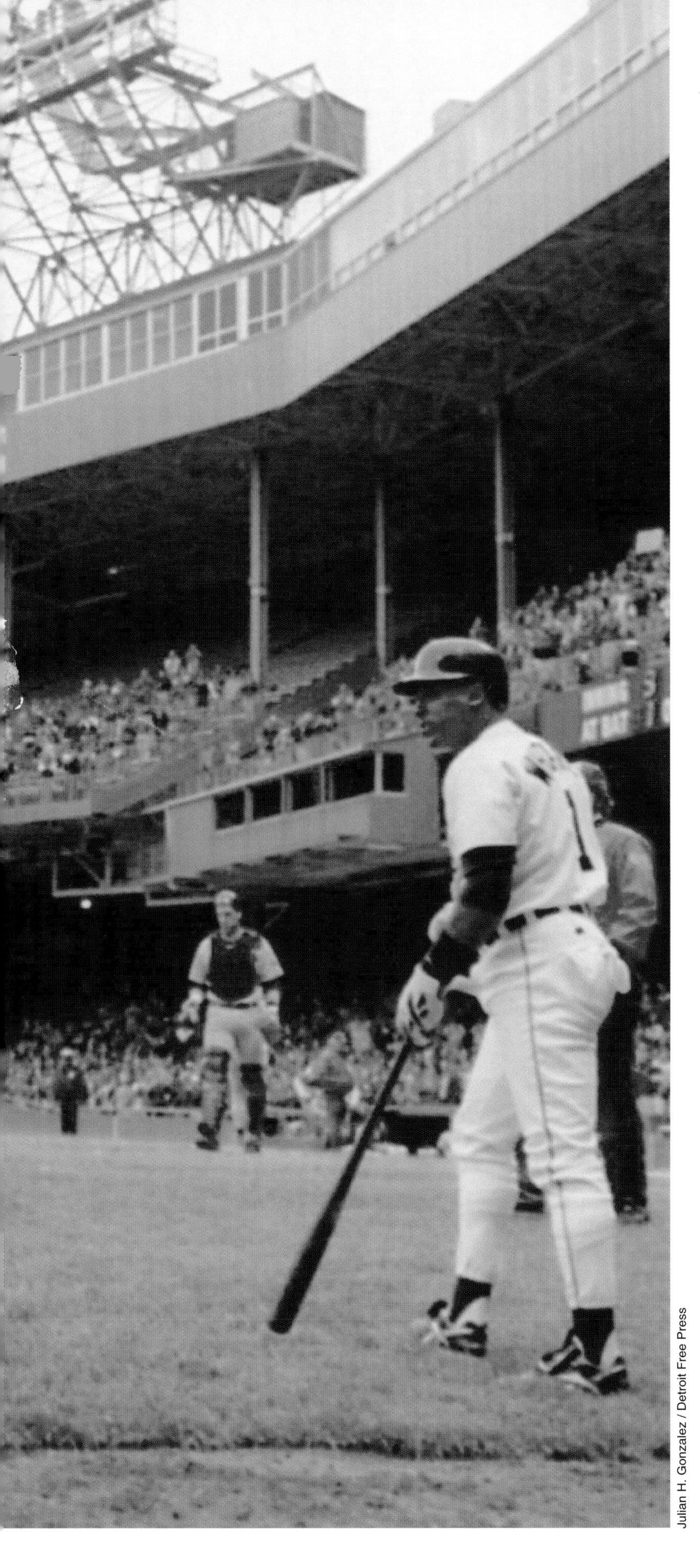

Julian H. Gonzalez / Detroit Free Press

CHAPTER 10

The green, green grass of home

For Frank Rashid, the best thing about the ballpark today is its yesterdays.

"The story of a person's first visit to Tiger Stadium is like an urban myth in Detroit," said the Marygrove College professor, a founding member of the Tiger Stadium Fan Club.

"It's not just my story, it's everybody's story who went from my generation. Because back then there were no color photos in the newspapers, and only the very fortunate had a color TV. The ballgames were broadcast in black and white anyway. So seeing the game in color was what really took your breath away.

"As you'd walk through the long catwalks and finally out into the stadium itself, what shocked you was the hugeness of the place, the greenness of the

Tony Spina / Detroit Free Press

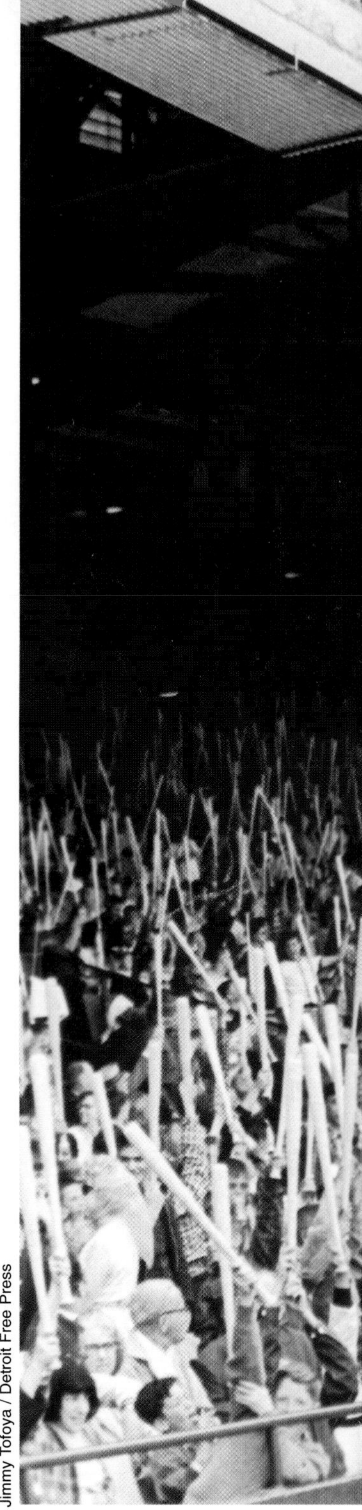

Jimmy Tofoya / Detroit Free Press

field. It was something I was just not prepared for."

As with most things in life, that original feeling of wonderment became diluted with age, but the sense of community that a few hours at The Corner offered remained strong. Here, at least, people could set aside their differences and lose themselves in a children's game played with fury and finesse by grown men. That their parents and uncles and great-grandparents did the exact same thing on the exact same site back in 1956, 1934 or 1912 made the experience that much more special.

At its best The Corner has served as a place where fans and players feed off each other's passion, their synergy lifting the game to a higher plane of communal meaning. This mystical connection between the city and its ball team was at its greatest in 1968, when the never-say-die Tigers did their part in mending a torn community desperately looking for something to believe in, if only temporarily.

The '68 Tigers were a truly cosmopolitan team. For the first time, a Detroit pennant winner fielded several black stars, including slugging leftfielder Willie Horton, pitcher Earl Wilson and pinch-hitter extraordinaire William (Gates) Brown.

"I knew that what we were doing was special," Brown told the Free Press in 1998, when the team credited with saving a city reassembled for a 30th-anniversary reunion at The Corner. "But I never realized how special it was until I went into the neighborhoods and heard people talking Tigers nonstop. None of the other stuff mattered, at least for the time being."

The "other stuff" in 1968 included the assassinations of Martin Luther King Jr. and Robert Kennedy, a fresh round of urban riots,

and continuing dissent over Vietnam. At times it seemed as if the world outside Tiger Stadium was unraveling.

The Tigers' therapeutic heroics came on the heels of a turbulent summer that saw Detroit ripped apart by a riot that claimed 43 lives and left chunks of the inner city in smoldering ruins. Violence also had visited The Corner in 1967 as bitterly disappointed fans tore up the park after the Tigers lost the pennant on the last day of the season.

"I don't want to use the word 'hatred,'" Brown said, "but everywhere I went in the summer of '67, people were just against everything connected with the city – anti-black, anti-white, anti-police, anti-Tigers. And in the following summer, we were able to give people a positive diversion."

It was 1968, an unforgettable, rollicking summer of champions, great and small, black and white. The country followed the exploits of Denny McLain, whose high, hard fastball

Fans went batty on Bat Day 1965, and a young fan displays pennant fever in 1967.

As Bill Freehan's thumbs-up and Denny McLain's postgame preening demonstrated, confidence never was lacking during the "sockit to 'em" season of 1968.

Both: Courtesy Bill Dow

Sockit to 'em Tigers

© D.L. Bonnell April 1968

"McLain throws a fastball that Powell hits like a bullet right back at him. He catches it, throws directly to second, then the throw goes to first. Triple play. And the fans are going crazy."
Bill Freehan

was threatening to make him the first pitcher since Dizzy Dean in 1934 to win 30 games.

The 24-year-old right-hander certainly had Dean's blend of talent, cockiness and showmanship. He guzzled Pepsi by the case, played his Hammond X-77 organ in clubs, and breezily bantered with the hosts of prime-time television shows.

Unfortunately, McLain lacked the common sense God gave ol' Diz's mule. He would be named MVP and win the first of two straight Cy Young Awards in 1968, but down the road were a string of problems involving gambling and juvenile behavior that earned him one-half year's suspension in 1970 and a ticket out of town at the end of the season. His post-baseball career was characterized by lawsuits, bankruptcies, shady dealings and criminal charges. As the final season at The Corner opened, McLain was serving yet another stint in prison, this time for draining an established family firm of its pension fund, forcing the company to close.

For one summer, though, McLain was the premier pitcher in baseball. Bill Freehan remembered a game McLain pitched against Baltimore late in the year, when the Orioles were "pressing us just a bit." While Tigers fans fidgeted in their seats, manager Mayo Smith gave the catcher the sign to go out to the mound to buy some time while help warmed up in the bullpen.

"Boog Powell was coming to the plate with guys on first and second," Freehan said. "I start walking out there slowly and McLain walks halfway in to me and says, 'What the hell are you going to tell me that I don't already know?'

"I told him, 'There's a guy up in the bullpen and I've got a feeling if you don't get this guy out, you're out of here.' He said, 'You get back behind the plate, I'll think of something.'

"So I get back there and put a signal down and McLain throws a fastball that Powell hits like a bullet right back at him. He catches it, throws directly to second, then the throw goes to first. Triple play. And the fans are going crazy.

"He walks off with this big grin on his face and says to me, 'See, I told you I'd think of something.' "

McLain went after his 30th victory on Sept. 14 at Tiger Stadium. Down by a run to Oakland in the bottom of the ninth, the Tigers scored twice, giving McLain his milestone win. It was one of 30 games they won in their last at-bats that season.

Three nights later, the Tigers clinched their first pennant in 23 years at The Corner. This prompted a citywide celebration that had 13-year-old fan Bill Dow and his buddies pouring cans of Coke over their heads in emulation of their champagne-guzzling heroes.

The celebrating got sillier and stickier when the Tigers went on to defeat St. Louis in one of the classic World Series comebacks. Down three games to one, the Tigers roared back to win behind timely hitting by Al Kaline, Norm Cash and Jim Northrup, and

John Collier / Detroit Free Press

MEMORIES AL KALINE

I'd never seen anything like it, being just out of high school

I became a Tiger in June 1953, when I was 18. I joined the team in Philadelphia and then we went to St. Louis, then came back to Detroit. At that time we landed at Willow Run Airport and took a bus back to Detroit. That was before the expressways were finished. We came down Michigan Avenue. I was sitting next to Johnny Pesky and he said, "Now I'm going to show you what Briggs Stadium looks like."

It was about 1 or 2 o'clock in the morning and he said, "It's going to look like a big ol' battleship." And sure enough, I looked out there through the darkness and it looked like a big ol' battleship.

Pesky said, "We call it 'The Old Lady.' "

The next day was the first time I went into the stadium. I was staying downtown at the Wolverine Hotel and I walked to the park with a guy named Johnny Bucha, a catcher. I walked out on the field right away, before I went into the locker room, and it was all green. It was unbelievable how beautiful it was. All the seats were green. It was magnificent. I'd never seen anything like it, being just out of high school.

Of course, since I was a kid they put me in the last locker all the way in the back. They had very few young guys at that time. Everybody spent a lot of time in the minor leagues before they got a chance at the majors, so I wasn't greeted too well. We had a lot of guys who were 26 or 27 years old, and that seemed pretty old to me at the time.

When I first joined the club, we only had 12 or 14 night games a year. It was amazing; every time – it didn't matter whether it was the Washington Senators or the New York Yankees – we had a full house. We had 50,000 people.

Maybe my biggest memory there was of hitting three home runs in one game, two in the same inning, one Sunday afternoon against the A's in 1955.

And I remember Reggie Jackson hitting a home run in the '71 All-Star Game. You had to know the situation in that game. He had two strikes on him, and to be that aggressive with two strikes is just phenomenal. Usually you back off a little bit so you don't strike out. Boy, when he hit that ball and it went all the way out there to the transformer, I didn't believe it. He hit it off Dock Ellis.

Of course, there are a lot of memories, too, after I quit playing and began broadcasting.

I had a difficult time at first, no question about it, because a lot of the guys on the team were still my friends. There were three guys in the booth, and I didn't know when to talk. The "professional" announcer would say something about the game and even though I thought it was wrong, I didn't correct it and sort of let it ride. But I finally decided I couldn't do that, that I had to correct it and say exactly what I thought was going on.

When the team moves, it's going to be very sad for me personally because Tiger Stadium's the only place I've ever worked – every summer of my life since I've been out of high school. ◆

Hall of Famer Al Kaline played 22 seasons at The Corner before settling into the broadcast booth.

Jimmy Tafoya / Detroit Free Press

AL KALINE'S HALL OF FAME JOURNEY BEGAN IN 1953 AND CULMINATED 21 YEARS LATER AT THE CORNER WITH A BARROWFUL OF SILVER DOLLARS, COMMEMORATING THE FIRST 3,000 OF HIS 3,007 CAREER HITS.

Courtesy The Designated Hatter

MEMORIES BILL DOW

What a thrill seeing No. 6 for the first time

My interest in baseball began in 1961, when I was 6 years old and listening to Ernie Harwell and George Kell on WKMH between Wiffle ball games with the neighborhood gang in Dearborn. The following season, Al Kaline became my hero after I watched him save a game with an amazing catch against the Yankees on television. That was the famous catch where he broke his collarbone, probably costing the Tigers a pennant. With my Kaline crew cut, I'd imitate his tumbling grab for anyone who'd watch.

My father died when I was 3, so I was always hoping that a friend's dad would take me to a game. One July day in 1962, my neighborhood pal, Craig Smith, asked if I'd like to go to a Tigers-Orioles game with him and his dad. Would I? I ran around the house screaming with joy.

Associated Press

Courtesy Dow family

IN 1962, BILL DOW HAD A CREW CUT LIKE HIS HERO, AL KALINE, WHO BROKE HIS COLLARBONE MAKING THIS CATCH AGAINST THE YANKEES.

To this day, I can recall crossing red-bricked Michigan Avenue holding Mr. Smith's hand and looking up at the giant light towers and team flags waving high atop the stadium. Entering the park released the most intense sensory magic I had experienced in my young life.

I remember walking up the runway and hearing the vendor yelling, "Scorecards, lineups, get your scorecards!" as I inhaled that wonderful aroma of hot dogs, popcorn, peanuts and cigar smoke. As we walked to our reserved seats between home and first base, I caught my first glimpse of the vivid green grass, dotted with the snow-white uniforms worn by the Tigers, who were completing fielding practice.

Even though Kaline was still sidelined with his broken collarbone, he was in uniform. What a thrill seeing No. 6 for the first time! He was standing on the dugout steps, his back to me, looking into the stands. I wondered if he knew that his biggest fan was coming to the game.

Many years later, I went to the library and copied the Free Press' account of my first game. It stirred so many memories of that glorious day. A member of the marching band fainting from the heat. Norm Cash's two home runs, including one into the bleachers. Jake Wood taking a lead off first base while the crowd chanted, "Go, go, go!" Today, my scorebook from that first game and my first souvenir, a bobbing-Tiger-head figurine, sit on a shelf over my 7-year-old son's bed.

To me, Tiger Stadium has always been a second home. Sitting in the stands, I often look out at various seats where I witnessed so many memorable moments. I watched Kirk Gibson's second homer in Game 5 of the '84 World Series sail over my head and out of sight. I gave Darrell Evans a standing ovation at the '87 playoffs less than 24 hours after he was picked off third base at a crucial moment. I saw Mark McGwire clear the leftfield roof a second after saying I would like to see him hit one out.

I also ponder that all of my memories cover only 36 years in the life of this century-old playing site. Just think about all those fans who could tell their friends that they had seen Ty Cobb steal home the afternoon Navin Field opened in 1912. Or those who saw Ted Williams' ninth-inning homer in the '41 All-Star Game. The sheer number of games and personalities associated with The Corner boggles my mind.

Although stadium hugs, lawsuits and lobbying ultimately failed to save Tiger Stadium, I'll always celebrate the joy of this great ballpark in my heart. ◆

Bill Dow, a Birmingham attorney, was a member of the Tiger Stadium Fan Club.

MEMORIES GEORGE PUSCAS

Courtesy Bill Dow

A RECORD PERFORMANCE: IN 1963, ANY FAN WITH A TURNTABLE COULD HEAR AL KALINE'S LIFE STORY.

Kaline … threw with a fury that lifted him off his feet

Among keen baseball observers, there is no player of his time rated higher in all-around fielding brilliance than Al Kaline. Not Mickey Mantle or Willie Mays, who were mighty fine indeed, not Tony Oliva or Jackie Jensen, who were recognized as fly-chasing thoroughbreds.

You get little argument when you say Kaline and Joe DiMaggio, for all-around fielding brilliance, rate among the dozen or so best outfielders in the history of the game.

We are talking some hallowed names, you know: Sam Crawford, Tris Speaker, Johnny Mostil, Harry Hooper. Do not tell me about Mays' catch in the 1954 World Series or Joe Rudi's miracle grab in '72.

Ask me the greatest play I ever saw an outfielder make and I will spot you all the catches you ever saw, and they can't beat one throw Kaline made.

It is a day when Mantle bombs one off the roof and out of Tiger Stadium and the crowd is still talking about it two innings later, when the Yankees put a runner on third with one out.

A fly goes deep into the corner, along the foul line in rightfield, and it is high and deep enough so that everyone can anticipate the run will score after the catch – but that Kaline will try to prevent it anyway.

With the baseball professionals, it is almost unanimous that nobody ever got into better position on a ball, in stride, in rhythm, in position to throw the instant the ball is secure, than Kaline. It was never truer than here.

He came flying over toward the foul-line barrier, then slackened his stride, timing his approach, preserving the momentum because he would have to pivot and throw instantly.

I remember glancing at the Yankee on third, and he is literally in a crouch, like a trackman at the starting blocks, and he is watching Kaline, realizing it will be no trot home, even though Kaline is almost against the rightfield wall.

Kaline made the catch in full circling stride toward the plate and threw with a fury that lifted him off his feet.

I have never seen a throw like that one. I can see it now. I see it every time people want to talk about the great plays they have seen in sports.

That ball is never more than eight feet off the ground during its flight, and Norm Cash looks it in the eye as it streaks past first base, whirring, whistling in the bright sun, and it pops right there into the catcher's mitt, right at his shoetops.

There is a mighty collision at the plate and the dust flies, and the umpire throws his fist into the air, and nobody can believe what they have seen.

It is a mighty close play indeed, and all the Yankees leap out of the dugout, but they do not scream at the umpire. They stand there in front of the dugout looking to rightfield, because they saw the throw, too, purring as it rocketed past their eyes, and they know only a howitzer could have propelled a ball 300 feet and more like that.

A few of them wave to Kaline. Some shake their heads in disbelief, but they will not debate the call at the plate. ◆

George Puscas is a retired sports columnist; his memory of Kaline first appeared in the Free Press in 1974.

MEMORIES **EARL WILSON**

The fans … could see your face, and you could hear 'em

I came up to the big leagues with Boston, but my first major league start was in Tiger Stadium. After that I always said that if I was ever traded, I wanted it to be to Detroit.

Back home in Louisiana, I had never seen black people who owned things. When I came to Detroit, I saw people own businesses; they had big homes; just a lot of things I wasn't accustomed to. I just fell in love with the Tigers and knew this was the place I wanted to be.

Tiger Stadium was a wonderful place to play and a wonderful place to watch a game. I remember when we won the pennant in '68, all the people running on the field, the joy and the happiness.

Personal memories? Oh, winning my 20th game there (in 1967) was big. And I remember one game against Baltimore, it was around the 12th or 13th inning, and they put me in to pinch-hit, and I hit a home run that won the game.

Just the whole atmosphere around the park was special. I came into a winning situation, as opposed to when I was in Boston, where it was just playing the game and getting out. But, oh, I remember too, that old stadium could be cold even in July.

The thing about Tiger Stadium was the fans. Even when you go to places like New York, which is supposed to have the biggest fan base, you don't get any better fans than Detroit's. I haven't played in almost 30 years, and people around town still recognize me. That's amazing to me.

In Tiger Stadium, the fans were close enough to get involved. They could see your face, and you could hear 'em. The worst thing you could do back then was pitch the second game of a doubleheader in July and give the fans a chance to drink that beer and you're not doing very well.

That's when you could really hear 'em. ◆

Earl Wilson – the last of an American League breed, a pitcher who could hit – retired in 1970.

Mike McClure / Detroit Free Press

Craig Porter / Detroit Free Press

Earl Wilson, all business on the mound, later shared laughs at The Corner with former teammates (from left) Pat Dobson, Willie Horton and John Hiller during a 10-year reunion honoring the '68 champs.

the mound magic of Mickey Lolich. The portly southpaw had won 17 games pitching in McLain's shadow. But while McLain faltered, losing two of three decisions, Lolich spun three complete-game gems, including the seventh-game showdown with the seemingly invincible Bob Gibson.

The clincher came in St. Louis, which gave 50,000 fans enough time to gather at Metropolitan Airport in anticipation of greeting their returning heroes. A million more took to the streets around the city, a communal embrace that crossed racial and economic lines.

"You could say that team provided a much-needed pressure valve for the city," Earl Wilson said. "Let's be realistic. A baseball team isn't going to cure the racial ills affecting a community. But we made everyone temporarily forget our differences and provided a little pride and a little hope."

The nucleus of the championship team was still around in 1972, when the Tigers edged Boston by one-half game for a half-pennant. Although he wasn't on the roster, McLain should have gotten a share of the postseason dough. General manager Jim Campbell had traded the troublesome pitcher and three other players to Washington before the 1971 season for pitchers Joe Coleman and Jim Hannan, shortstop Eddie Brinkman and third baseman Aurelio Rodriguez. Coleman, Brinkman and Rodriguez were instrumental in pushing the Tigers over the top in '72.

It had only been four years since the Year of the Tiger, but already minor corruptions had made their way into the modern game. The leagues had split into two divisions each, so the Tigers' Eastern Division crown only earned them the right to play (and lose) a playoff with Oakland, the Western Division champs. And a players strike – the first of many to plague the game in coming years – produced a shortened season. Around the bend were designated hitters and free agency. The baseball world would never be the same, though the Tigers' conservative front office continued to spit into the winds of change until John Fetzer sold the club to Tom Monaghan after the 1983 season.

Richard Bak Collection

Demonstrative manager Billy Martin fired up the Tigers, leading them to a 91-win season in 1971 and a first-place East finish in 1972.

All of this served to make the legacy of the '68 Tigers that much greater. Many members of the club stayed in the Detroit area after their playing days were over – something that was not the case with the Tigers' other championship teams.

"We, as a team, embodied what this city was all about," said Lolich, who opened a doughnut shop.

"We were a blue-collar, working-class team who loved being a part of this city. We were family then, and we're still very close. A lot of us still live in the area. There's a connection with the community with this team that's not there with the '84 championship team. There's a bond there that's impossible to break."

Detroit went through much of the 1970s and '80s with a "Kick Me" sign taped to its back. The national media were happy to oblige, often describing the city in Third World terms. Not that it was all undeserved. Oakland pitcher Paul Lindblad, who liked to spend afternoons before games at The Corner poking around with a metal detector, once found five spent bullets in the outfield grass. But the social and economic ills were hardly unique to Detroit. Lindblad's discomforting discovery aside, temporary relief from everyday problems could still be found with-

Bob Scott / Detroit Free Press

Generation gap: Club ownership passed from John Fetzer to Tom Monaghan in 1983.

Detroit Free Press

MEMORIES NADINE SCODELLARO

Courtesy Nadine Scodellaro

NADINE SCODELLARO AND DARYL, THE GUY SHE MARRIED "THE JUNE AFTER WE WON THE WORLD SERIES."

You stuck by your team through thick and thin

I went to my first Tigers game in 1966, when I was 14. I lived in Southfield, which in those days was still pretty much the country. I went with a couple of girlfriends on the bus from Northland. We were given a transfer ticket when we got on the bus but had no clue what it was for. When the bus stopped at the shopping area – I remember a Marianne's and a Winkleman's – we just walked the rest of the way to the park.

After that we'd go down on Saturdays for Ladies Day, when general admission seats were 50 cents. That's when the ballpark had those green wood seats that made such a wonderful racket when everyone banged them up and down.

That first year we made the bullpen our special cause and once brought a cake that was decorated to read, "To the Unsung Heroes." We got to the park early and gave it to an usher who swore he'd give it to the guys in the bullpen. We were so thrilled!

After the games we always waited around by the entrance where the players drove out, and we'd cheer them as they left. Then we'd walk back to where the stores were to pick up the bus home. I still have most of the scorebooks and ticket stubs from those games.

I remember sending Dick McAuliffe a get-well card when he had back surgery. And I remember how amazed I was when I took my first typing class and realized Don Wert's last name was spelled out on the keyboard.

Goofy, maybe, but you have to understand that these guys were our team. They were our heroes. We lived and died with each game. And each game counted even when we were stuck in fifth place and knew the best we could do was maybe move up to fourth. You stuck by your team through thick and thin. I guess that's what made the good years so very good, because they sure didn't come easy.

It's amazing how much baseball meant back when there were 10 teams in each league and only one team was going to end up on top. The devotion lasted all season long. Wherever we'd go we'd hear Ernie Harwell's voice on the radio. It was just a natural part of summer, like opening up the windows.

When the Tigers won it all in 1968, it was just the most glorious time. God bless Mickey Lolich! We took it all so personally. I still have the reply the Tigers sent me saying that World Series tickets were not available yet – I had sent the letter in July!

I remember feeling bad that Hank Aguirre wasn't a Tiger that year – he'd been traded after the '67 season – because I always liked him and thought he was a good pitcher (but a terrible batter).

Nineteen-eighty-four was such an incredible year, from that first long winning streak right down to Kirk Gibson's two homers in the fifth game of the World Series. I can't tell you how proud we were – and still are.

That's the thing. You don't forget your guys, your team. I'll always recall the year I got married, 1985, as "the June after we won the World Series."

Now the ballpark is the only link that's left. All those wonderful memories. I wonder what it'll be like at the new park, but no matter how fancy the food is or how many amenities it has, it won't be Tiger Stadium. ◆

Nadine Scodellaro is a magazine editor living in Royal Oak.

in the aging walls of Tiger Stadium.

At no time was this more true than in 1976, that storybook summer when a skinny, fidgety, frizzy-haired pitcher named Mark (The Bird) Fidrych took The Corner – and the rest of America – by storm.

Fidrych, less than two years out of high school, had unexpectedly made the trip north from spring training. After a couple of relief appearances, he got his first start on a drizzly Saturday afternoon against Cleveland. He tossed a two-hitter for his first big-league win, a performance that impressed manager Ralph Houk as much as it charmed the soggy spectators at Tiger Stadium.

Fidrych pitched good, fast and goofy. The only time he wasted between deliveries was spent manicuring the mound, patting and smoothing the dirt until it felt just right. Otherwise, it was pitch, get the ball back from the catcher, get the sign, pitch again.

At 21, he retained the natural exuberance of a child. He flailed his pencil-like arms and stomped around like the ungainly giant fowl he was named after, Sesame Street's Big Bird. He applauded his fielders for even the simplest play and raced to and from the mound. He talked to the ball, trying to coax it into cooperating: "Get down, ball. Get down. Stay low, ball. Stay low."

The antics obscured his skills. In a tight game, the Bird was, well, unflappable.

"He could throw the ball in an area this small (showing how small with his hands), one pitch after the other," Houk remembered. "The ball would just naturally sink, and he would put it right in there, over and over again."

Fidrych's defining moment came in a nationally televised Monday night game against New York on June 28. Bird mowed down the first-place Yankees, 5-1, running his record to 8-1. Afterward, as Tiger Stadium quaked with chants of "We Want Bird!" he was interviewed by sportscaster Bob Uecker.

"Where's Curt Gowdy?" he asked, referring to NBC's longtime announcer.

"This is ABC," Uecker said.

"Well, where's Curt Gowdy?"

"I'm sorry," Uecker said. "He's not here."

"He does 'Monday Night Baseball,' " Fidrych insisted.

"You got the wrong network, Bird."

That game turned a local sensation into a national phenomenon. Fidrych began appearing on magazine covers and was the second rookie pitcher chosen to start the All-Star Game. The media portrayed him as a refreshing change from the game's emerging

Both: Alan R. Kamuda / Detroit Free Press

Tiger Stadium was never so well-groomed as when Mark Fidrych was pitching. The Bird won only 29 games in Detroit, but few players are more fondly remembered.

DAY OF THE DEAD MILKMEN

BY MITCH ALBOM

Let's go back to 1987 for a day in the life of the Tigers' latest hero: Jim Walewander.

Uh, that's W-a-l-e-w-a-n-d-e-r.

Right. OK. He is a rookie. He has played in 23 big-league games. Here is how he learned he was starting Sunday: Lou Whitaker, the Tigers' second baseman, came in at noon and said he couldn't play. Bad back. The game was nine minutes away. A call went out from Sparky Anderson's office, a call to arms, a call to destiny.

"GET ME WALEWANDER!"

This had already been a special day for Jim Walewander. Earlier in the morning, he had met his favorite punk rock group. Perhaps you've heard of it. The Dead Milkmen? Yeah. Well. Maybe not. Anyhow, on Saturday night, the Dead Milkmen played a gig in Hamtramck, if it's called a "gig" in Hamtramck. I'm not sure about this.

Anyhow, Walewander had gone to see his idols. He had gone alone. Why? I'll let you figure that out. And now, during batting practice, they were returning the favor.

Here they stood, on the Tiger Stadium field, dressed in their Sunday-best combat boots. They posed for photos. It was great fun, and Walewander was having the time of his life, especially when they signed a poster. One member wrote: "To Jim – Satan is My Master, (signed) Rodney." You can imagine how special that must have felt.

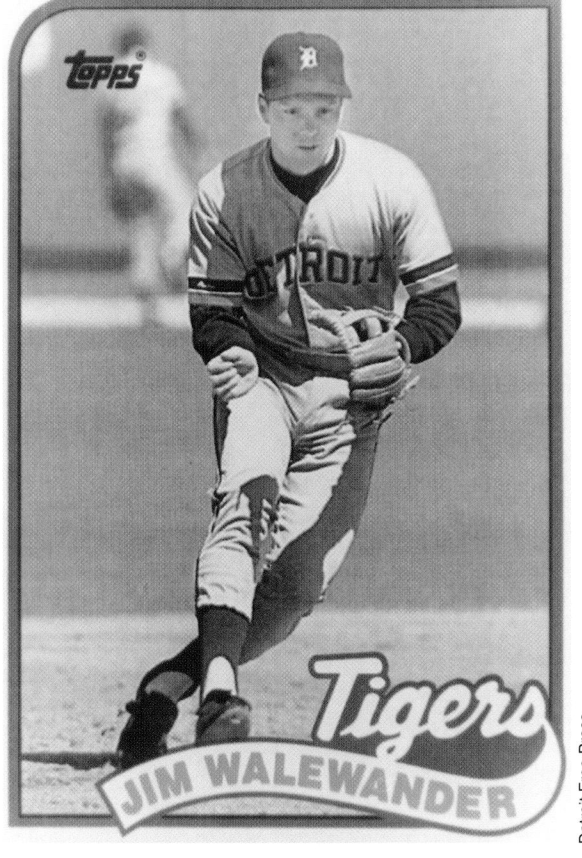

Detroit Free Press

And then the Dead Milkmen got to meet Sparky Anderson. I missed that, but Sparky related this story after the game: "One of them had on combat boots, a camouflage army shirt and an earring. I told him, 'Son, don't take no prisoners.' "

You gotta love a manager like that.

For most of us, meeting the Dead Milkmen would be enough for one day. Or maybe a week. But there was more in store for Walewander. He came to bat in the sixth inning with Chet Lemon on first and the Tigers clinging to a 2-1 lead over the California Angels. This was an important game. If the Tigers won and the Yankees lost, Detroit would move into first place for the first time all year.

And what did Walewander do? He cracked a fastball high into right-centerfield, up, up – it slammed off the upper deck! The crowd went crazy! His first major league homer! Goodness. As we reporters watched him circle the bases, we thought about this and the Dead Milkmen in one day, and, well, we got all choked up – mostly when we thought about the Dead Milkmen.

And the Tigers went on to win the game, 6-2, and stay right on the Yankees' tails. And in the clubhouse after the game, Walewander, the hero, was given his home run ball and the privilege of choosing the music to dress by. He chose one of the Dead Milkmen's more mellow numbers, something just right for the moment. "Bomb the Sewage Plant," I think it was called.

"What will you do with the ball?" someone yelled, trying to be heard over the bass guitar.

A once-in-a-millennium convergence at The Corner: The Dead Milkmen – Dean Clean, Joe Jack, Rodney Anonymous and Dave Blood – share hallowed ground with Sparky Anderson (the guy on the right).

Capitol Records, Inc.

"Put it in my glove compartment," he yelled back, "along with my first major league hit."

"How many balls do you have in there?"

"Just these two for now," he said. "When I fill it up, I'll be able to buy myself a new car."

He grinned like a high-schooler, which is about how old he looks. His T-shirt featured a smiling cartoon cow. A cow? Yes. A gift from – oops! The music changed! A new number.

"What's this one called?" he was asked.

" 'Take Me to the Specialist,' " he said.

Gotcha.

So the day was a real thrill, as any music lover can imagine. And baseball fans enjoyed it, too. After all, one telltale sign of a pennant contender is winning games with your No. 9 hitter blasting a home run, while your starting pitcher (in this case, the inimitable Walt Terrell) goes all the way.

Good stuff. Promising stuff. This is simply the hottest team in the major leagues right now. There is no telling who today's hero will be, where he will come from, what size combat boots he will wear. But no matter. The fact is, the Tigers are getting something out of just about everybody.

And Sunday, it was a perfectly timed debut homer by Walewander, who figured his biggest thrill already had come before the starting call.

"Did the Dead Milkmen stay for the game?"

"Nah," he said. "They had a gig somewhere."

Livonia, perhaps? ◆

Mitch Albom is a Free Press columnist.

plutocracy. He had a rock-star following, with crowds of mostly young fans chanting "Go, Bird, Go!" and demanding curtain calls when he won. Girls raided barber shops to get locks of his curly hair and sent him presents by the sackload. His locker inside Tiger Stadium was crammed with cakes, cookies, letters, pictures, stuffed animals, balloons and flowers. Teammate Rusty Staub said: "I've never seen a city turned on like this."

Fidrych finished the year with a 19-9 record, completed a league-high 24 of 29 starts and rang up a 2.34 ERA, best in the majors.

Throughout, he remained generally unaffected by all the commotion caused by his fresh and free-spirited ways. He continued to drive his Dodge Colt from his unfurnished apartment to the ballpark, and to ration his $16,500 salary to cover essential purchases like T-shirts and bottles of Stroh's. Meanwhile, the Tigers made a financial killing. Attendance increased 40 percent at The Corner, a spike solely attributable to The Bird's popularity.

Sadly, Birdmania evaporated nearly as quickly as it appeared. The following spring, he sustained torn cartilage in his left knee while shagging fly balls and underwent an operation. The injury affected his pitching motion and ultimately ruined his arm. Despite occasional flashes of brilliance, The Bird never was the same. He won only 10 games during the next four seasons before drifting into the minors and then out of baseball. He returned to his native Northboro, Mass., got married and settled down to a life of raising pigs and horses. The Bird was philosophical. "When it's gone," he said, "all you can say is it's gone, and this is what I got out of it."

Mary Schroeder / Detroit Free Press

Is that Jack Frost warming up or Jack Morris cooling off on a wintry April day in Detroit? Morris, like teammate Lou Whitaker (facing page), arrived at The Corner in 1977.

As Fidrych passed from the scene, others destined to become part of Tiger Stadium lore checked in at The Corner. Sparky Anderson, the white-haired bane of grammar teachers everywhere, became manager on June 14, 1979, and stayed through 1995. The man who "never got no A in English" nonetheless rewrote the Tigers' record book with his 17 seasons and 1,331 wins in Detroit.

Two other models of longevity, Alan Trammell and Lou Whitaker, arrived in 1977. The textbook shortstop from San Diego and whisper-quiet second baseman from Brooklyn, N.Y., became the peanut butter and jelly of baseball, in 1988 becoming the longest-running keystone combination in history. By the time Trammell retired in 1996, one year after Whitaker, the perennial All-Stars had turned more than 1,200 double plays, combined for nearly 5,000 base hits and spent 19 seasons as teammates.

"Not only have they been excellent players defensively and as a duo, but boy, they've

Julian H. Gonzalez / Detroit Free Press

"Where do you find a shortstop and a second baseman who can hit 20 home runs a year for you? Drive in 80-plus runs? And steal bases?"
LOU PINIELLA

he ran around the clubhouse like he had hit two grand slams and stole the mustard off somebody's hot dog." Morris, on the other hand, "had his own kind of ugly. He had the stubbornness of a mule and the grace of a thoroughbred."

Morris' batterymate for eight seasons was Lance Parrish, an Arnold Schwarzenegger in shin protectors. His 32 homers in 1982 were a league record for backstops for 14 years. Parrish, Gibson and Morris eventually would leave The Corner via free agency. But not before helping to produce the Roar of '84.

That season the Tigers exploded out of the gate, winning 35 of their first 40 games. After that it was only a matter of waiting to see who their opponents in the postseason were going to be.

Having gone 16 years without a championship, the city was baseball-mad, crazier than at any other time since the Year of the Bird. A new attendance record was set, with more than 2.7 million fans pouring into the park. They amused themselves with innovative twists of a cheer known as the wave, by slapping beach balls at each other, and by exchanging chants in the bleachers. Good, clean fun (if one didn't mind the occasionally profane chants), but Sparky was the only person in Detroit not enjoying himself. The fast start had jacked up expectations among fans, writers and players.

Anderson, who had skippered Cincinnati to a pair of World Series championships, was consumed with becoming the first manager to win a World Series in both leagues. He later admitted that he felt more pressure in 1984 than he did in 1989, when the team lost 103 games.

"When you start 35-5, you have to win," Anderson said. "Every time a visiting manag-

been offensive producers, too," marveled Lou Piniella, who saw them break in when he was playing for the Yankees. "Where do you find a shortstop and a second baseman who can hit 20 home runs a year for you? Drive in 80-plus runs? And steal bases?

"They can do everything on the field while they're playing except manage a ballgame. They're both class people – I like the way they play."

Pitcher Jack Morris and rightfielder Kirk Gibson, as grouchily competitive a pair of teammates as ever shared a locker room, came along about the same time.

In Anderson's view, Gibson was a Hall of Fame performer, someone who hit more game-winning home runs than anybody he had seen during his 26 years of managing.

"Half of Gibby's game plan was to intimidate the opposition," Anderson wrote in "They Call Me Sparky." "He was the ultimate team player. When he went 3-for-4 and we lost, he could bite off the head of a rattlesnake. When he went 0-for-4 and we won,

MEMORIES KIRK GIBSON

The green seats, the wooden chairs, banging my bat

The biggest vision I have of the stadium is of when I was a little kid. My birthday's in May, and I remember going down there for that. Earl Wilson, Mickey Lolich, Mickey Stanley, Willie Horton, Bill Freehan, Dick McAuliffe, Norm Cash – that's the era that really sticks out in my mind. I remember watching them in the World Series. I think I was in the sixth grade.

Bat Day always used to take place right around my birthday. I remember sitting in the green wooden seats in the upper deck just above third base, banging my bat on the cement floor and with my free hand smashing the vacant chair next to me and screaming, "Let's go, Tigers!"

That's my first memory of Tiger Stadium. The green seats, the wooden chairs, banging my bat. When they switched over to orange and blue plastic, it looked good, but I'll never forget the green.

The memories go back so far. The things on the field are so obvious. The whole '84 World Series scene was awesome, seeing the whole place packed and the excitement. I'll never forget when the sod got ripped up. That was just Detroit. I didn't see anything negative in that.

I remember the Opening Day when I lost the ball in the sun and it hit me. No clouds in the sky. Tiger Stadium is known for that. I remember one ball that just missed the overhang, and I lost sight of it, and it got me.

I'll always remember things like the short rightfield porch with the overhang ... the small dugout, where you'd always bump your head when you were excited and jumped up ... the proximity of the fans to the players ... things that were incredible and probably will never be recaptured.

And one more thing. I remember seeing Lions games there. I remember when Chuck Hughes died on the field. They should have a football game there before they close it for good. ◆

Kirk Gibson grew up in Waterford.

Ira Rosenberg / Detroit Free Press

David C. Turnley / Detroit Free Press

Kirk Gibson always had the heart of a Tiger, even if he happened to be playing for the Dodgers or the Royals or the Pirates. At left, just a cub, Gibby signs a Tigers contract in 1978 in the presence of his approving parents. In 1985, he married JoAnn Sklarski while best bud Dave Rozema wed JoAnn's sister, Sandra. Gibson abandoned the Tigers in 1988 but closed out his playing days at The Corner in 1993-95.

Julian H. Gonzalez / Detroit Free Press

MEMORIES BILL McGRAW

The air was thick with the smell of marijuana

Some of the weirdest things I've ever witnessed in public took place in the Tiger Stadium bleachers – nudity, fisticuffs, food fights, obscene chants and dozens of flying beach balls.

It wasn't easy being a bleacher creature, as fans who sat there came to be known. The seats were uncomfortable and wedged closely together, and the upper deck was open to the elements. All 10,000 bleacher seats were poorly served by vendors and concession stands, and home plate was more than 440 feet away.

Nonetheless, the bleachers, especially those in the upper deck, could be a pleasure. With a small crowd on a warm summer's night, you could stretch across a couple of benches and gaze upon the entire field, in all of its emerald splendor, and the city's lights would be twinkling at your back. Until the Tigers modernized, you also could stand on the last row of the bleachers, under the old scoreboard, and talk to the two guys who sat inside and ran it.

The lower-deck bleachers were shady, peaceful and a little claustrophobic, scrunched as they were under the upper-deck stands. I sat there with my friend Mark for the 1971 All-Star Game. We were within shouting distance of two of the greatest outfielders in history, National Leaguers Willie Mays and Roberto Clemente. Mays endeared himself to fans by tossing a warm-up ball into the bleachers. Reggie Jackson smashed a ball against the light tower high above us, but we couldn't see where it landed until we saw the paper the next morning.

BLEACHER CREATURES, CONSIDERED BY MANY THE GAME'S MOST KNOWLEDGEABLE FANS, WEREN'T ALWAYS CHASING BEACH BALLS.

While the bleachers could be tranquil, especially during the many seasons the Tigers were out of the running by June 1, they were long associated with rowdyism. In 1960, a fan was convicted in Recorder's Court of throwing eggs from the bleachers at Cleveland outfielder Jimmy Piersall, who suffered emotional problems and often was the target of fan abuse. I saw bleacher fans throwing cherry bombs at Yankees rightfielder Joe Pepitone in the early 1960s, and others have disrupted games from the bleachers by tossing such mean-spirited weapons as bolts, seat parts, golf balls and hammers.

By 1974, the bleachers became known for mass nudity.

I took another friend, Sue, to Opening Day that year, and we sat in the upper deck. It was a bitter 38 degrees, not counting windchill, but that didn't stop fans from taking off their clothes.

This was the heyday of streaking, that short-lived fad in which otherwise normal young men – and sometimes women – would run naked through a public place. Given the anything-goes atmosphere of the bleachers, it was not surprising that we would have seen a streaker or two. But we saw about 20 of them, all men.

Nudes ran up and down the aisles. They slid (sidesaddle) down the railings. They swung to and fro while hanging from the bottom of the scoreboard. One naked guy just sat on the frigid bench, nonchalantly watching the game. Sue thought the bleachers were more interesting than the game, which the Tigers lost to the Yankees.

A decade later, beach balls began to cause turmoil.

The upper-deck bleachers by this time had become an attraction in themselves for young people, and rather than control it and market the fun atmosphere as White Sox owner Bill Veeck did in Chicago, the unimaginative Tigers management failed to get a handle on the frivolity, and it got out of hand.

Beach balls fluttering to the field stopped play about a dozen times during a nationally televised game in August 1983. I was in the bleachers the next game as a reporter, watching as fans smuggled in dozens of balls and inflated many right after the first pitch. Suddenly, the bleachers took on the atmosphere of a wild Easter weekend in Ft. Lauderdale. The crowd let out war whoops as the balls bopped crazily from one section to another. People who reached out across the packed seats to smack a ball spilled beer on their neighbors. The air was thick with the smell of marijuana.

Inevitably, some poor soul would fail to keep a ball in the air, and a security guard would rush out and seize it. Angry at losing the ball to a rent-a-cop, dozens of crowd members would chant a vulgar, two-syllable insult while pelting that person (and nearby fans) with mashed food, warm beer and crushed cups. Some fans would throw garbage back.

During the fifth inning, security guards were attempting to drag a man through the chanting crowd when someone near the top of the bleachers threw a small bottle that bounced off the prisoner and broke on the ground, cutting a nearby man and a youngster with flying glass. In all, police arrested five fans that night, ticketed six others and ejected six more.

Before long, the problem became cuss words.

The bleacher creatures began chanting a profane version of the "Less filling! Tastes great!" TV beer commercials. One side would scream: "Eat s - - - !" The other side would respond: "F - - - you!" The foul language shocked even players. "I was sort of saying to myself, 'What are they saying? No, it can't be,' " said Chicago centerfielder Daryl Boston. But they were. By 1985, profanity had become so loud and frequent that the Tigers closed the bleachers for eight games and erected signs that forbade chanting.

I will not miss vulgar chants or naked guys, but I will miss the merriment of a bleacher crowd and the all-encompassing view from centerfield as Alan Trammell and Lou Whitaker turned a double play 300 feet away. While some of the behavior was crude, stupid and dangerous, a lot of it was fun.

I laugh when I recall the reaction of bleacher creatures to Yankees slugger Dave Winfield, who arrived in Detroit after having thrown a ball in Toronto that killed a sea gull. Whenever Winfield came to bat, nearly everyone in the upper-deck bleachers stood and flapped their arms. Entertainment like that is hard to find. ◆

Bill McGraw is a Free Press reporter.

Bill DeKay / Detroit Free Press

ASSUME THE POSITION

During the 1987 playoffs, guards searched patrons entering the bleachers in an attempt to cut down on rowdyism at The Corner. But the practice raised the hackles of fans who said getting into the game had all the charm of a police lineup. Several minutes before a Sunday game, the crowd outside Gate 8 at Trumbull and Kaline Drive spilled into the street and disrupted traffic. "Open the doors," some shouted. "Let us in." Men and women were split into separate lines and searched for alcoholic beverages. Guards were observed frisking children. Many fans were angry. "It was the most demeaning experience I've had in my whole life," fumed a 40-year-old schoolteacher from Novi. "A stadium security guard felt inside my thighs, around my buttocks – there wasn't a crevice in my body that this man didn't go over. Imagine standing in front of your wife and being treated like a criminal." ◆

Detroit Free Press

DURING TIGER STADIUM'S FINAL DECADE, ONE'S VIEW COULD BE OBSTRUCTED AS BEFORE, BUT FANS COULD TURN TO TV MONITORS FOR THE INSTANT REPLAY.

er came to Detroit after that, I told them to take a look at that flagpole in centerfield. If we don't win, there's only gonna be one person hanging from it."

Willie Hernandez, whose airtight relief pitching earned him MVP and Cy Young honors, was one of several veterans brought in to round out the Tigers' cast of young talent. Dave Bergman, a valuable pinch-hitter and utility player, was part of the three-team trade with San Francisco that brought Hernandez from Philadelphia.

First baseman Darrell Evans, the Tigers' biggest free-agent acquisition to that point, contributed as much in the locker room as he did on the field. Evans' signing also served as a message from owner Monaghan – the Domino's Pizza magnate who had bought the team for $53 million from Fetzer – that the club needed to be more aggressive if it expected to win in the modern era of free agency.

Anderson expertly blended his core group of youngsters and veteran acquisitions with role players such as Marty Castillo, Rusty Kuntz, Johnny Grubb and Ruppert Jones.

"You never knew when he was going to call on somebody at any point of the game," Trammell said. "He was so sharp that he knew a certain player in just the right situation could mean the difference in a game. It didn't matter if it was early in a game or late, everybody better be ready. That kept everybody sharp. When the playoffs and World Series rolled around, everybody was at their peak. Nobody was tired."

Fatigue set in only after the Tigers completed a remarkable season with a sweep of Kansas City in the playoffs and a five-game win over San Diego in the World Series.

As was the case with the '68 champions, the dynasty many envisioned after the World Series win of 1984 never happened. The Tigers came close in '87, edging Toronto in a torrid race that wasn't settled until Frank Tanana blanked the Blue Jays, 1-0, at The Corner on the last day of the season. Despite accumulating the most wins in the majors, Anderson considered it a squad of overachievers. His judgment proved right on the money when Minnesota blew the Tigers out of the playoffs in five games.

Ten years after the Roar of '84, only Trammell and Whitaker remained of the original crew that had thrilled Detroit. Gibson, who had left town in a huff after Monaghan refused to give him more than a one-year deal, returned after the pizza baron sold the team to his competitor, Little Caesars owner Mike Ilitch, for an estimated $85 million before the 1993 season.

Ilitch inherited a wrecking crew led by Cecil Fielder, the rotund first sacker who had left Japan to hit 51 home runs in 1990. For three straight years, 1990-92, "Big Daddy" led the majors in RBIs, a feat previously accomplished only by Babe Ruth. Ilitch, a former Tigers farmhand, made the mistake of throwing boxcars of cash at Fielder and several free agents. By 1994, he had one of the most expensive lineups in baseball. His $42.7 million bought him a fifth-place club before the game shut down for the year in the longest, most contentious strike yet.

With the likes of Fielder, Gibson, Mickey Tettleton, Rob Deer, Tony Phillips and Travis Fryman in the lineup, the Tigers generally fielded an interesting but noncompetitive

Julian H. Gonzalez / Detroit Free Press

CLEVELAND'S SANDY ALOMAR JR. KICKS JOHN DOHERTY IN THE BREADBASKET AFTER A BRUSHBACK PITCH IN JUNE 1992.

team for much of the gray '90s. The roof caved in when Ilitch, hemorrhaging $20 million a year because of a bloated payroll and poor attendance, started jettisoning Fielder and other high-priced veterans. The younger, cheaper and suddenly pathetic Tigers lost a whopping 109 games in 1996 under new manager Buddy Bell. They were so awful that they became the butt of late-night jokes by David Letterman and Jay Leno.

For Ilitch, the embarrassing season was made more palatable by the knowledge that, after a bitter, drawn-out debate that featured more posturing than a fashion runway in Milan, a new stadium would be built on Woodward Avenue. Taxpayers would pay $115 million of the expected $295 million cost for the 42,000-seat, open-air stadium, which would be owned by the city and county and leased back to the Tigers. To help finance his projected $180 million share, Ilitch sold the naming rights to Comerica Bank for $66 million. That an individual was allowed to keep every cent paid to name a publicly owned facility evidently bothered nobody except the Tiger Stadium Fan Club, which had been formed in 1988 to ask

Duane Burleson / Associated Press

ATTENDANCE HIGHS AND LOWS

DAY GAME

High: 57,588 – Sept. 26, 1948 vs. Cleveland

Low: 150 – Sept. 16, 1897 vs. Grand Rapids

NIGHT GAME

High: 56,586 – Aug. 9, 1948 vs. Cleveland

Low: 2,173 – Aug. 20, 1964 vs. Los Angeles

DOUBLEHEADER

High: 58,369 – July 20, 1947 vs. New York

Low: 500 – Sept. 6, 1898 vs. Columbus

OPENING DAY

High: 54,500 – April 22, 1938 vs. Cleveland

Low: 2,700 – April 29, 1898 vs. Indianapolis

WORLD SERIES GAME

High: 55,500 – Oct. 5, 1945 vs. Chicago

Low: 6,210 – Oct. 14, 1908 vs. Chicago

SEASON

High: 2,704,794 – 1984

Low: 78,950 – 1898

◆ **Led league in attendance:** 1919, 1934, 1935, 1937, 1940, 1944, 1945, 1968, 1972, 1973, 1984.

◆ **Last in league in attendance:** 1905, 1994.

uncomfortable questions about the need for publicly financing a new ballpark.

With blossoming stars like Bobby Higginson, Tony Clark and Justin Thompson, the Tigers regained respectability in '97, only to fall back into the cellar the following year. The backsliding cost Bell his chance to manage the Tigers in their final season at The Corner. He was replaced by Larry Parrish, who shared his players' excitement about the impending move into Comerica Park.

"I've never been able to call one of those nice, new parks as the place where I play," second baseman Damion Easley said.

"That's something a lot of us are looking forward to."

There's no need to rehash the arguments for and against the new stadium. It is permissible, however, to strike a melancholic note when pondering The Corner's central role in the lives of so many people during the past century. The smells, the personalities, the shared moments all get wadded into a nostalgic ball.

"Tiger Stadium, for me, was just a nice place to be in general," Wilson said. "Even now, when I pass there, the memories always come over me. For me, the memories are mostly of the people. When you talk about Tiger Stadium, you cannot do it without thinking about Al Kaline, Denny, Gates, Northrup or Freehan, McAuliffe, Cash, Willie ... That was Tiger Stadium to me. It was our home."

Tiger Stadium's fate is uncertain and generally undiscussed. The city, which bought the stadium for one dollar in 1977 in exchange for a 30-year lease with the club, owns it. However, because of prohibitive maintenance and security costs and the city's long history of demolition by neglect, it seems likely the once-proud park will become a crumbling eyesore that, like the Hudson's building and the Monroe Block, will stand sad and empty for years while its destiny is periodically debated. It's a safe bet that the Ilitch regime, which has been criticized for marketing nostalgia as if it was pizza, will strip it clean of seats and anything else that can be sold as souvenirs, including the grass. Afterward, the only things restlessly moving through the silent, gutted stands will be rodents and … ghosts.

Think of the history: Three-quarters of the players in the Baseball Hall of Fame played at The Corner. No other venue, not even such celebrated golden-age parks as Fenway and Yankee Stadium, can say as much.

"The ghosts … more than anything, that's what I think about when I remember Tiger Stadium," said Evans, recollecting his first visit to The Corner one December day in 1983.

"I'd been in the National League 15 years before going to the Tigers," he said, "and just getting an opportunity to walk on that field was special. Of course, I had seen the stadium on TV, but there's nothing like walking into it. It was empty, it was cold, and there was snow on the infield. But it was warm for me, just imagining Kaline and Colavito and Cash and Cobb and Gehringer and the Babe and Gehrig and all those guys playing there.

"I was at the last game at Atlanta-Fulton County Stadium and, of course, that doesn't have near the tradition of Tiger Stadium, but we were all a little misty-eyed because of that being torn down.

"Tiger Stadium, Fenway and Yankee Stadium are what baseball's all about as far as I'm concerned. There's so many more things than just going out there and playing.

"Winning it all in '84 was a great memory, but when the fans gave me a standing ovation after being picked off of third base in the '87 playoff game against Minnesota – well, you can't pay for that. You can't ever plan on something like that happening.

"I was worried about having things thrown at me. It was such an important thing. God, it gives me chills just to think about that again. There's not many places, maybe no other place, where the fans would have done that."

The torrent of memories concluded with a simple rhetorical question.

"When the Tigers move," he asked, "where are the ghosts going to go?" ◆

FACING PAGE: BOBBY HIGGINSON, DETROIT'S MOST EXCITING PLAYER IN THE LAST HALF OF THE '90S, THRILLED FANS WITH HIS BAT (.320 IN 1996, 101 RBIS IN 1997) AND HIS GLOVE. BELOW: TONY CLARK SCALED THE 30-HOMER AND 100-RBI MARKS IN THE LATE '90S WHILE DISPLAYING AGILITY AT FIRST BASE.

Kirthmon F. Dozier / Detroit Free Press

PHOTOSTORY BY ALAN R. KAMUDA

When the field is empty and the stands are silent, the stadium comes alive. The personality of the house that sits on The Corner clouds over the events that have visited it.

Yesterday becomes today when I walk the wide concrete corridors that haven't changed in the three decades I've been shooting pictures at the stadium. Ty Cobb, Babe Ruth and Al Kaline were here yesterday, and parts of them will always be here. I can look at the empty seats and see people I saw 30 years ago sitting in them. I can sit by myself in the bleachers and feel the crowd's roar. My mind can hear a bat's loud crack and see the ball fly into the stands.

I never feel lonely in Tiger Stadium and always say hi when I pass by. The stories the park has to tell make for damn good company.

Alan R. Kamuda is a Free Press photographer and photo editor of "The Corner."

WHERE SPIRITS ROAM

COBB
GEHRINGER
COCHRANE
FAMERS

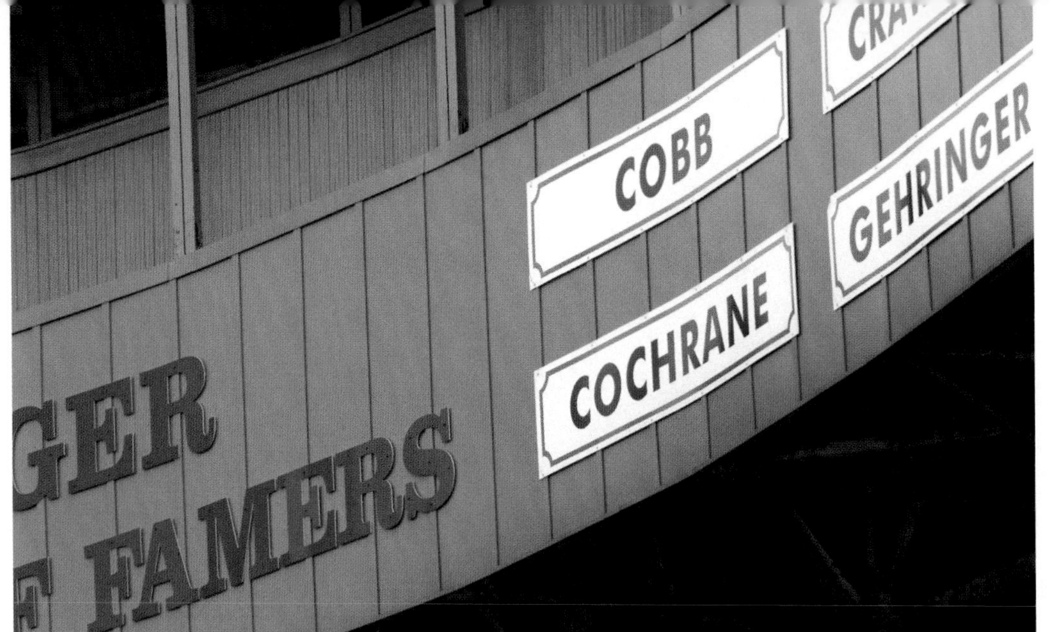

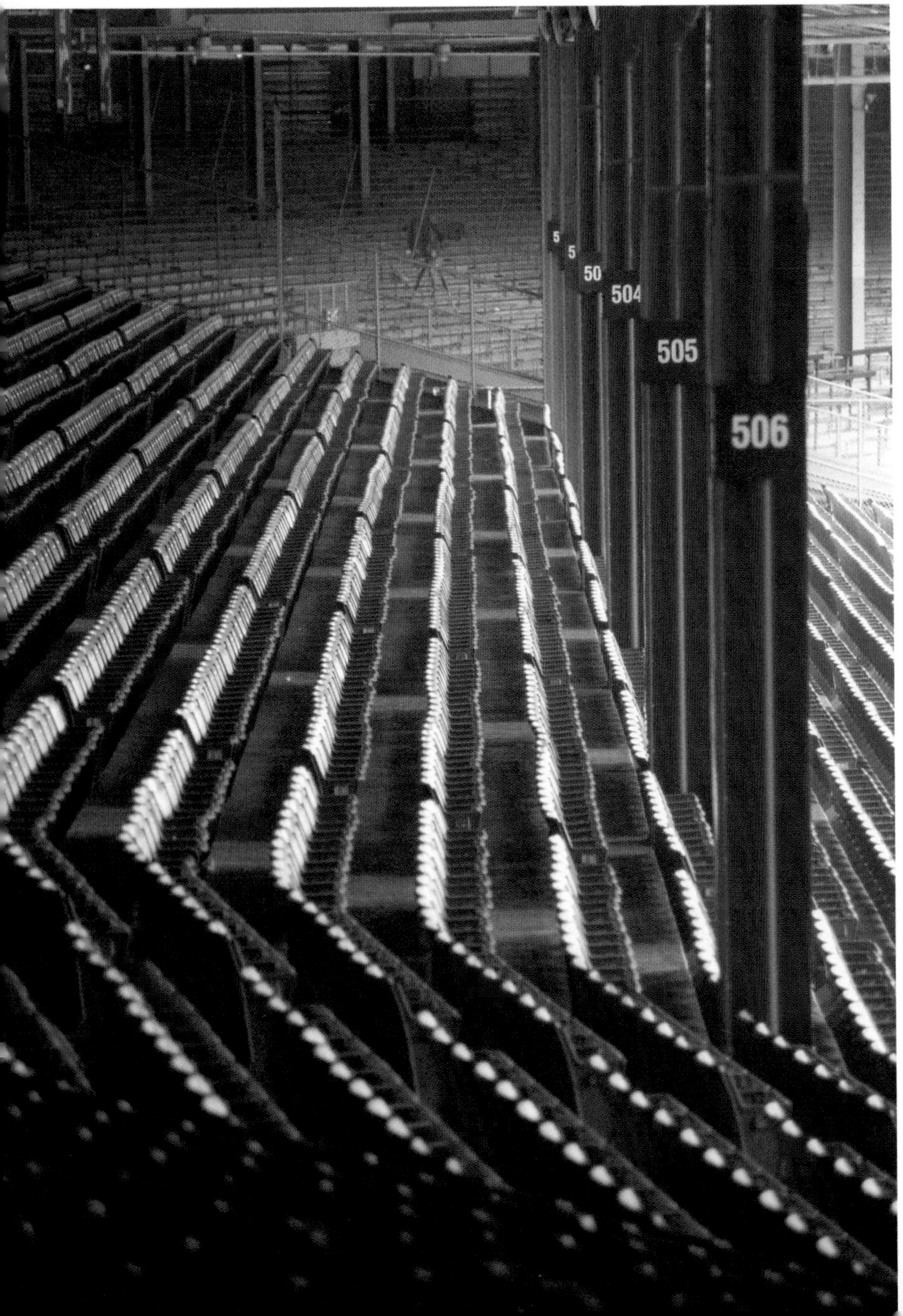
504
505
506

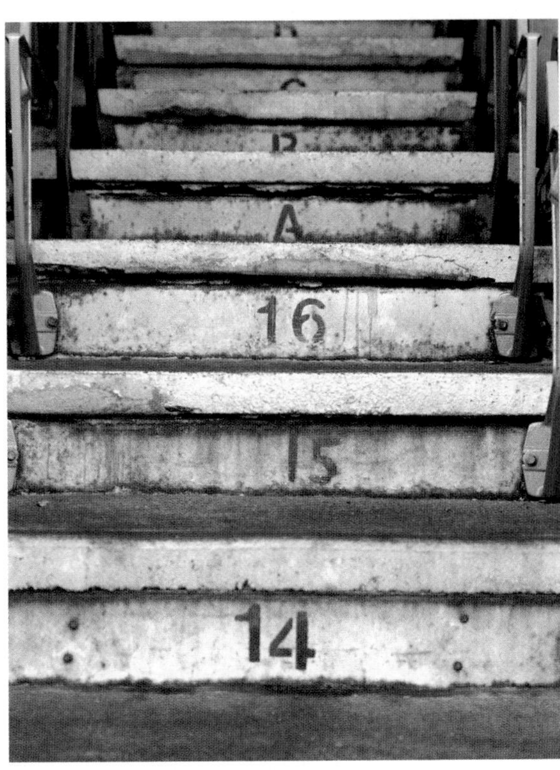

A
16
15
14

TIGERS DEN
8

EXIT
COCHRANE
&
KALINE

TIGERS
2 5 6 16
42
CONFIDENCE
BUD LIGHT BUD LIGHT
DTE Energy
325
Office DEPOT
325

TIME ◆ LINE

1896-1999

By Richard Bak

1896

April 28. Bennett Park opens on the northwest corner of Michigan and Trumbull, previously the site of a municipal haymarket. The Detroit Tigers, members of the Western League, beat Columbus, 17-2, in the first professional baseball game at The Corner. Tigers captain George Stallings hits the first home run.

May 31. Looking to skirt the local ordinance banning Sunday ball, Tigers owner George Vanderbeck rents Athletic Park in Mt. Clemens for a game. A crowd of 3,483, the largest since Opening Day, watches second-place St. Paul beat the first-place Tigers, 6-2. Vanderbeck abandons the experiment after two more Sunday dates in 1897.

July 4. The first doubleheader at Bennett Park, a twin bill with Grand Rapids, attracts a capacity crowd of 5,000.

Sept. 24. The Tigers and Cincinnati Reds play an exhibition game under portable lights, the first night game at The Corner.

Oct. 3. The Detroit Athletic Club plays a high school squad, the Seaforths, in the first of many soccer matches at Michigan and Trumbull.

1897

May 31. On Memorial Day against Minneapolis, the Tigers play their first morning-afternoon doubleheader. Sixteen-hundred rooters attend the first game; another 5,000 watch the second. The split twin bill becomes a holiday tradition that continues well into the new century.

Aug. 6. In a game against Kansas City, Detroit catcher Pat McCauley becomes the first player to hit for the cycle at Michigan and Trumbull.

Sept. 16. A game with Grand Rapids draws 150 fans, the smallest crowd ever to watch a game at The Corner.

1898

Sept. 6. A doubleheader with Columbus attracts 500 people, the lowest figure ever for a twin bill at Michigan and Trumbull.

Nov. 12. The University of Michigan plays its first of several football games at The Corner, beating Illinois, 12-5, before 3,500 fans.

1899

April 30. The Tigers play their first of nine Sunday games at River Rouge Park in Ecorse.

1900

Jan. 1. Western League owners vote to rename their circuit the American League. It remains a minor league.

March 6. George Vanderbeck sells the team for $12,000 to Tigers manager George Stallings and local sportsman Jim Burns.

April 20. Chicago's Doc Amole no-hits the Tigers, 8-0, as Detroit inaugurates American League play.

May 6. The Tigers play the first of an eventual 34 Sunday games through 1902 at Burns Park in Springwells Township, losing to Indianapolis, 11-5, before a rowdy overflow crowd.

Oct. 14. Owners of several key American League teams, including Charles Comiskey and Connie Mack, vote to reorganize the circuit as a major league in direct competition with the established National League.

1901

April 25. In the city's first major league game since 1888 and the greatest ninth-inning rally in big-league history, the Tigers score 10 runs to beat Milwaukee, 14-13.

July 13. Leftfielder Doc Nance, batting seventh in the order, has six hits in six at-bats in the Tigers' 19-12 victory over

KEEPING SCORE ◆ CYCLING

A dozen players — half of them Tigers — hit for the cycle at The Corner after Detroit catcher Pat McCauley did it first in an 1897 Western League game against Kansas City.

DATE	PLAYER
July 28, 1993	**Travis Fryman**, Detroit vs. New York
Aug. 3, 1982	Frank White, Kansas City
Sept. 3, 1976	Mike Hegan, Milwaukee
Sept. 7, 1950	**Hoot Evers**, Detroit vs. Cleveland
Aug. 2, 1940	Joe Cronin, Boston
May 27, 1939	**Charlie Gehringer**, Detroit vs. St. Louis
April 20, 1937	**Gee Walker**, Detroit vs. Cleveland
July 26, 1928	Bob Meusel, New York
Sept. 26, 1926	**Bob Fothergill**, Detroit vs. Boston
June 27, 1922	Ray Schalk, Chicago
Aug. 13, 1921	George Sisler, St. Louis
Sept. 17, 1920	**Bobby Veach**, Detroit vs. Boston
Aug. 6, 1897	**Pat McCauley**, Detroit vs. Kansas City

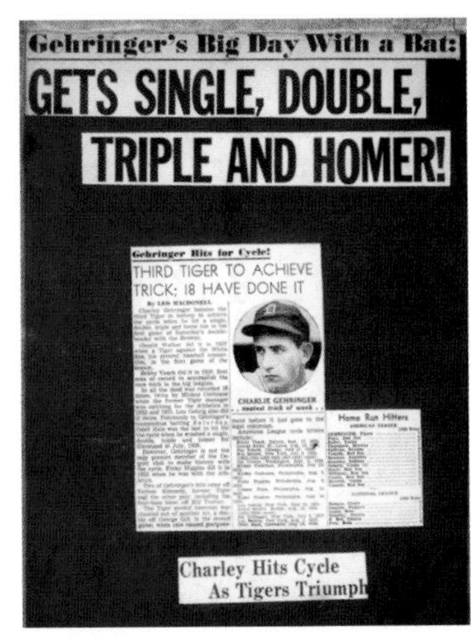
Gehringer's Big Day With a Bat:
GETS SINGLE, DOUBLE, TRIPLE AND HOMER!
THIRD TIGER TO ACHIEVE TRICK; 18 HAVE DONE IT
Charley Hits Cycle As Tigers Triumph

Courtesy Bill Dow

A fan's scrapbook records Gehringer's feat.

Richard Bak Collection

BATTER UP AT BENNETT PARK IN 1911, ITS WANING DAYS.

Cleveland, tying an American League record for most hits in a nine-inning game.

Sept. 15. Detroit ends the season with a 21-0 thumping of Cleveland at Burns Park, the worst shutout loss in the big leagues.

Nov. 2. The largest crowd to attend a football game in the state up to that time, 8,000 fans, packs Bennett Park to watch Fielding Yost's famous "Point-a-Minute" Michigan squad beat Pop Warner's Carlisle team, 22-0.

Nov. 14. League president Ban Johnson forces the sale of the Tigers to a syndicate headed by local insurance man Samuel F. Angus.

1904

Jan. 22. Samuel Angus sells the Tigers to millionaire lumber heir William H. Yawkey for $50,000. Frank Navin, a clerk in Angus' office, gets a 10 percent share of the team for brokering the deal.

1905

July 24. The Tigers lose to Boston, 7-1, at Neil Park in Columbus, Ohio. The game marks the Tigers' 51st and final neutral-site game since 1896. All but one were played on Sunday.

Aug. 30. Ty Cobb makes his major league debut with a double off the New York Highlanders' Jack Chesbro.

Sept. 6. Chicago's Frank Smith no-hits Detroit, 8-0.

1907

June 29. Ty Cobb steals home for the first time, victimizing the Cleveland battery of Heinie Berger and Howard Wakefield.

Aug. 18. A turnout of 9,635 sees the Tigers and New York Highlanders play the first Sunday game at Michigan and Trumbull.

Sept. 24. Frank Navin acquires a half-interest in the Tigers for $20,000 and is named president. Bill Yawkey remains co-owner until his death in 1919.

Oct. 11. A crowd of 11,306 watches the Chicago Cubs beat the Tigers, 6-1, on a rainy Friday in the first World Series game at The Corner.

1908

April 17. A major expansion of Bennett Park is readied for Opening Day. A 2,000-seat bleacher section and expansion of the main grandstand doubles the seating capacity to 10,000.

Oct. 14. The smallest crowd in World Series history – 6,210 – watches the Cubs close out a second straight championship over the Tigers with a 2-0 win.

1909

July 16. Ed Summers goes the distance in an 18-inning, 0-0 tie with Washington, the longest scoreless tie in league annals.

Aug. 24. Ty Cobb spikes Philadelphia third baseman Frank Baker, igniting national controversy over his playing style.

Oct. 12. The Tigers win their first World Series game at home, beating Pittsburgh, 5-0.

Oct. 16. Pittsburgh beats Detroit in Game 7 of the World Series, 8-0.

1910

April 14. The season opens with additions to the main grandstand, increasing Bennett Park's seating capacity from 10,000 to 13,000.

Sept. 17. Ed Summers becomes the first pitcher in modern baseball history to hit two home runs in a game, victimizing Philadelphia with a pair of two-run shots.

1911

April 13. The Tigers open the season with permanent bleacher sections in rightfield and leftfield.

June 18. The Tigers overcome a 12-run deficit, rallying to beat Chicago, 16-15, after trailing, 13-1, in the fifth inning.

1912

April 20. Navin Field, built at a cost of $300,000, opens before a capacity crowd of 23,000. The Tigers beat Cleveland, 6-5, on George Mullin's single in the 11th inning.

July 4. Mullin celebrates his 32nd birthday with a 7-0 no-hitter against St. Louis – the first by a Tiger at The Corner.

Aug. 30. Earl Hamilton of St. Louis no-hits Detroit, 5-1.

1915

June 20. St. Louis arrives at Navin Field without uniforms. The Tigers lend the Browns their spares, then beat them, 1-0.

1917

July 11. Boston pitcher Babe Ruth one-hits the Tigers, 1-0. He also collects two of the five hits off losing pitcher Hooks Dauss.

Nov. 11. A benefit football game between the Camp Custer All-Stars and the Detroit Heralds attracts 16,000 to Navin Field. The All-Stars win, 13-0.

1918

June 3. Hub Leonard of Boston no-hits Detroit, 5-0.

1920

Sept. 20. Bobby Veach goes 6-for-6 and is the first American League Tiger to hit for the cycle in a 12-inning win over Boston.

1921

Oct. 9. In the first National Football League game at Michigan and Trumbull, the Detroit Tigers beat the Dayton Triangles, 10-7.

1922

April 30. Unheralded rookie Charlie Robertson of Chicago pitches a perfect game against Detroit, 2-0.

1923

April 26. Thirty-six thousand fans attend the Tigers' home opener, which has been delayed a week so that the double-decking of the grandstand can be completed. The expansion increases seating capacity from 23,000 to 29,000, though crowds in excess of 40,000 can be accommodated through temporary bleacher sections and outfield overflows.

Both: Burton Historical Collection

FACES IN THE CROWD ON OPENING DAY 1923 ... RECOGNIZE ANYONE?

1925

Aug. 29. Thirty thousand fans turn out for Ty Cobb Day at Navin Field, honoring his 20th anniversary as a Tiger. Cobb receives a new car and other gifts at home plate before the game, then contributes two hits in a 9-5 win over Philadelphia.

Sept. 27. The Detroit Panthers become the second NFL team to play their home schedule at Michigan and Trumbull, beating Columbus, 7-0, in the season opener.

1926

June 8. Babe Ruth hits the longest home run of his career, a 626-foot wallop off Lil Stoner.

Sept. 26. Heinie Manush gets six hits in a season-ending doubleheader against Boston at Navin Field and edges Babe Ruth for the batting title, .378 to .372.

HEINIE MANUSH

1927

April 20. Ty Tyson begins radio broadcasts of Tigers games over station WWJ.

May 31. Tigers first baseman Johnny Neun preserves a 1-0 victory over Cleveland with an unassisted triple play in the ninth inning.

July 19. Ty Cobb, now with Philadelphia, collects his 4,000th career hit – a first-inning scratch double off the glove of Harry Heilmann.

Oct. 2. On the final day of the season, Harry Heilmann pounds out seven hits in a doubleheader sweep of Cleveland and edges Philadelphia's Al Simmons for the batting crown, .398 to .392.

1928

Sept. 25. A game with last-place Boston attracts 404 people, the Tigers' smallest American League crowd ever.

1933

Dec. 12. The cash-strapped Philadelphia Athletics send catcher Mickey Cochrane to the Tigers for $100,000 and catcher Johnny Pasek.

1934

April 24. With the repeal of Prohibition, beer is sold in Navin Field for the first time. Several fans are arrested for public intoxication.

July 13. Babe Ruth hits the 700th home run of his career, off Tommy Bridges.

Sept. 10. Hank Greenberg, after widespread discussion about whether he should play on the Jewish holy day of Rosh Hashanah, decides to suit up. In the bottom of the ninth, he hits his second home run of the game to beat Boston, 2-1.

Oct. 9. St. Louis wins a hotly contested World Series as Dizzy Dean shuts out the Tigers, 11-0, in Game 7. A riot by Detroit fans causes the commissioner, Judge Kenesaw Mountain Landis, to order the Cardinals' Ducky Medwick out of the game.

1935

June 8. Nine thousand attend the production of "The Student Prince," launching

Opera Under the Stars, a summer-long outdoor series created by Frank Navin and local theater owner J. J. Shubert.

Oct. 7. The Tigers win their first world championship, beating Chicago, 4-3, on Goose Goslin's single in the ninth. Catcher-manager Mickey Cochrane scores the winning run.

Nov. 13. Frank Navin suffers a fatal heart attack while horesback riding. Industrialist Walter O. Briggs, a silent partner since 1920, purchases the team from Navin's estate for $1 million.

1936

April 17. The season opens with a double-decked grandstand extending down the first-base line into rightfield. The upper deck is widened 10 feet in both directions, resulting in the famous "porch" overlooking rightfield and a bulge in the park's outer wall along Trumbull Avenue. This first stage of expansion increases Navin Field's seating capacity to 36,000.

1937

Aug. 14. The Tigers pound out 36 runs in a doubleheader, beating the St. Louis Browns, 16-1 and 20-7.

Oct. 3. On the final day of the season, Jake Wade pitches a one-hitter and beats Cleveland's Johnny Allen (15-0 entering the game), ending Allen's quest for a record-tying 16th consecutive win. Hank Greenberg knocks in the only run of the afternoon but falls one short of equaling Lou Gehrig's league record of 184 RBIs.

1938

April 22. Briggs Stadium is dedicated before a record Opening Day crowd of 54,500. During the winter, a two-story grandstand was completed in leftfield and centerfield, making the field the first in baseball to be completely encircled by two decks.

July 26-27. Hank Greenberg becomes the fourth major-leaguer to homer in four consecutive official at-bats, turning the trick with a pair of two-homer games against Washington.

Aug. 6. Mickey Cochrane is fired as manager of the Tigers.

Oct. 18. The Detroit Lions lose to Washington, 7-5, in their first game at The Corner.

Nov. 26. Catholic Central beats heavily favored Hamtramck, 19-13, in the first Goodfellows Game matching champions of the Catholic and Public School leagues.

1939

May 2. Lou Gehrig's consecutive-games playing streak stops at 2,130.

May 4. Ted Williams becomes the first player to homer over the rightfield stands since it was double-decked, connecting off Bob Harris.

Sept. 20. Joe Louis knocks out Bob Pastor in the 11th round of their heavyweight title fight. Attendance is 33,000.

1940

Oct. 6. Bobo Newsom beats Cincinnati, 8-0, in Game 5 of the World Series as 55,189 look on.

1941

July 8. Ted Williams' ninth-inning home run off Claude Passeau gives the American League a dramatic 7-5 victory over the National League in the first All-Star Game played in Detroit.

1943

June 23. In the aftermath of a bloody race riot, 350 armed troops guard the stadium during a Detroit-Cleveland doubleheader.

July 25. Satchel Paige's All-Stars play the Motor City Giants in one of scores of contests involving Negro leagues teams between 1916 and the 1950s.

Nov. 7. The Lions and New York Giants play to a 0-0 deadlock, the last scoreless tie in NFL history.

Detroit Free Press

TY TYSON WAS BEHIND THE MIKE FOR THE TIGERS' FIRST RADIO BROADCAST IN 1927 AND THE CLUB'S FIRST TV BROADCAST IN 1947.

1944

Oct. 1. Last-place Washington beats Detroit, 4-1, depriving the Tigers of a tie for the pennant with St. Louis.

1945

July 1. Hank Greenberg hits a home run against Philadelphia in his first game since returning from four years in the military.

Oct. 5. The biggest turnout for a post-season baseball game in Detroit, 55,500, watches the Cubs beat Detroit, 3-0, in Game 3 of the World Series. Claude Passeau surrenders one hit, a single by Rudy York.

1946

April 16. The warning track, a narrow strip of crushed brick installed between the edge of the outfield grass and the walls, makes its debut in the home opener against Cleveland.

May 24. While Philadelphia is in town for a series, Connie Mack trades third baseman George Kell to Detroit for centerfielder Barney McCosky.

1947

June 3. Ty Tyson of WWJ handles the first televised broadcast of a Tigers game, a 3-0 loss to New York. At the time there are only 2,000 televisions in the Detroit area.

July 20. A doubleheader with the Yankees draws the largest baseball crowd in Detroit, 58,369. Detroit wins twice, 4-1 and 12-11 (11 innings).

1948

June 15. Detroit beats Philadelphia, 4-1, before 54,480 fans in the first official game played under the lights at The Corner.

June 30. Cleveland's Bob Lemon no-hits the Tigers, 2-0, in the first no-hitter played under the lights in American League history.

Aug. 9. A Detroit-Cleveland game attracts 56,586 fans. It's the largest night crowd in club history.

Sept. 26. An afternoon contest with Cleveland attracts 57,588, the greatest turnout ever for a single day game in Detroit.

1949

June 16. Jake LaMotta wins the middleweight crown with a 10th-round knockout of Marcel Cerdan in front of a disappointing crowd of 22,183.

Sept. 8. The Tigers host their first day-night doubleheader, beating Cleveland twice.

Oct. 3. George Kell's two hits off Cleveland's Bob Lemon in the last game of the season allows the Tigers' third baseman to edge Ted Williams for the batting title, .3429 to .3427.

1950

June 23. The Tigers and Yankees set a record by combining for 11 home runs. The final one, an inside-the-parker by Hoot Evers in the ninth, gives Detroit a 10-9 victory.

Oct. 5. The University of Detroit loses to Notre Dame, 40-6, before 52,331 football fans.

1951

July 10. In the second All-Star Game in Detroit, the National League beats the American League, 8-3, before 52,075. Tigers George Kell and Vic Wertz account for two of the record-setting six home runs hit in the game.

1952

Jan. 17. Walter O. Briggs dies. Walter (Spike) Briggs Jr. succeeds his father as president. After a probate court rules that the club is not a prudent investment and orders it sold, Spike Briggs unsuccessfully tries to buy the team from the estate.

May 15. With many Detroiters attending a downtown parade for Gen. Douglas MacArthur, only 2,215 watch Virgil Trucks no-hit Washington, 1-0, behind Vic Wertz's two-out, ninth-inning home run.

Richard Bak Collection

Tom Venaleck / Detroit Free Press

They might not have known his name at first, but Ozzie Virgil left his mark at The Corner, as did Roger Maris.

Dec. 21. On a foggy Sunday afternoon, the Lions beat Los Angeles, 31-21, in a special playoff to advance to the NFL title game against Cleveland.

1953

July 23. The Tigers end the practice of having both teams share the centerfield bullpen by moving the batteries to the outfield corners. General manager Charlie Gehringer explains that it's meant to cut down the time required for changing pitchers.

Sept. 22. Rookie Al Kaline makes his first start at The Corner, collecting a single while playing centerfield in a 7-3 loss to the St. Louis Browns.

Oct. 31. Forty-five thousand turn out to hear preacher Billy Graham in the largest Protestant rally ever in Michigan.

Dec. 27. The Lions win their second straight NFL championship with a 17-16 victory over Cleveland in front of 54,577.

1954

April 13. Ernie Harwell, radio voice of the Baltimore Orioles, broadcasts from The Corner for the first time.

July 23. Briggs Stadium hosts a concert featuring Perry Como, Patti Page, Sarah Vaughan and Nat King Cole. Tickets cost the 25,000 music fans $4.50 each.

1955

April 17. Al Kaline hits three home runs in a 16-0 rout of Kansas City. Two come in the sixth inning, making him the first American Leaguer since Joe DiMaggio in 1936 to homer twice in an inning.

July 19. Rookie Babe Birrer becomes the first relief pitcher to homer twice in a game at The Corner, slamming a pair of three-run shots in his only two at-bats during a 12-4 victory over Baltimore.

1956

June 18. Yankees slugger Mickey Mantle, en route to winning batting's Triple Crown, becomes the second player to clear the rightfield stands, connecting off Paul Foytack.

July 3. A syndicate headed by radio-television magnates Fred Knorr and John Fetzer buys the Tigers for $5.5 million. Their sealed bid is $200,000 better than the one submitted by former St. Louis and Cleveland owner Bill Veeck.

1957

April 18. The Tigers televise the home opener for the first time, resulting in an unusually small turnout of 31,227.

April 26. Spike Briggs is forced to resign as general manager, ending 37 years of

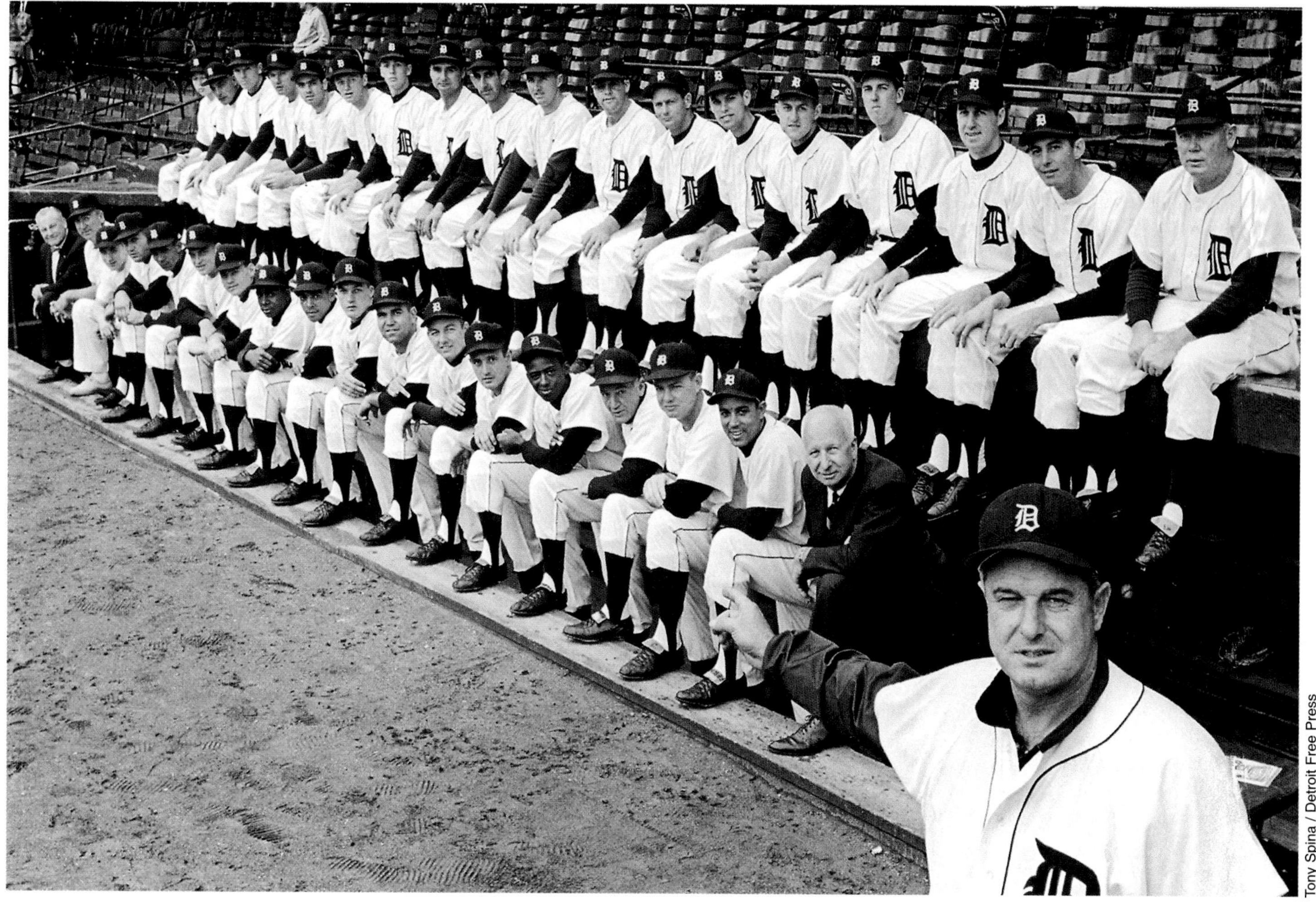

Tony Spina / Detroit Free Press

THE TIGERS OF 1961, MANAGED BY BOB SCHEFFING, WON 101 GAMES BUT FINISHED SECOND TO THE YANKEES.

family involvement with the team.

Dec. 29. As 55,263 delirious fans look on, the Lions annihilate Cleveland, 59-14, claiming their third NFL title in six years.

1958

June 17. Ozzie Virgil, the Tigers' first black player, makes his Briggs Stadium debut by going 5-for-5 against Washington.

1959

May 3. Charlie Maxwell ties a big-league mark by hitting four home runs in a doubleheader sweep of the Yankees.

1960

April 22. Home run champion Rocky Colavito, acquired from Cleveland in a controversial trade for batting champ Harvey Kuenn, homers in his first Tigers at-bat at Briggs Stadium.

Sept. 10. Mickey Mantle hits a ball over the rightfield roof that travels an estimated 643 feet, the longest home run ever measured.

1961

Jan. 1. Briggs Stadium is renamed Tiger Stadium.

April 26. New York's Roger Maris hits his first of a record-breaking 61 home runs for the season, a bases-empty blast off Paul Foytack. Maris goes on to hit numbers 23, 24, 57 and 58 at The Corner.

June 11. Norm Cash becomes the first Tiger to hit a home run over the rightfield roof. Washington's Joe McClain is the victim.

June 27. The Tigers and White Sox square off in front of 57,271, the largest Detroit crowd for a twi-night doubleheader.

Nov. 14. John Fetzer buys out the interest of the recently deceased Fred Knorr from Knorr's estate and becomes sole owner of the Tigers.

1962

June 24. Jack Reed hits the only home run of his career in the 22nd inning, leading New York past Detroit, 9-7. The seven-hour marathon sets a record for the longest game in big-league history.

Aug. 3. Minnesota's Harmon Killebrew becomes the first player to hit a home run over the leftfield roof, connecting off Jim Bunning.

Nov. 22. On Thanksgiving Day, a national television audience of 32 million watches the Lions thrash previously unbeaten Green Bay, 26-14.

1964

Aug. 9. The first Bat Day promotion draws 46,342 to a doubleheader with Kansas City.

Aug. 20. A game with the Los Angeles Angels attracts 2,173, the smallest night crowd in team history.

1967

June 17. Kansas City and Detroit establish the league record for the longest doubleheader: 9 hours, 5 minutes. Detroit wins the rain-delayed first game, 7-6, and drops the nightcap, 6-5, in 19 innings.

July 25. A riot forces postponement of the Detroit-Baltimore game; the balance of the three-game series is shifted to Baltimore.

Sept. 10. Chicago's Joel Horlen no-hits Detroit, 6-0.

Oct. 1. On the final day of the season, California beats Detroit, 8-5, in the second game of a doubleheader, dashing the Tigers' hopes of tying Boston for the pennant.

1968

May 19. Al Kaline's pinch-hit home run off Washington's Steve Jones is the 307th of his career and allows him to pass Hank Greenberg as the team's all-time leader.

Aug. 11. The game's premier pinch-hitter, Gates Brown, wins both games of a doubleheader against Boston with a 14th-inning homer in the opener and a ninth-inning single in the nightcap.

Aug. 22. Dick McAuliffe, enraged by a brushback pitch, gets into a brawl with Tommy John and severely injures the Chicago pitcher's shoulder. McAuliffe is suspended for five games and fined $250.

Sept. 14. The Tigers rally for a pair of ninth-inning runs against Oakland and make Denny McLain the majors' first 30-game winner since Dizzy Dean in 1934.

Oct. 7. The Tigers rally to beat the Cardinals, 5-3, in Game 5 of the World Series. Lou Brock's failure to slide on a close play at the plate is the turning point of the game and the Series.

1969

May 23. Mickey Lolich breaks Paul Foytack's 1956 club record with 16 strikeouts in a 6-3 win over California.

Aug. 28. Dancing groundskeeper Herbie Redmond entertains the home crowd for the first time.

THE CORNER IN 1970: AT FIRST GLANCE, AL KALINE THOUGHT IT LOOKED LIKE A BIG OL' BATTLESHIP; YEARS LATER IT REMINDED ALAN TRAMMELL OF A WAREHOUSE.

1970

July 1. A crowd of 53,863 turns out for Denny McLain's first game since being suspended in February for his involvement in a bookmaking operation. McLain doesn't make it out of the sixth inning against New York but gets no decision.

1971

July 13. Detroit's third All-Star Game sees a record-tying six home runs, including a massive blast by Oakland's Reggie Jackson that hits the light tower on the rightfield roof. The American League wins, 6-4, in front of 53,559.

Aug. 28. Les Cain homers in the fifth inning off Chicago's Tom Bradley, the last Tigers pitcher to reach the seats before the advent of the designated-hitter rule in 1973.

Oct. 24. Lions receiver Chuck Hughes dies on the field in the last minute of a 28-23 loss to Chicago.

1972

Jan. 12. Owner John Fetzer announces that the team has signed a 40-year lease (at $450,000 a year) for a planned $126-million domed riverfront stadium. Plans for the combined baseball-football facility die in the face of a failed bond issue, lawsuits and the Lions' decision to build a football-only stadium in Pontiac.

April 15. The Tigers open the first strike-delayed season with a 3-2 victory over Boston in front of 31,510 fans.

Sept. 28. Mickey Lolich is the victim as Lindy McDaniel of the Yankees becomes the last pitcher to homer at Tiger Stadium.

Oct. 10. Joe Coleman sets a league playoff record with 14 strikeouts in a 3-0 win over Oakland.

Oct. 12. Oakland defeats Detroit, 2-1, in the fifth and decisive game of the league playoffs.

1973

April 27. Kansas City's Steve Busby no-hits Detroit, 3-0.

July 15. Nolan Ryan of California strikes out 17 Tigers in 6-0 no-hit win.

1974

Sept. 1. Reggie Sanders becomes the first

Ira Rosenberg / Detroit Free Press

Tiger to homer at Michigan and Trumbull in his first big-league at-bat, hitting one off of Oakland's Catfish Hunter.

Nov. 28. The Lions play their final game at Tiger Stadium, losing to Denver, 31-27, on Thanksgiving Day.

1975

June 18. Boston rookie Fred Lynn collects a single, triple and three home runs and drives in 10 runs as the Red Sox romp, 15-1.

1976

May 15. Mark Fidrych wins his first major league start, a 2-1 two-hitter against Cleveland.

June 28. Fidrych's 5-1 victory over the Yankees in a nationally televised night game sets off "Birdmania."

1977

Feb. 1. A fire destroys the Tiger Stadium press box and part of the third deck.

July 13. Mayor Coleman Young announces that the Tigers have agreed to sell the stadium to the city for $1 and lease it back for 30 years. The move allows the city to apply for a federal grant to renovate the park.

1980

June 17. The Tigers close the bleachers after several incidents of rowdyism. They're reopened June 30 after the club initiates tighter security measures and limits beer sales.

Aug. 17. Al Kaline becomes the first Tiger to have his uniform number (6) officially retired.

1982

May 18. After homering in his final at-bat against Minnesota two days earlier, Larry Herndon extends his home run streak to four with blasts in the first, third and fifth innings against Oakland.

1983

June 12. The Tigers retire the uniform numbers of Hank Greenberg (5) and Charlie Gehringer (2) in a ballpark ceremony.

Oct. 10. John Fetzer sells the franchise to Domino's Pizza owner Tom Monaghan for $53 million.

1984

Oct. 5. The Tigers wrap up a three-game sweep of Kansas City and advance to the World Series with 1-0 victory.

Oct. 14. Kirk Gibson's two home runs power Detroit past San Diego, 8-3, and clinch a five-game World Series win.

1987

Sept. 2. The Tiger Stadium Fan Club is founded by five longtime fans inside a Buddy's Pizzeria.

Oct. 4. Behind Frank Tanana's pitching and Larry Herndon's home run, the Tigers beat Toronto, 1-0, edging the Blue Jays for the Eastern Division pennant.

Oct. 10. Pat Sheridan's home run produces a 7-6 win over Minnesota, Detroit's sole victory in a surprising five-game playoff loss to the underdog Twins.

1988

April 20. Before a game with Boston, more than 1,000 fans encircle the ballpark for the first "stadium hug."

Oct. 1. The team holds its first Fan Appreciation Day.

Detroit Free Press

MIKE ILITCH, WHO PLAYED BASEBALL AS A MARINE AND IN THE TIGERS' FARM SYSTEM, BOUGHT THE CLUB IN 1992.

1990

June 28. African National Congress leader Nelson Mandela speaks about apartheid in South Africa before 49,000 people.

Aug. 25. Cecil Fielder becomes the first Tiger to homer over the leftfield roof; Oakland's Dave Stewart is the pitcher.

1991

April 22. New club president Bo Schembechler gives his infamous "rusted girder" speech at the Economic Club of Detroit, demanding that civic leaders come up with plans to build a new stadium.

June 10. Tiger Stadium becomes the first sports facility to be placed on the National Trust for Historic Preservation's annual list of most endangered historic places.

1992

April 6. A no-smoking policy limits puffers to designated areas on the main and third-floor concourses.

Aug. 26. Tom Monaghan sells the team to Little Caesars Pizza magnate Mike Ilitch for $85 million.

1993

April 13. Tiger Stadium opens with a reported $8 million in improvements, including a new food court called Tiger Plaza, carved out of what had been the players' parking lot alongside Michigan Avenue.

Sept. 14. The Tigers fall to Toronto, 14-8, in four hours, 12 minutes, a club-record time for a nine-inning game.

Sept. 25. Rod Stewart performs the first major concert at The Corner since the 1950s.

1994

July 6. Matthew Duprey, 11, of Novi is selected as the team's 100 millionth fan. He throws out the first pitch, receives free merchandise and tickets, and sits in the dugout and the owner's suite.

Aug. 11. Detroit loses to Milwaukee, 10-5, in the last game before the players strike over the issue of a salary cap. The rest of the season and the World Series are subsequently canceled.

1995

May 2. In a contentious opener to the Tigers' 100th season at The Corner, 34 people are arrested for disorderly conduct.

May 28. The Tigers and White Sox combine for a record 12 home runs in Chicago's 14-12 victory. The teams also establish a league standard with 21 extra-base hits.

June 18. Detroit beats Baltimore, 10-8, giving Sparky Anderson the 2,158th managerial win of his career, placing him third behind Connie Mack and John McGraw.

July 8. Detroit and Kansas City players wear throwback uniforms of the Detroit Stars and Kansas City Monarchs in the first annual salute to the Negro leagues.

Sept. 20. In a key decision, board members of the Michigan Strategic Fund vote to contribute $55 million to help finance a new stadium. Tigers owner Mike Ilitch's original vision of an 80-acre, $400-million retail, entertainment and sports complex called Foxtown is whittled down to a $230-million ballpark to be built with a mix of city, state and private money. The Tigers' announced contribution is $145 million.

David C. Turnley / Detroit Free Press

NELSON MANDELA, HERO OF THE STRUGGLE AGAINST APARTHEID IN SOUTH AFRICA, PACKED 'EM IN FOR A 1990 RALLY AT THE CORNER.

Oct. 28. Ilitch and Mayor Dennis Archer unveil details of a new 40,000-seat stadium.

1996

April 24. Tigers give up a club-record number of runs in a 24-11 loss to Minnesota.

Aug. 21. Members of the Ilitch and Ford families, together with Detroit and Wayne County executives, jointly announce a $505-million plan for side-by-side downtown, baseball and football stadiums on the east side of Woodward, across from the Fox Theatre.

Sept. 18. Boston's Roger Clemens matches his major league record by striking out 20 Tigers.

Sept. 19. Tony Clark's strikeout in the first inning against Boston's Tom Gordon is Detroit's 1,186th of the season, breaking the league record set by the Tigers in 1991.

Sept. 25. Toronto beats Detroit, 4-1, as the Tigers set a franchise mark with 105 losses.

1997

June 16. Detroit loses to the Florida Marlins, 7-3, in the first regular-season home game against a National League team.

June 30-July 1. During the course of two games against the New York Mets, Bobby Higginson hits home runs in four consecutive official at-bats.

Oct. 29. Hal Newhouser throws out the first pitch to Little Leaguer Brandon Glenn as ground is ceremoniously broken on the new stadium in a parking lot across the street from the Fox Theatre.

1998

June 25. Sammy Sosa of the Chicago Cubs hits his 19th home run of the month, breaking Rudy York's 1937 major league mark.

Dec. 21. The Tigers announce they have sold the naming rights to the new stadium to Comerica, the biggest Michigan-based bank, for $66 million. The $285-million facility will be known as Comerica Park.

1999

April 12. The Tigers lose to Minnesota, 1-0, in 12 innings, in their 104th – and final – home opener at Michigan and Trumbull.

Alan R. Kamuda / Detroit Free Press (1988)

K of P
BADGES
FOR SALE HERE
HAVE YOU HAD YOUR FORTUNE TOLD
TELL ME
WHAT'S YOURS
IF YOU WANT TO
Shake FOR DRINKS
GO SIT ON THE
ICE PALACE
NO!
THE BEER PIPES
ARE NOT FROZEN
THERE ARE OTHERS
GET YOUR SKATES ON
HERE
TIVOLI BREWING COS.